IFIP Advances in Information and Communication Technology

636

Editor-in-Chief

Kai Rannenberg, Goethe University Frankfurt, Germany

IFIP – The International Federation for Information Processing

IFIP was founded in 1960 under the auspices of UNESCO, following the first World Computer Congress held in Paris the previous year. A federation for societies working in information processing, IFIP's aim is two-fold: to support information processing in the countries of its members and to encourage technology transfer to developing nations. As its mission statement clearly states:

IFIP is the global non-profit federation of societies of ICT professionals that aims at achieving a worldwide professional and socially responsible development and application of information and communication technologies.

IFIP is a non-profit-making organization, run almost solely by 2500 volunteers. It operates through a number of technical committees and working groups, which organize events and publications. IFIP's events range from large international open conferences to working conferences and local seminars.

The flagship event is the IFIP World Computer Congress, at which both invited and contributed papers are presented. Contributed papers are rigorously refereed and the rejection rate is high.

As with the Congress, participation in the open conferences is open to all and papers may be invited or submitted. Again, submitted papers are stringently refereed.

The working conferences are structured differently. They are usually run by a working group and attendance is generally smaller and occasionally by invitation only. Their purpose is to create an atmosphere conducive to innovation and development. Refereeing is also rigorous and papers are subjected to extensive group discussion.

Publications arising from IFIP events vary. The papers presented at the IFIP World Computer Congress and at open conferences are published as conference proceedings, while the results of the working conferences are often published as collections of selected and edited papers.

IFIP distinguishes three types of institutional membership: Country Representative Members, Members at Large, and Associate Members. The type of organization that can apply for membership is a wide variety and includes national or international societies of individual computer scientists/ICT professionals, associations or federations of such societies, government institutions/government related organizations, national or international research institutes or consortia, universities, academies of sciences, companies, national or international associations or federations of companies.

More information about this series at https://link.springer.com/bookseries/6102

Jason Staggs · Sujeet Shenoi (Eds.)

Critical Infrastructure Protection XV

15th IFIP WG 11.10 International Conference, ICCIP 2021
Virtual Event, March 15–16, 2021
Revised Selected Papers

 Springer

Editors
Jason Staggs
University of Tulsa
Tulsa, OK, USA

Sujeet Shenoi
University of Tulsa
Tulsa, OK, USA

ISSN 1868-4238   ISSN 1868-422X (electronic)
IFIP Advances in Information and Communication Technology
ISBN 978-3-030-93513-9   ISBN 978-3-030-93511-5 (eBook)
https://doi.org/10.1007/978-3-030-93511-5

This Springer imprint is published by the registered company Springer Nature Switzerland AG
The registered company address is: Gewerbestrasse 11, 6330 Cham, Switzerland

Contents

Contributing Authors

Irfan Ahmed is an Associate Professor of Computer Science at Virginia Commonwealth University, Richmond, Virginia. His research interests include cyber security, digital forensics, malware, cyber-physical systems and cyber security education.

Prashant Anantharaman is a Ph.D. student in Computer Science at Dartmouth College, Hanover, New Hampshire. His research interests include smart grid and Internet of Things protocol security, and eliminating input-handling vulnerabilities in code.

Adeen Ayub is a Ph.D. student in Computer Science at Virginia Commonwealth University, Richmond, Virginia. Her research interests include device firmware and network protocol reverse engineering, digital forensics and vulnerability discovery in industrial control systems.

David Balenson is a Senior Computer Scientist in the Infrastructure Security Group at SRI International, Arlington, Virginia. His research interests include critical infrastructure protection, experimentation and testing, and technology transition.

Qi Cao is an Assistant Professor of Computing Science at the University of Glasgow, Glasgow, United Kingdom. His research interests include virtual reality, augmented reality, signal processing, data analytics and computational intelligence.

Anmol Chachra recently completed his M.S. degree in Computer Science at Dartmouth College, Hanover, New Hampshire. His research interests include applications of neural networks and web development.

Chun-Fai Chan is a Ph.D. student in Computer Science at the University of Hong Kong, Hong Kong, China. His research interests include penetration testing, digital forensics and Internet of Things security.

Raymond Chan, Vice Chair, IFIP WG 11.10 on Critical Infrastructure Protection, is an Assistant Professor of Information and Communications Technology at Singapore Institute of Technology, Singapore. His research interests include cyber security, digital forensics and critical infrastructure protection.

Kam-Pui Chow is an Associate Professor of Computer Science at the University of Hong Kong, Hong Kong, China. His research interests include information security, digital forensics, live system forensics and digital surveillance.

Yu Han Chu is a Business Integration Architecture Analyst at Accenture, Singapore. His research interests include location-based systems, cyber security and cyber-physical systems.

Bogdan Copos is a Software Engineer at Google in Sunnyvale, California. His research interests include systems security with a focus on using side channels to monitor systems.

Stephen Dunlap is a Cyber Security Research Engineer at the Air Force Institute of Technology, Wright-Patterson Air Force Base, Ohio. His research interests include embedded systems security, cyber-physical systems security and critical infrastructure protection.

Tim Ellis is a Senior Principal Research Engineer at SRI International, San Diego, California. His research interests include critical infrastructure protection and information system privacy and security.

Scott Graham is an Associate Professor of Computer Engineering at the Air Force Institute of Technology, Wright-Patterson Air Force Base, Ohio. His research interests include embedded and communications systems security, vehicle cyber security and critical infrastructure protection.

Janne Hagen is a Special Advisor at the Norwegian Water Resources and Energy Directorate, Oslo, Norway; and an Associate Professor at the Institute for Informatics, University of Oslo, Oslo, Norway. Her research interests include cyber security, critical infrastructure protection and security governance.

Kyle Hintze recently completed his M.S. degree in Computer Engineering at the Air Force Institute of Technology, Wright-Patterson Air Force Base, Ohio. His research interests include computer communications, avionics security and critical infrastructure protection.

Jordan Johnson is a Cyber Security Technical Professional in the Embedded Systems Security Group at Oak Ridge National Laboratory, Oak Ridge, Tennessee. His research interests include intrusion detection systems and industrial control system testbed development.

Rohan Kela recently completed his B.E. (Hons.) degree in Computer Engineering at Birla Institute of Technology and Science, Pilani, India. His research interests include formal models, software engineering and critical infrastructure protection.

Sye Loong Keoh is an Associate Professor of Computing Science at the University of Glasgow, Glasgow, United Kingdom. His research interests include cyber security for the Internet of Things, cyber-physical systems and trusted artificial intelligence.

Rajesh Kumar is an Assistant Professor of Computer Science at Birla Institute of Technology and Science, Pilani, India. His research interests include information security risk management, and safety and security risk analysis using formal models and model checking.

Michael Locasto is a Principal Computer Scientist at SRI International, Princeton, New Jersey. His research focuses on understanding system failures and developing fixes.

Robert Mellish recently completed his M.S. degree in Computer Engineering at the Air Force Institute of Technology, Wright-Patterson Air Force Base, Ohio. His research interests include industrial control systems, embedded systems security and critical infrastructure protection.

Michael Millian is a Ph.D. student in Computer Science at Dartmouth College, Hanover, New Hampshire. His research interests include bootloader security and trusted parsers.

Syed Ali Qasim is a Ph.D. student in Computer Science at Virginia Commonwealth University, Richmond, Virginia. His research interests include digital forensics, cyber security and industrial control system threat intelligence.

Indrakshi Ray is a Professor of Computer Science and the Director of Colorado Center for Cybersecurity at Colorado State University, Fort Collins, Colorado. Her research interests include cyber security and cyber analytics in various domains, including transportation, energy, healthcare and information technology.

Brandt Reutimann recently completed his M.S. degree in Computer Science at Colorado State University, Fort Collins, Colorado. His research interests include cyber security, industrial control systems and critical infrastructure.

Chee Kiat Seow is an Assistant Professor of Computing Science at the University of Glasgow, Glasgow, United Kingdom. His research interests include localization methodologies and algorithms, physical cyber security, big data, artificial intelligence and machine learning.

Siddhant Singh recently completed his B.E. (Hons.) degree in Computer Engineering at Birla Institute of Technology and Science, Pilani, India. His research interests include cyber-physical systems security, software engineering and critical infrastructure protection.

Shikhar Sinha recently completed his A.B. degrees in Computer Science and Economics at Dartmouth College, Hanover, New Hampshire. His research interests include network security and low-latency systems.

Sean Smith is a Professor of Computer Science at Dartmouth College, Hanover, New Hampshire. His research interests include industrial Internet of Things security, trusted computing and human-computer interaction security.

Patrick Sweeney is an Assistant Professor of Computer Engineering at the Air Force Institute of Technology, Wright-Patterson Air Force Base, Ohio. His research interests include avionics security, critical infrastructure protection and embedded systems security.

Soon Yim Tan is an Associate Professor of Electrical and Electronic Engineering at Nanyang Technological University, Singapore. His research interests include propagation models, indoor localization and inertial navigation systems.

Tim Tang recently completed his B.Eng. degree in Computer Science at the University of Hong Kong, Hong Kong, China. His research interests include information security, digital forensics and machine learning.

Oyvind Toftegaard is a Senior Advisor at the Norwegian Energy Regulatory Authority, Oslo, Norway; and a Ph.D. student in Information Security and Communications Technology at the Norwegian University of Science and Technology, Gjovik, Norway. His research interests include cyber security governance of advanced metering infrastructures and electric power supply.

Kai Wen is a Research Fellow in the School of Electrical and Electronic Engineering at Nanyang Technological University, Singapore. His research interests include indoor localization and tracking, inertial navigation systems and cyber security.

Ken Yau is a Ph.D. student in Computer Science at the University of Hong Kong, Hong Kong, China. His research interests are in the area of digital forensics, with an emphasis on industrial control system forensics.

Siu-Ming Yiu is a Professor of Computer Science at the University of Hong Kong, Hong Kong, China. His research interests include security, cryptography, digital forensics and bioinformatics.

Preface

The information infrastructure – comprising computers, embedded devices, networks and software systems – is vital to operations in every sector: chemicals, commercial facilities, communications, critical manufacturing, dams, defense industrial base, emergency services, energy, financial services, food and agriculture, government facilities, healthcare and public health, information technology, nuclear reactors, materials and waste, transportation systems, and water and wastewater systems. Global business and industry, governments, indeed society itself, cannot function if major components of the critical information infrastructure are degraded, disabled or destroyed.

This book, *Critical Infrastructure Protection XV*, is the fifteenth volume in the annual series produced by IFIP Working Group 11.10 on Critical Infrastructure Protection, an active international community of scientists, engineers, practitioners and policy makers dedicated to advancing research, development and implementation efforts related to critical infrastructure protection. The book presents original research results and innovative applications in the area of critical infrastructure protection. Also, it highlights the importance of weaving science, technology and policy in crafting sophisticated, yet practical, solutions that will help secure information, computer and network assets in the various critical infrastructure sectors.

This volume contains twelve selected papers from the Fifteenth Annual IFIP Working Group 11.10 International Conference on Critical Infrastructure Protection, which was held virtually on March 15–16, 2021. The papers were refereed by members of IFIP Working Group 11.10 and other internationally-recognized experts in critical infrastructure protection. The post-conference manuscripts submitted by the authors were rewritten to accommodate the suggestions provided by the conference attendees. The twelve selected papers were subsequently revised by the editors to produce the final chapters published in this volume.

The chapters are organized into four sections: (i) themes and issues; (ii) industrial control systems security; (iii) telecommunications systems security; and (iv) infrastructure security. The coverage of topics show-cases the richness and vitality of the discipline, and offers promising avenues for future research in critical infrastructure protection.

This book is the result of the combined efforts of several individu-als and organizations. In particular, we thank David Balenson for his tireless work on behalf of IFIP Working Group 11.10. We also thank the National Science Foundation, U.S. Department of Homeland Secu-rity, National Security Agency and SRI International for their support of IFIP Working Group 11.10 and its activities. Finally, we wish to note that all opinions, findings, conclusions and recommendations in the chapters of this book are those of the authors and do not necessarily reflect the views of their employers or funding agencies.

JASON STAGGS AND SUJEET SHENOI

I

THEMES AND ISSUES

Chapter 1

CYBER SECURITY REQUIREMENTS IN THE NORWEGIAN ENERGY SECTOR

Janne Hagen and Oyvind Toftegaard

Abstract   This chapter discusses ongoing developments in cyber security regulations in the Norwegian energy sector through research and government-
industry cooperation. The focus is on cyber security policies for Norwegian electric power supply entities at the strategic, tactical and operational levels. The chapter promotes the integration of regulatory
requirements with traditional cyber security standards tailored to electric power supply entities and highlights how the integration contributes
to effective cyber security governance and risk management.

Keywords: Cyber security regulations, Norway, energy sector, electric power supply

1.   Introduction

Norway has a population of about 5.5 million people and land area
of roughly 385,000 km^2. It has temperate coastal and continental sub-
arctic climates that contribute to risks associated with floods, storms,
landslides and avalanches. Extreme weather events and human threats
following World War II and the Cold War have motivated continuous
efforts at building a hydroelectric power system under state and munici-
pal control that is resilient to various natural, technological and anthropogenic hazards.

Norwegian sector-specific contingency regulations have existed since
1948. The regulations include various security requirements, including
redundancy and contingency planning. In 2003, the regulations were revised based on research conducted by the Norwegian Defense Research
Establishment (FFI) [3, 4], which recommended mitigation measures to
address the vulnerabilities of the electric power supply system. The new
regulations provide a holistic security regime for electric power supply
contingencies, and cover physical, personnel and organizational security,

© IFIP International Federation for Information Processing 2022
Published by Springer Nature Switzerland AG 2022
J. Staggs and S. Shenoi (Eds.): Critical Infrastructure Protection XV, IFIP AICT 636, pp. 3–21, 2022.
https://doi.org/10.1007/978-3-030-93511-5_1

redundancy, maintenance capacity, restoration ability, information technology security and industrial control systems security. In 2014, three Norwegian electric power sector entities created KraftCERT, the first energy computer emergency response team (CERT) in Europe.

The Norwegian Water Resources and Energy Directorate (NVE) regulates security and contingency planning in the hydroelectric power supply and district heating (thermal energy) systems. The goal is to minimize the power outage risk in order to reduce adverse primary and secondary societal consequences. Due to the focus on security and contingency, the Norwegian power supply system is highly reliable and delivers 99.99% of the annual energy demand. The few power outages that occur are primarily due to natural hazards such as extreme weather events and, less frequently, technical failures.

Meanwhile, cyber security awareness has increased as a result of data breaches in the Norwegian Parliament [14], ransomware attacks on several Norwegian businesses and the SolarWinds and Microsoft Exchange attacks of 2021. Although cyber attacks have not caused power outages in Norway, the threat is growing. A recent report from Norway's Office of the Auditor General [4, 12] emphasizes the need for continuous improvements in cyber security.

This chapter discusses how NVE develops regulatory requirements pertaining to cyber security, how the regulatory requirements are transformed to corporate policies and procedures, and how compliance is controlled. It stresses the importance of a holistic approach that covers physical security, cyber security, redundancy, people and processes to create a cyber-resilient power supply infrastructure.

2.   Norwegian Electric Power Sector

The Norwegian power grid is associated with the European Union through the European Economic Agreement and is part of the European electricity market. Among European countries, Norway generates the largest percentage of electricity from renewable sources and has the lowest power sector emissions. At the end of 2020, Norwegian electricity generation amounted to 153 TWh. The vast majority of the generation capacity is hydroelectric. Wind power accounts for approximately 10% of the generation capacity and dominates investments. District heating (thermal energy) amounts to 4%.

A special feature of the Norwegian hydroelectric power generation system is its high storage capacity – Norway has half of Europe's reservoir storage capacity. Furthermore, more than 75% of the Norwegian electric power generation capacity is flexible. Hydroelectric power generation can be rapidly increased or decreased on demand at low cost. Balancing power supply and demand is vital to achieving resilience; imbalances in power production and consumption can lead to outages. The need for flexibility is underscored by the growing share of intermittent generation technologies such as wind and solar power.

The Norwegian electric power generation system plays a key role in the "green shift" towards clean energy and low carbon dioxide emissions. NVE [16] projects that the complete electrification of the transportation sector – road, rail and ferries – will require about 20 TWh and will not be realized until at least 2050. There are no signs that the importance of electric power supply will decrease in the coming decades.

Norway's electric power generation system leverages about 1,000 water storage reservoirs located up in the mountains. The reservoirs are essentially energy batteries that are interconnected through rivers and tunnels. Tunnels and pipes connect the reservoirs to hydroelectric power generation plants located downstream in the valleys. The power plants transform kinetic energy from flowing water to electricity.

Electricity is stepped up to a high voltage level for transmission by transformer stations located outside the hydroelectric power generation plants. Transformer stations step down electricity to a lower voltage level before delivery to consumers. As of 2021, Norway had more than 1,600 hydroelectric power plants and over 50 wind farms. While hydroelectric power generation is adjusted easily, electricity generation in wind farms depends on wind velocity. Variations in wind velocity make it difficult to ramp up or ramp down electricity generation at wind farms to meet demand.

Electricity generation and consumption must be balanced continuously and the alternating current frequency must be kept at 50 Hz. Norway has overhead power line and direct current cable connections to neighboring countries. Electricity generated by Norwegian hydroelectric plants, which is easily adjusted based on demand, is traded in the European energy market via energy stock exchanges. The energy market plays an important role in balancing Norwegian domestic electric power generation and consumption. During emergency situations, Statnett, Norway's national transmission system operator can override market mechanisms to balance generation and consumption, preventing cascading problems and outages. In surplus situations, Norway exports electricity. In deficit situations, Norway imports electricity.

Information technology is essential to managing Norway's electric power supply system. Maximum and minimum water levels in reservoirs and rivers are monitored and managed by NVE to protect fish stocks and prevent flooding. Power generation entities optimize electricity production according to market needs, constraints on water use, and generation and transmission capacity. Decisions are supported by industrial process control systems or supervisory control and data acquisition (SCADA) systems. Industrial control systems are also used to manage electricity transmission in the grid that crosses fjords, mountains and valleys. In addition to supervisory control and data acquisition systems, power generation entities and distribution system operators use commodity information technology products to support business operations. These myriad systems collectively constitute the digital infrastructure that enables the operation of Norway's complex electric power supply system.

Supply chain risk is an increasing concern because the vast majority of information technology products and applications are developed and distributed by transnational enterprises. Meanwhile, cyber attacks such as those on SolarWinds and Microsoft Exchange impact commodity information technology systems. When new vulnerabilities are recorded in the Common Vulnerabilities and Exposures (CVE) database [8], it is important to address them quickly. However, as demonstrated by the SolarWinds incident, a patch can be turned into a cyber weapon. The important point is that detection capability is effective at reducing risk. Immediately after the SolarWinds and Microsoft Exchange incidents were announced, KraftCERT broadcasted information about vulnerabilities and mitigation measures to Norwegian energy sector entities. As a result, the incidents did not impact the security of the Norwegian electric power supply.

The information technology and operational technology infrastructures in the electric power supply system can be protected by enforcing diversity, redundancy and defense-in-depth measures, along with contingency plans and recovery capabilities that enable normal operations to be established quickly after incidents. Additionally, various physical, personnel, technical and organizational measures are required to achieve resilience. These measures are included in the Norwegian contingency regulations for the electric power supply system.

Figure 1 shows the digital value chain of the Norwegian electric power supply system. The Norwegian power supply system has deployed new digital technologies in electricity generation, transmission and distribution. A prominent example in the transmission side is the positioning of sensors on power lines to collect physical parameters such as temperature and vibration data [5]. Meanwhile, advanced metering (smart meter) infrastructures have been constructed across the country to manage power distribution to customers.

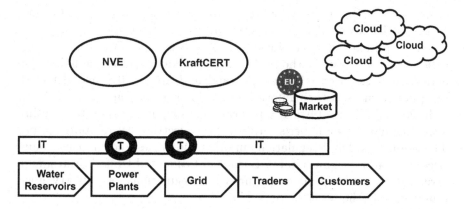

Figure 1. Digital value chain of the Norwegian elctric power supply system.

A study on innovation and the use of Internet of Things devices reports that several electric power sector entities intend to utilize sensors and data analytics for real-time control and effective operations and maintenance [15]. The study points to two trends. First, many projects are demonstrations, so large-scale implementations are still in the future. Second, vendors have expanded their services by offering innovative software solutions for data transmission, cloud services and data analytics, in addition to hardware. Extensive use of digital services and chains involving third parties increase system complexity and cyber security challenges. On one hand, they enable the electric power sector to apply innovative solutions to enhance operability and potential profits. On the other hand, the complexity and new dependencies induce latent, emergent risks.

3.   Cyber Security Regulation Development

The Norwegian Ministry of Petroleum and Energy is responsible for energy policy. NVE's mandates are to ensure the integrated and environmentally-sound management of water resources, promote efficient energy markets and cost-effective energy systems, and contribute to efficient energy use. Also included are the responsibilities for national flood contingency planning and maintenance of the national electric power supply. NVE's Audit and Contingency Department oversees electric power infrastructure construction, security and contingency planning of water and energy facilities, technical energy installations and cyber security.

A 2015 report by the Norwegian Commission on Digital Vulnerabilities devoted an entire chapter to digital vulnerabilities in the electric power sector [7]. However, in 2016, few cyber security incidents were registered by NVE, although electric power sector entities are required to report all extraordinary incidents. A subsequent NVE study of the cyber security status in the sector revealed that at least one-half of all entities had experienced Internet fraud and about 40% had detected computer viruses in their information technology systems [9].

In 2016, NVE established a project that sought to revise the contingency regulations on cyber security for the electric power supply sector. The project explored regulations in other industries and in other countries, regulatory regimes in the European Union and United States, and arranged workshops on cyber security and regulations for industry, government and other stakeholders.

NVE's final report recommended new regulations on traditional information technology systems. Industrial control systems were already well regulated; in fact, regulations inspired by the U.S. Federal Energy Regulatory Commission (FERC) [18] have existed since 2003 and they were revised extensively in 2013. The cyber security principles were generally regarded as valid, but they were continually being challenged by innovations in information technology and operational technology. It was clear that a new regulatory regime was required.

In 2018, NVE sought to formalize the cyber security regulations. The NVE team members had backgrounds in electrical engineering, cyber security and law. The team considered whether certification should be conducted based on international standards or statutory regulations. In Europe, the ISO/IEC 27001 standard is commonly used for information security management. While the efforts of a standardization committee comprising technical experts who attempt to comply with national regulations around the world are appreciated, certification according to an information security management standard only implies the existence of systems and procedures; it does not guarantee that security measures are implemented correctly. ISO/IEC 27001 also demands that entities perform risk assessments and choose appropriate security controls according to their levels of acceptable risk. Although this is good in principle, it does not enforce a minimum security level as in the case of compulsory regulatory requirements.

However, two advantages were discerned if NVE were to require certifications based on ISO/IEC 27001. First, NVE would not have to do audits, but instead collect certificates, check their validity and possibly sanction electric power supply entities with invalid certificates. The second advantage is that the information technology community would be familiar with the standards.

The NVE team produced two draft regulations. One draft was inspired by information security regulations in the Norwegian financial sector that build on the Control Objectives for Information Technologies (COBIT) framework [6]. The second draft drew from the efforts of the Norwegian National Security Authority (NSM), the responsible entity under the Norwegian Security Act, which has developed security baselines for Norwegian businesses based on *inter alia* international security standards. The Norwegian Energy Act and its contingency regulations cover various hazards, including natural, technological and intentional and unintentional anthropogenic hazards. However, the Norwegian Security Act, with its focus on intentional threats, does not apply to Norway's electric power supply sector.

Ultimately, the NVE team decided to base the cyber security regulatory requirements on the NSM baseline information technology security guidelines. The regulations do not explicitly mention the security baselines, but incorporate general security requirements that referred to international standards and norms. Nevertheless, the guidelines associated with the regulations link to NSM's baseline security requirements and other standards.

This approach provides an opportunity to leverage updated national baseline cyber security guidelines in the future. NVE released the revised regulations with the new requirements in an open hearing with a request for comments to be made within a few months. Minor changes to the regulations were made as a result of the hearing. Industry largely agreed that stricter regulation of information technology security were needed. The new regulations came into force on January 1, 2019.

4.   New Cyber Security Contingency Regulations

The new Norwegian contingency regulations on cyber security cover requirements for securing information technology systems. According to the new regulations, entities shall:

- Secure digital systems to maintain confidentiality, integrity and availability

- Implement security measures

- Apply baseline security according to recognized standards and norms, including the following actions:

    - Identifying and documenting services and systems
    - Performing risk assessments
    - Securing systems and detecting security incidents

- Managing and restoring systems after attacks and failures

- Maintaining or increasing the security level when outsourcing tasks

- Performing security audits

Temporary guidelines followed the new regulatory requirements. On NVE's request, Energi Norge, an association of electric power supply entities, arranged to offer four courses on the regulations. Personnel from NVE, NSM, Norwegian University of Science and Technology (NTNU) and Elvia, Norway's largest distribution system operator, gave lectures on the new regulations and provided practical guidance on complying with the new requirements. NVE also arranged a seminar in Oslo that focused on the main changes in the new regulations. The seminar was well attended by Norwegian energy sector entities.

Changing regulations will not effect change on its own. It is vital to communicate the changes and disseminate information to industry entities. Familiarity with the new regulations is not enough. As discussed below, the intent of the regulations and their requirements must be understood and accepted by the stakeholders.

5.   Development of Guidelines

In 2019, NVE established a working group and appointed a multidisciplinary team to revise the guidelines according to the new regulations. The coverage included cyber security, industrial control systems security, electrical engineering, risk management, emergency preparedness and legal issues. The effort had to balance the specificity of recommendations against the risk of becoming outdated and losing relevance in the long run. Guidelines that are frequently changed provide unstable frameworks, which are neither useful to industry nor the regulator to ensure compliance over time.

The final guidelines developed by NVE comprised eight chapters with one sub-chapter for each section in the regulations [11]. Each section presented the regulatory requirements, NVE's interpretation of the requirements and examples based on advice given to industry on the interpretations of the requirements. User-friendly "Attention!" and "Learn More!" boxes were incorporated. The "Learn More!" boxes provided links to international standards, guidelines and relevant reports produced by Norwegian authorities as well as foreign organizations like the U.S. National Institute of Standards and Technology (NIST). Standard symbols were used throughout the guidelines. Cross-references were provided to other sections in the regulations. The guidelines attempt to

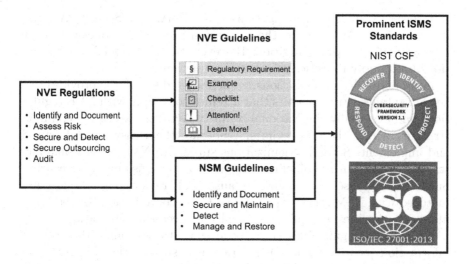

Figure 2. Alignment of NVE regulations with the NSM, NIST and ISO/IEC regimes.

communicate conflicts between standards, guidelines and statutory requirements. When conflicts occur, the statutory requirements always prevail.

The new guidelines were published in December 2020. In January 2021, a webinar was conducted to disseminate the guidelines to the stakeholders. Industry was given three months to study and comment on the guidelines. As it turned out, NVE received a few comments and minor changes were made to the guidelines.

6. Interoperability Principles

To ensure that cyber security regulations are timely, functional and relevant, NVE has attempted to make them compatible with other regulatory frameworks, guidelines and international security standards. Since entities in the energy sector may be subject to other regulations related to data privacy and national security imposed by the Norwegian Data Protection Authority and NSM, respectively, it is important that the NVE regulatory requirements and guidelines do not conflict with these and other requirements, as well as guidelines that would hinder compliance.

Figure 2 illustrates the alignment of the core content of NVE's contingency regulations with the NSM's security baseline guidelines and the prominent information security management standards. The security principles presented in the NSM guidelines are introduced as the first step towards fulfilling the obligations of the Norwegian Security Act and its regulations. At this time, the Norwegian Security Act does not apply to power supply system entities. However, the NVE and NSM regulations both apply to critical community functions.

Interoperability of regulations, guidelines and standards provides two key advantages. First, entities that attempt to comply with NVE regulations and eventually the National Security Act can discern the common structure across the two regimes, rendering them easy to understand and implement. Second, organizations subject to NVE regulations may still use NSM security guidelines effectively to establish baseline security. Such crossover use is simplified because NVE regulations are carefully matched with NSM security principles. Close coordination between regulatory authorities is required to facilitate successful integration.

NSM security guidelines are also designed to dovetail with common information security management standards such as the U.S. National Institute of Standards and Technology Cyber Security Framework (NIST CSF) and ISO/IEC 27001 Information Security Management Standard (ISMS). As shown in Figure 2, the main principles of the NSM security guidelines are similar to the main principles of the NIST CSF framework. In addition, the NSM security guidelines are designed to enable entities to populate the guideline sub-categories with detailed security measures in the ISO/IEC 27001 ISMS standard. To assist entities that comply with the ISO/IEC 27001 ISMS standard, NSM has prepared a matching list that mirrors its guidelines and content in the ISO/IEC 27001 ISMS standard.

7.   Cyber Security Policy Implementation

The understanding of the term policy varies between industry and academia. In this context, the term policy is a statement of objectives, rules, practices and/or regulations that governs the behavior of entities and/or the activities of individuals in a given context [13].

The distinction between public policies and corporate policies must be clarified. Public policies are systems of laws, regulatory measures, courses of action and funding priorities concerning topics promulgated by governmental entities or their representatives [2]. Regulatory requirements, such as laws, have a central role in public policy because they are often used to enforce policy compliance.

In contrast, corporate policies include strategies, rules, guidelines and procedures. It is common to divide corporate policies into three hierarchical levels, strategic, tactical and operational [19]. Strategic policies address corporate risks while complementing applicable laws; they

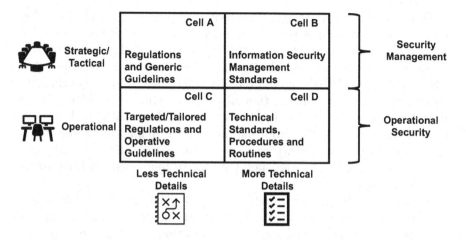

Figure 3. Relationships between public and private sector policies.

provide high level objectives with regard to security. Tactical policies include plans for extraordinary incidents such as contingency and crisis management plans, security maturity models, risk assessments, asset evaluations and information classification and other ways of guiding security implementations. Operational policies include routines and checklists for day-to-day monitoring and implementation of security requirements, such as permitting and revoking access rights, updating firewall rules, updating encryption protocols and installing security updates.

The level of detail is typically greater at the operational level and more generic at the strategic level. While the focus at the strategic level is on management and business processes, the focus at the operational level is on the technological aspects. Note that NVE does not regulate operational aspects such as the choice of information technology.

Figure 3 illustrates the relationships between public and private sector policies related to security management, operational security and level of technical detail. Regulations are in many cases generic and manifest long-term perspectives. Therefore, regulations are placed in Cell A, reflecting less technical detail at the managerial level. Crafting and approving regulatory requirements require considerable time and effort, and they should not be changed too often. Reducing the pace at which regulations are modified gives industry entities legal stability while they work on complying with the regulations. When requirements are specific and stipulate details, such as a specific technological solution, they may risk becoming obsolete and irrelevant.

Guidelines that specify generic activities also belong in Cell A. In this case, the effectiveness of security measures may be in focus. Examples are guidelines pertaining to asset management and risk assessment.

Asset management and risk assessment are also covered in the NIST CSF and ISO/IEC 27001 standards. Although these standards primarily specify management policies, they also cover technical security aspects in detail. Therefore, these standards are placed in Cell B in Figure 3. Organizations may utilize information security management standards to systematize their security regulation compliance efforts. NVE also requires organizations in the energy sector to implement security management systems.

Standards differ from regulations in that they are not intrinsically compulsory. NVE as a regulatory authority has little influence on the security controls from the various standards that Norwegian energy sector entities choose to implement. It is common for a standard such as ISO/IEC 27001 or NIST CSF to encourage entities to follow a risk-based approach and select controls from the standard that meet their risk assessment results and risk acceptance levels. However, NVE can enforce controls from standards through regulation. If NVE were to choose such a path, active participation in the standardization committees and their working groups could ensure some influence on the content of the requirements in the standards.

Although information security management standards may be detailed, they still reside at the managerial level and do not explain how the security measures should be implemented in practice. Therefore, entities may have to develop their own detailed procedures and routines or look to strictly technical standards such as IEC 62443 for industrial control system security or IEC 62351 for authentication. This is necessary to obtain the right level of detail for implementing the most technical requirements at the operational level. Cell D in Figure 3 contains the most technical and operational content that would support system operators in their daily security activities.

Tailored regulations and operative guidelines are placed in Cell C. These may be quite specific and feasible to follow at the operational level. However, as with other regulations and guidelines, they are made to last, and, therefore, do not discuss specific technological solutions. As an example, consider a hypothetical requirement that certain communications should be encrypted. Then, an entity with an information system that switches to encrypted communications on a mouse click could incorporate the requirement in an operational policy as a checklist entry. An entity without an information system with an encryption option would have to select an encryption standard in Cell D to implement

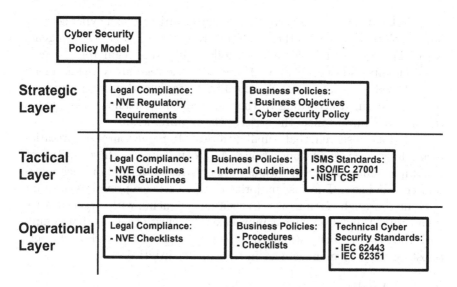

Figure 4. Hierarchical cyber security policy model.

the requirement. An advantage with this setup is that if the encryption standard chosen by the entity were to become obsolete, the tailored regulation or operative guideline in Cell C would still be relevant. Only the encryption standard in Cell D would have to be changed by the entity to satisfy the requirement.

8.   Regulatory Requirement Compliance

Figure 4 shows a cyber security policy model with hierarchical layers of legal compliance, business policies and security standards. The policy model illustrates the principle of integration of regulatory requirements with traditional security standards tailored to the specific business roles of entities. The incorporation of cyber security regulatory requirements in business entity policies, supported by security standards where beneficial, may be key to successful and cost-effective security governance while ensuring legal compliance.

Norway has about 115 electric utilities. According to the European Union's definition of small enterprise [1], 88 Norwegian utilities would be small enterprises. Around 50 of these small utilities have less than 7,000 customers and struggle to have dedicated security staff. NVE has observed that some of these utilities comply with the minimum cyber security regulatory requirements and have minimal security governance. This often means that they merely have a general cyber security management policy that addresses strategic security objectives, a cyber security handbook that addresses the regulatory requirements and a contingency plan. These small utilities have to follow the same regulatory baseline requirements as larger utilities. However, some regulatory requirements differ based on utility size. Specifically, systems and infrastructure assets are classified according to their size and importance. The greater the size and importance, the stricter the requirements.

NVE has observed that small utilities often outsource information technology services and operations. As a consequence, these entities often implement the security frameworks of their information technology service providers. The vast majority of these service providers have undergone thorough vetting prior to their engagements with larger utilities. As a result, they often have comprehensive security regimes that comply with the cyber security standards at the managerial and technical levels, boosting security management in the smaller utilities.

9.   Audits

NVE oversees the effectiveness of cyber security governance in electric power supply entities via audits. Before the COVID-19 pandemic, NVE performed about 50 audits annually covering various parts of the contingency regulations. The major findings were related to risk assessment and contingency planning, but other issues were also identified by NVE during the audits.

An electric power supply entity is informed by mail about an impending audit. NVE requests documents related to the specific audit and the documents are thoroughly examined before the NVE site visit. The audit methodology uses standard checklists based on the sector regulations. NVE controls entity compliance using a selection of sections in the regulations. The audit is neither a certification nor a full revision nor a penetration test. During the daylong session involving discussions with and questions posed to electric power supply entity personnel, deviations from the selected sections of the statutory regulation are identified. A tradeoff exists between the level of detail to which NVE can investigate the security framework of a single entity and the number of entities that can be audited during a given period. At this time, the trend has been to audit more entities at lower levels of detail, inevitably hindering the identification of all possible deviations and vulnerabilities.

An NVE study has investigated the use of digital tools to improve the auditing process. For example, efficient auditing may be achieved by using open-source intelligence tools to monitor the release of sensitive information on the Internet [10]. This task could be performed by the entities themselves after being trained in workshops or seminars, enabling NVE to enhance the quality and quantity of its audits. Scripts and vulnerability scanning tools would be employed to enhance the detection of technical vulnerabilities. However, such tools are not widely used by Norwegian authorities due to the potential negative impacts on the systems being evaluated [17].

NVE personnel would need to have the requisite technical skills to use digital tools in audits. If such skills do not exist in-house, NVE would have to hire a third-party for this purpose. This issue is being considered and a decision has yet to be made.

During its audits, NVE has mainly observed deviations related to risk assessments and their connections to contingency planning. There is also the potential for improving logging and log analytics for industrial control systems. NVE visits and audits have helped increase security awareness among top management that often participates in the meetings. Thus, the audits contribute to the creation of security cultures at the entities as well as increased investments in cyber security. Electric power supply entities are typically given three months to address issues identified in audits. Longer timeframes are given when large investments have to be made.

10.   Potential Improvements

The Office of the Auditor General monitors the Norwegian public sector. In March 2021, the Office of the Auditor General [12] published a report about NVE's efforts in the energy sector. The report critiques the cyber security and contingency planning efforts and provides recommendations for improvement.

A key recommendation with regard to security governance is that NVE should improve the audit methodology. The report also recommends efforts focused on developing guidelines for the statutory requirements; this is important because statutory regulations currently do not apply to vendors with the exception of the requirements that protect sensitive information. Furthermore, the report highlights supply chain issues as a systemic risk. Supply chain security is regulated via private contracts between entities. NVE plans to explore ways in which its regulatory role may be leveraged to enhance supply chain security.

11.   Conclusions

Developing prescriptive and flexible regulations that accommodate technological advances and organizational innovation is challenging. The impacts of technological advances and organizational innovation on security should be investigated along with the relevance of current statutory requirements. NVE's experience reveals that small electric power supply entities prefer prescriptive regulations and highly specific advice whereas larger entities prefer functional regulations that give them the freedom to develop security policies and manage risk.

NVE's principal objective in regulating cyber security is to reduce the electric power outage risk and minimize adverse impacts on society. The Norwegian power supply system is highly reliable and delivers 99.99% of the country's annual electricity demand. Power outages in Norway are rare – they are primarily caused by extreme weather events and technical failures to a lesser degree. However, cyber security incidents are on the rise and demand increased attention and resources. As of 2021, cyber threats have been mitigated without any power outages. Nevertheless, this chapter argues that statutory regulations built on knowledge and international standards, with guidelines referring to standards, expert reports and subject matter expertise, can reduce the exposure to hidden and emergent risks associated with the digitalization of the electric power supply system. In addition, external audits are necessary to reveal deviations and improving auditing methods is a priority.

Successful governance requires an active regulator that conducts audits and sanctions electric power supply entities for non-compliance. This has contributed in part to the reliability of the electric power supply in Norway. Natural hazards are currently the dominant threats, but this will change as information technology increases its penetration in the electric power supply infrastructure. This is why updating regulations, guidelines and auditing methods in a timely manner, and communicating them to the various stakeholders are important. It is also important to keep abreast of advances in cyber security research and development and use the knowledge to update regulations and requirements. NVE looks to leading experts for advice and guidance, and has instituted partnerships with researchers from universities in Norway and the Nordic and Baltic countries, as well as in the United States to advance it energy regulation mission.

In conclusion, regulations are often viewed as hindrances by innovative business entities that seek to engage novel cyber technologies. However, it is prudent to carefully assess the current and emergent risks to the electric power supply system and implement security measures based on statutory requirements before going full speed ahead on the cyber highway.

Acknowledgements

The authors wish to thank their colleagues at the Norwegian Water Resources and Energy Directorate, Head Engineer Helge Ulsberg and Head Engineer Amir Zaki Messiah, for providing valuable comments, and Ph.D. candidate Jenny Sjastad Hagen of the University of Bergen and the Bjerknes Center for Climate Research for her critical reading and language vetting.

References

[1] European Commission, Internal market, industry, entrepreneurship and SMEs, Brussels, Belgium (`ec.europa.eu/growth/smes/sme-definition_en`), 2021.

[2] S. Evans (Ed.), *Public Policy Issues Research Trends*, Nova Science Publishers, Hauppauge, New York, 2008.

[3] H. Fridheim, J. Hagen and S. Henriksen, A Vulnerable Electrical Power Supply – Final Report from Protection of Society (BAS3) (in Norwegian), Norwegian Defense Research Establishment, FFI Report 2001/02381, Oslo, Norway (`publications.ffi.no/nb/item/asset/dspace:3605/01-02381.pdf`), 2001.

[4] J. Hagen, Securing the energy supply in Norway – Vulnerabilities and measures, presented at the *NATO Membership and the Challenges from Vulnerabilities of Modern Societies Workshop of the Norwegian Atlantic Committee and the Lithuanian Atlantic Treaty Association*, 2003.

[5] Heimdall Power, The power of knowing, Sandnes, Norway (`heimdallpower.com`), 2021.

[6] Information Systems Audit and Control Association, COBIT – An ISACA Framework, Schaumburg, Illinois (`www.isaca.org/resources/cobit`), 2021.

[7] O. Lysne, K. Beitland, J. Hagen, A. Holmgren, E. Lunde, K. Gjosteen, F. Manne, E. Jarbekk and S. Nystrom, Digital Vulnerabilities – Safe Society (in Norwegian), NOU 2015:13, Norwegian Government Security and Service Organization, Oslo, Norway (`www.regjeringen.no/contentassets/fe88e9ea8a354bd1b63bc0022469f644/no/pdfs/nou201520150013000dddpdfs.pdf`), 2015.

[8] MITRE Corporation, Common Vulnerabilities and Exposures (CVE), Bedford, Massachusetts (`cve.mitre.org`), 2021.

 [9] Norwegian Water Resources and Energy Directorate, The State of Information Security in the Power Supply Sector (in Norwegian), NVE Report no. 90-2017, Oslo, Norway (`publikasjoner.nve.no/rapport/2017/rapport2017_90.pdf`), 2017.

[10] Norwegian Water Resources and Energy Directorate, Method for Identifying Power Supply Sensitive Information on the Internet (in Norwegian), NVE Factsheet no. 11 09/2019, Oslo, Norway (`publikasjoner.nve.no/faktaark/2019/faktaark2019_11.pdf`), 2019.

[11] Norwegian Water Resources and Energy Directorate, Power Supply Contingency Regulations – Guidelines (in Norwegian), Oslo, Norway (`www.nve.no/nytt-fra-nve/nyheter-tilsyn/rettleiar-til-kraftberedskapsforskrifta`), 2020.

[12] Office of the Auditor General of Norway, The Office of the Auditor General of Norway's Study of NVE's Work with ICT-Security in the Power Supply Sector (in Norwegian), Document 3:7 (2020–2021), Oslo, Norway (`www.riksrevisjonen.no/globalassets/rapporter/no-2020-2021/nves-arbeid-med-ikt-sikkerhet-i-kraftforsyningen.pdf`), 2021.

[13] A. Oldehoeft, Foundations of a Security Policy for Use of the National Research and Educational Network, NISTIR 4734, National Institute of Standards and Technology, Gaithersburg, Maryland, 1992.

[14] Reuters Staff, Norway's Parliament hit by new hack attack, *Reuters*, March 10, 2021.

[15] M. Royksund and A. Valdal, An Exploratory Study of the Application of Internet of Things (IoT/IIoT) in the Norwegian Power Supply Sector (in Norwegian), NVE External Report no. 2/2020, Norwegian Water Resources and Energy Directorate, Oslo, Norway (`publikasjoner.nve.no/eksternrapport/2020/eksternrapport2020_02.pdf`), 2020.

[16] D. Spilde and C. Skotland, How Could Extensive Electrification of the Transportation Sector Influence the Power Supply System? (in Norwegian), NVE Note, Norwegian Water Resources and Energy Directorate, Oslo, Norway (`beta.nve.no/Media/4117/nve-notat-om-transport-og-kraftsystemet.pdf`), 2015.

[17] T. Svensen, K. Kallseter and S. Husabo, Application of Digital Tools in ICT-Security Audits (in Norwegian), NVE Report no. 38/2020, Norwegian Water Resources and Energy Directorate, Oslo, Norway (`publikasjoner.nve.no/rapport/2020/rapport2020_38.pdf`), 2020.

[18] Technical Support Working Group, Securing Your SCADA and Industrial Control Systems, Version 1.0, U.S. Department of Homeland Security, Washington, DC, 2005.

[19] R. Wies, Policy definition and classification: Aspects, criteria and examples, *Proceedings of the IFIP/IEEE International Workshop on Distributed Systems: Operations and Management,* 1994.

Chapter 2

CYBER SECURITY AWARENESS REQUIREMENTS FOR OPERATIONAL TECHNOLOGY SYSTEMS

Tim Ellis, David Balenson and Michael Locasto

Abstract   Recent events have demonstrated that critical infrastructure assets operated by networked industrial control systems are vulnerable to cyber attacks. The first step to addressing the threats is to establish and maintain reliable monitoring of the cyber security health of systems so that their true cyber security states are known. For current operational technology systems, there is growing, but limited, availability of technologies and tools that provide the needed cyber security awareness. This chapter summarizes recent efforts conducted in collaboration with members of the U.S. natural gas distribution sector to develop a set of recommended functional requirements for cyber security health monitoring and awareness of operational technology systems. The design-driven process is described and the resulting nine key recommendations for securing operational technology systems are presented.

Keywords: Operational technology, cyber security health, monitoring tools

1.   Introduction

Cyber actors have demonstrated their willingness to target critical infrastructure by exploiting Internet-accessible industrial control systems and other operational technology assets. These attacks, including spear phishing, ransomware, control logic modification and denial of service, have caused significant interruptions, loss of visibility and/or control of operational technology systems as well as potential damage. In response, the National Security Agency (NSA) and Cybersecurity and Infrastructure Security Agency (CISA) recently issued an alert to the critical infrastructure community to take specific actions to strengthen operational technology defenses and monitoring [1]. A recent study iden-

© IFIP International Federation for Information Processing 2022
Published by Springer Nature Switzerland AG 2022
J. Staggs and S. Shenoi (Eds.): Critical Infrastructure Protection XV, IFIP AICT 636, pp. 23–44, 2022.
https://doi.org/10.1007/978-3-030-93511-5_2

tified a broad range of failure scenarios in the natural gas distribution infrastructure and provides a framework for evaluating potential system threats and mitigations [11].

The first step in addressing cyber threats is to establish and maintain reliable monitoring of the cyber health of a system, so that the true cyber security state of the system is known. The Transportation Security Administration (TSA) Pipeline Security Guidelines provide baseline cyber security measures that pipeline owners and operators should deploy at all facilities, including technical and/or procedural controls for cyber intrusion monitoring and detection [19]. For current operational technology systems, there is growing, but still limited, availability of monitoring technologies and tools that could provide cyber security awareness.

The authors of this chapter have worked collaboratively with a consortium of natural gas distribution utilities to develop requirements and recommendations for a monitoring tool called the Cyber Analytics Dashboard for Operational Technology (CADOT) that could be deployed in natural gas distribution systems to enhance monitoring and cyber security awareness. The CADOT tool is intended to provide initial indications of potential cyber security threats and, in coordination with existing operational technology tools, quickly and effectively distinguish malicious events from common electrical and mechanical malfunctions, ensuring that the proper and most efficient responses can be conducted.

Drawing on the CADOT experience, this chapter describes the efforts to gather and define cyber security awareness needs and capabilities to enable industrial control system owners and operators to effectively monitor and assess the cyber security states of their operational technology systems. The process used to collect and develop the operational technology cyber security awareness recommendations are presented, along with the recommendations themselves.

2.   CADOT Concept

Figure 1 presents the CADOT monitoring concept. CADOT is intended to provide a means for connecting and monitoring cyber-related data and processing activities across an operational technology system, potentially at physically-distributed substations, and aggregating and displaying the information for cyber security analyses by operational technology personnel. The CADOT design includes trusted monitoring capabilities embedded in the operational technology fabric of distributed substations. The capabilities would leverage embedded software agents in programmable logic controllers (PLCs) and remote terminal units (RTUs) to monitor processing, memory and communications, function-

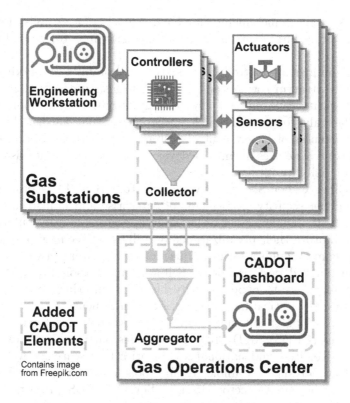

Figure 1. CADOT monitoring concept.

ality embedded in sensors and actuators, and network tools (e.g., serial test access points (TAPs) and network switch port analyzers (SPANs)) to monitor message traffic. The cyber data would be combined by a local collector at each substation and sent via secure channels to a central operations center. At the operations center, the substation cyber data would be aggregated and analyzed for possible alert conditions and displayed on a dashboard for operations personnel.

3.   Related Work

This research focuses on the design of a reliable operational technology cyber security health monitoring and awareness capability for natural gas distribution systems. A number of government and commercial activities are aligned with this effort.

As mentioned above, the Transportation Security Administration has provided comprehensive risk-based security guidelines for natural gas pipeline systems, which include a recommendation for establishing technical and procedural controls for cyber intrusion monitoring and detection [19].

CISA's industrial control systems strategy commits to working with critical infrastructure owners and operators to institute industrial control system security capabilities. The strategy is built around four pillars. One pillar calls for technological developments that harden the cyber security defenses of legacy control systems, build security into new industrial control devices during the development stage and increase lower-level data visibility [2].

The CISA Cyber Security Evaluation Tool (CSET) is designed to perform cyber security assessments of enterprise and industrial control systems [3, 4]. It helps asset owners and operators identify vulnerabilities and improve their organizations' overall cyber security postures by guiding them through a series of questions that cover network security requirements and best practices. Self-assessment tools like CSET can lead organizations to cyber security health monitoring and awareness capabilities, the critical first step in risk management.

The U.S. Department of Energy's Cybersecurity for Energy Delivery Systems (CEDS) R&D Program leverages partnerships between industry, universities and national laboratories to research, develop and demonstrate advanced technologies and tools for operational technology systems in the energy sector [15–17]. Several CEDS projects are exploring advanced monitoring and situational awareness capabilities for operational technology systems in the electric grid and, in some cases, natural gas pipeline systems. The Schweitzer Engineering Laboratories Project Ambassador is developing a capability to manage trust and data sharing between multiple software applications to improve awareness and visualization of enterprise and operational technology systems in electric utilities [7]. The Texas A&M CYPRES Project is designing a next-generation cyber-physical energy management system intended to detect and prevent malicious events by fusing cyber and physical data and to facilitate online control actions that couple cyber and physical systems [5]. The Dragos Neighborhood Keeper Project seeks to develop a no-trust, low cost, interconnected sensor network for the rapid sharing of non-sensitive threat information from operational technology networks across multiple enterprises [6]. The GE Research Cyber-Physical Protection for Natural Gas Compression Project is developing a cyber-physical protection capability deployed at the edge to provide near real-time asset protection and situational awareness focused on prime mover, control and compressor systems [14]. The CADOT concept is well positioned to leverage or align with the novel capabilities resulting from these projects.

The 2017 Liberty Eclipse Exercise brought together energy suppliers, trade associations and government agencies to review plans, policies and procedures for responding to and recovering from a cyber incident that affects the energy infrastructure in a major region of the United States. The results of the exercise highlighted the need to improve information sharing and coordination during emergencies and incidents [18]. The CADOT effort intends to provide high-quality information to feed such activities.

In 2017, Idaho National Laboratory conducted a survey to identify tools that could be used to prevent, detect, mitigate and investigate cyber attacks in industrial control environments and to show the coverage of applicable tools [10]. While the survey found a growing number of tools suitable for industrial control systems, it identified gaps related to controller local area networks and field input/output devices, partial coverage for network traffic anomaly detection devices and very few or untested tools for outlier analysis, log reviews and system artifact reviews. The survey identified several multi-purpose tools with network and system monitoring functions; the current generations of many of these tools are considered in this work. However, the efforts did not test the tools for suitability or verify vendor claims. Many tools for industrial control environments have been developed in recent years and the community would greatly benefit from a new study that identifies security tools and evaluates their coverage and suitability.

Responding to the need for a more comprehensive approach to situational awareness with (near) real-time cyber security monitoring, the National Institute of Standards and Technology (NIST) National Cybersecurity Center of Excellence (NCCoE) developed and documented an exemplar solution targeted at the electric grid [13]. The solution uses commercial products, including network intrusion detection systems in the operational technology space, to provide a converged view of sensor data across the information technology, operational technology and physical access control systems in a utility. While the solution is focused on the electric grid, the underlying concepts are applicable to natural gas distribution pipelines and could help realize the desired CADOT capability.

Finally, several current commercial technologies and tools can be leveraged to address the recommended CADOT requirements and design features. These technologies and tools and their coverage of the CADOT recommendations are discussed later in this chapter.

4.   Cyber Security Awareness Requirements

A collaborative design-driven approach was employed to identify gaps in cyber security monitoring capabilities for industrial control systems and to gather key CADOT functional requirements. The design-driven approach, developed at the Hasso Plattner Institute of Design at Stanford University [9], begins with an assessment of the desired user experience to determine user-facing needs for a product. Next, it combines requirements engineering processes to establish and maintain feasibility and product viability. Finally, it uses a collaborative agile development paradigm to iteratively prototype and evolve the product features and functions. This industry-standard process enabled the collective expertise of national gas distribution operations personnel to be leveraged in identifying the CADOT functional requirements.

The Gas Technology Institute (GTI) administers the Operations Technology Development (OTD) Cybersecurity Collaborative, a partnership between the U.S. Department of Homeland Security and industry to identify and mitigate cyber security capability gaps in the natural gas distribution sector. The collaborative seeks to address high-priority cyber security issues faced by members through focused outreach and education coupled with technology evaluation and transfer activities [8]. Company representatives in the collaborative include experienced engineers, researchers, system operators and security staff.

The process employed in this research began by conducting a survey of members of the collaborative. The survey questionnaire covered the following topical areas to establish general requirements guidelines:

- Overall CADOT objectives, constraints and utility participation interest (nine questions).

- Cyber security situational awareness needs and requirements (five questions).

- System integration requirements (two questions).

- Open question to collect unsolicited ideas (one question).

The survey results indicated strong agreement among the respondents for a centralized dashboard that can process, communicate and store the cyber security status of operational technology systems to improve cyber security awareness and trust during operations. In particular, there was general agreement for operators to be able to:

- Assess, analyze and maintain awareness of the cyber security state, including data and operations confidentiality, integrity and availability.

- Collect, analyze and monitor cyber security state properties, including higher-level synthesis (fusion) for improved understanding.

- Discover new and potentially useful correlations between cyber security state properties.

- Provide an active topological map of networks and devices, including dynamic active/inactive states of devices and components and their vulnerabilities to cyber attacks.

In addition, the survey respondents expressed a strong desire to leverage commercial technologies and tools where available, minimize lifecycle costs and take advantage of industry advancements.

The survey results were used in a live, interactive ideation workshop to develop the CADOT requirements. The workshop focused on four areas related to the CADOT requirements:

- **Users and Tasks:** Identify relevant cyber security actors and their associated roles.

- **Cyber Security Monitoring Rhythms:** Define cyber monitoring priorities and frequencies.

- **Malicious Scenarios:** Define cyber use cases to be detected and mitigated.

- **Normal Operations:** Establish normalcy baselines for cyber security monitoring.

In the workshop, personnel responsible for system operations and security (including cyber security) participated and provided first-person perspectives on the capability needs and gaps. Due to COVID-19 pandemic safety concerns, the ideation workshop was conducted virtually using the StormBoard collaborative tool and Zoom conferencing application. StormBoard provided a means for remote collaborative brainstorming to capture, organize and prioritize ideas. The Zoom breakout room feature was used to dynamically divide the participants into small working groups to foster interactions and idea creation before meeting as a single group to share and review incremental progress.

5.   Key Recommendations

The ideas, concepts and requirements generated in the workshop were assessed and distilled into a set of recommended functional requirements for cyber security health monitoring and awareness of operational technology systems. Table 1 lists the nine key recommendations, which are summarized in the following subsections.

Table 1. Key recommended functional requirements.

Recommendation 1:	CADOT should accommodate three high-level types of users or personnel.
Recommendation 2:	CADOT should provide multiple views into a potential cyber security situation based on the analytic needs of the moment.
Recommendation 3:	CADOT should operate with the notion of a baseline that expresses normal functioning.
Recommendation 4:	When a baseline deviation occurs, CADOT should attempt to provide information about possible external factors or influences.
Recommendation 5:	Some (mostly static) state information should be made visible immediately because it could signal important alert situations.
Recommendation 6:	CADOT should provide a means to interactively query the various interfaces and components.
Recommendation 7:	CADOT should provide a means to plug in arbitrary data streams.
Recommendation 8:	CADOT should provide a means to set arbitrary running rules for alerts.
Recommendation 9:	CADOT should be designed to accommodate the computational, power, network bandwidth and availability constraints on operational technology devices.

5.1   CADOT User Types

The first recommendation relates to CADOT user types:

- **Recommendation 1:** CADOT should accommodate three high-level types of users or personnel.

Different organizations have varying titles and responsibilities for their operational technology personnel. The three general user types identified are: (i) monitoring personnel responsible for continuously monitoring system operations from control rooms (remote and central), (ii) response personnel responsible for engineering maintenance, fixes and upgrades in the field as well as in control rooms and (iii) analytics personnel responsible for longer-term collection, analysis and planning of system configurations and operations. Note that these descriptions are

Table 2. Summary of CADOT user types.

	Users
Roles	**Monitoring:** SCADA administrator, field technician, operational technology cyber analyst
	Response: Local engineer, central engineer, operations/ incident manager (controller), cyber security investigator
	Analytics: Technical analyst, policy and compliance analyst
Responsibilities	**Monitoring:** Monitor health and configuration of SCADA systems, setup, configure and monitor controllers and electronic devices, analyze cyber security of operational technology systems
	Response: Assess status and causes of incidents in the field and control center, manage operations, measurements and incident resolution, coordinate mitigation actions, verify resolutions, investigate anomalous incidents
	Analytics: Analyze logs and after-action reviews, Prepare safety and security reports, verify compliance, provide decision support for workforce and operations policies
CADOT Usage	**Monitoring:** Monitor, validate and coordinate cyber settings changes, verify cyber mitigation actions
	Response: Identify and respond to cyber incidents, verify cyber security mitigations
	Analytics: Review device performance and stability, capture cyber baselines, maintain vendor device ratings

generalizations of the information provided by the workshop participants and may not reflect specific titles or staff positions at their organizations.

Table 2 summarizes the roles and responsibilities and the cyber-specific usage that the roles and responsibilities need from a CADOT capability. CADOT should provide cyber-specific capabilities to augment operational capabilities for the three types of system users.

The monitoring roles include SCADA administrator responsible for health monitoring and configuration validation of supervisory control and data acquisition (SCADA) systems. From a CADOT cyber security perspective, a SCADA administrator validates and coordinates field setting changes, and watches for unplanned changes to system operations. Another monitoring role is field technician responsible for the setup and configuration of controllers, including programmable logic controllers and remote terminal units, and other electronic measurement and instrumentation devices. From a CADOT cyber security perspective, a field technician monitors planned or unplanned changes to the aforementioned devices. The third monitoring role is cyber analyst (operational technology cyber security analyst) responsible for cyber security analysis of operational technology systems. This role focuses on detecting and investigating anomalous or malicious cyber activities as well as verifying the effectiveness of mitigation actions.

The response roles include local and central engineers responsible for assessing the status and causes of incidents in the field and at operations centers, respectively. The engineers' cyber-specific responsibilities include identification, response and follow-up monitoring of anomalous incidents. Another response role is operations manager, incident manager or simply controller responsible for managing operations, measurements and incident resolution activities. The cyber-specific responsibilities include monitoring operating trends and response times, coordinating with field personnel and verifying responses to mitigation actions. The third response role is cyber security (forensic) investigator responsible for identifying and investigating cyber security anomalies and verifying the effectiveness of mitigation actions.

The analytics roles have a longer-term perspective into meta-forensics and strategic reviews. One analytics role is technical analyst responsible for forensic analyses of digital logs and after-action reviews. The cyber-specific responsibilities include reviewing and assessing the performance and stability of systems and devices over time, understanding and capturing systemic cyber security state baselines and issues, and creating and maintaining cyber scores for rating vendors on operational and cyber security reliability. The second analytics role is policy and compliance analyst responsible for safety and security reporting, compliance verification and decision support to system managers about workforce and operations policies. The cyber-specific responsibilities include assessing and summarizing system downtime and cyber events related to system and component failures.

5.2   CADOT Data Access and Display Needs

The second recommendation relates to data access and display needs:

- **Recommendation 2:** CADOT should provide multiple views into a potential cyber security situation based on the analytic needs of the moment.

Monitoring and response personnel attempt to understand if something is different from the normal (baseline) operational state. The CADOT system should provide active and passive monitoring tools that provide information about the system state: pushed (active) notifications if something is abnormal and query-based (passive) requests for supporting investigative operations. When something appears to be abnormal, personnel need the capability to drill into the data to understand what has gone wrong and why (i.e., root cause determination). The investigation role can be part of the monitoring and response roles. However, analytics personnel require a longer-term view of the cyber security state and need data at multiple levels of temporal granularity (hours, days, weeks, months and years). The analytics role is more focused on helping make long-term decisions about equipment and operations, and the effectiveness of security policies. However, it is important not to add complexity to an already complex system. Therefore, an integrated systems approach to use and augment existing practices and tools is appropriate and preferred for CADOT, instead of simply adding more applications and displays that must be checked.

5.3   CADOT Cyber Security Baseline

The third recommendation relates to a cyber security baseline:

- **Recommendation 3:** CADOT should operate with the notion of a baseline that expresses normal functioning.

The concepts of baseline, system stability and normal operations are foundational to the CADOT concept. These could include historically-derived operational and performance levels over time for controllers and devices and should be further parameterized by vendor or manufacturer and include historical maintenance log data.

Baselines need to capture recurring rhythms of activity at multiple levels of temporal granularity for dynamic component data. For example, energy usage and network activity baselines could consider per-day variations in usage during a typical day, per-week variations that account for weekend versus weekday usage, and per-year variations that account for seasonal influences. The baselines might also consider environmental factors such as weather and component lifecycle phases. The baselines could be considered as windows of acceptable or normal variability captured as rolling averages or historical visualizations over time.

Figure 2 depicts a notional example of this concept. Historical baseline temporal patterns can provide more effective indicators of possible trouble while minimizing false positives. It would take time to establish these baselines because up to six months, or even one year, of historical baseline data may be needed to accurately establish baselines. Additionally, baselines may be multi-faceted and complex, involving multiple sensor inputs to establish meaningful metrics. However, the workshop

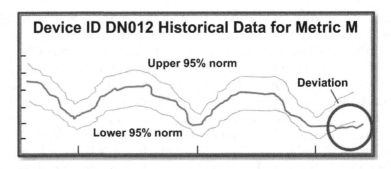

Figure 2. Notional use of historical baseline temporal patterns.

participants also cautioned that too many data sources or metrics should not be aggregated into one "all OK" sensor because it would be difficult to calibrate and would provide less meaningful information in investigations.

5.4   Relevant Additional Information

The fourth recommendation relates to deviations from the cyber security baseline:

- **Recommendation 4:** When a baseline deviation occurs, CADOT should attempt to provide information about possible external factors or influences.

Ideally, given a potential cyber security alert, CADOT should identify correlating events based on monitoring, and the SCADA management and control system. This would help determine the relevant issues and guide the investigation into possible causes. Additional relevant data could include device operational status, history and health, system operational and maintenance status, current and seasonal weather conditions, and other related historical or environmental data. This aspect admittedly implies a level of smarts that will need to be designed, developed and refined over time due to its inherent multi-variable nature. Potential external influences on deviations may be obvious or semi-predictable, and CADOT should do its best to provide this information immediately when possible.

The workshop participants preferred a three-level protocol for CADOT alerts when potentially harmful situations occur: green representing system OK, yellow representing a possible issue and red representing critical. This simple protocol would help operators prioritize responses.

Note also that a single root cause could cause multiple alerts, possibly at different levels and at different parts of a system.

Additionally, the workshop participants suggested that it would be very helpful if the CADOT system could guide the compliance process, such as the suggested or required order of responses, notifications and mitigation actions.

5.5   CADOT Monitoring Frequencies

The fifth recommendation relates to monitoring frequencies.

- **Recommendation 5:** Some (mostly static) state information should be made visible immediately because it could signal important alert situations.

The CADOT monitoring capability must be configurable to accommodate the urgency and importance of various cyber security situations. The workshop consensus was that general monitoring timeframes should be considered. For example, slow-changing items such as system configurations and logs may need long-term monitoring frequencies of days to weeks. More dynamic information, such as the health status of systems, networks and devices would need more frequent, short-term monitoring of minutes to hours. The health and status of critical devices and networks would need continuous, real-time monitoring in order to identify dangerous trends quickly. In the case of data that is typically unchanged except under controlled circumstances, such as device IDs, firmware versions and remote system logins, any change could indicate a serious problem and the CADOT tool must immediately issue alerts about these types of falling or rising changes. Finally, data that is only needed during investigations may not have to be monitored on a regular basis, but it should be available via interactive queries.

Table 3 summarizes the monitoring timeframes suggested for various data types. Note that some data items are listed in multiple timeframes due to differences in organizational policies and priorities. Therefore, the CADOT monitoring timelines must be configurable.

5.6   CADOT Query Support

The sixth recommendation relates to interactive query support:

- **Recommendation 6:** CADOT should provide a means to interactively query the various interfaces and components.

The CADOT system must provide an interactive query capability to support incident investigations and analyses. Query requests for data

Table 3. Suggested timeframes for monitoring data.

Timeframe	Data Type
Long Term (**Days/Wks.**)	**Boolean:** Firewall status, device integrity check
	Discrete: Device firmware number, last maintenance date, device last maintenance/inspection date
	Scalar: SCADA device baselines, SCADA safety system compromise indicators, network/bus states, device response latency
	Model: Weather conditions, maintenance logs, network changes, source/configuration changes, operating system artifacts, active/inactive attack surface
Short Term (**Mins./Hrs.**)	**Boolean:** Device availability, device integrity check, device performance level, device operation OK, device memory valid
	Discrete: Weather conditions, device performance level, last message from network device, device last login
	Scalar: Trend comparison with historical data, system operational status, network/bus states, device response latency
	Model: Weather conditions, device health
Immediate (**Real Time**)	**Boolean:** Device operation OK, device memory valid
	Discrete: Last message from network device
	Scalar: Device health, device operational status
On-Change	**Boolean:** Vendor/manufacturer diagnostic channels, device availability, device memory valid
	Discrete: Asset ID, device last login, device firmware last updated date
	Scalar: Device response latency
	Model: Device health, device firmware signature
On-Demand	**Boolean:** Device memory valid
	Discrete: Asset ID, device firmware version, device firmware last updated date
	Scalar: Trend comparison with historical data
	Model: Maintenance logs, weather conditions

vary based on response payload size and processing requirements. To avoid burdening the overall system, CADOT users will need assistance mechanisms to make decisions about interactively querying various interfaces and components depending on their needs. The assistance should enable users to create the most effective and efficient queries. Also, safeguards should be implemented to ensure that inadvertent large queries do not degrade system performance. CADOT query requirements depend on the root cause determination scenarios and processes that will have to be developed over time.

5.7 CADOT Data Extensibility

The seventh recommendation relates to data extensibility:

- **Recommendation 7:** CADOT should provide a means to plug in arbitrary data streams.

Sensors and devices continually evolve. Therefore, CADOT should future-proof itself as much as possible by considering sensor message handling for classes of data streams based on urgency and update frequency, nature of data and protocols, cost and benefit tradeoffs, and push versus pull data access. CADOT and its user interface should be able to handle new data streams that adhere to established rules, such as reusable widgets for similar data types, even if the sources differ. Other considerations include data interface type, temporal needs, API protocol and bus and network dependencies.

5.8 Configurable CADOT Alerting

The eighth recommendation relates to configurable alerts during deviations from baselines:

- **Recommendation 8:** CADOT should provide a means to set arbitrary running rules for alerts.

It is anticipated that operators will come to understand important nuances about what constitutes normal and emergency situations in their operational technology systems regardless of the level of automation employed by a mature CADOT implementation. Therefore, CADOT should include the ability to set customizable running rules that operators can define and manage interactively.

Figure 3 shows notional examples of user-definable running rules that alert based on simple one-metric thresholds (left) or more complex if-then rules based on multiple input metrics (right). The output alert levels are also definable.

5.9 CADOT Design Constraints

The ninth recommendation relates to accommodating device constraints:

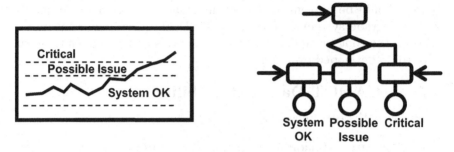

Figure 3. Notional examples of user-definable running rules.

- **Recommendation 9:** CADOT should be designed to accommodate the computational, power, network bandwidth and availability constraints on operational technology devices.

The heterogeneous nature of operational technology systems and devices means that their capabilities (or lack of capabilities) vary greatly. For example, devices with limited processing capacity may not be able to support encryption and authentication. Connections with network communications carriers may have downstream dependency implications on other parts of the networks. Devices also vary in their ability to communicate rapidly or continuously, which will require a range of update frequencies to be accommodated, from real-time/continuous to intermittent (e.g., hourly or daily) to on-demand only. CADOT should also define and leverage device interfaces to maximize compatibility and reuse.

6.   CADOT Key Design Features

The nine recommended requirements summarized above contributed to the specification of the following key design features to achieve an effective CADOT cyber security situational awareness capability:

- CADOT should strive to streamline operations and incident response with consistent cyber information. Duplication in monitoring displays and functionality should be avoided. Integration with existing tools and infrastructure should be maximized. Customizable groupings of related events and alerts should be provided.

- To render CADOT effective and adaptable, it should be able to establish and maintain baseline normal operation metrics of historical trends and cyber security metrics, establish normal limit thresholds and interactively manage user-defined running rules.

- CADOT displays and analysis support should be specialized for different user roles. This means that the CADOT user interface will have to be customizable, if not composable, by users. CADOT should support multiple temporal scales and user-defined running rules based on alerts, logs and associated data. To support near-term visual analytics until more advanced machine learning features can be developed, visualizations of current cyber security state data against historical trends and patterns at selectable temporal scales should be provided.

- Active (push-based information and alerts) and passive (query-based) monitoring should be implemented. CADOT users need the ability to drill down into issues from multiple perspectives. CADOT should provide access to all relevant data (e.g., environmental, associated metrics and historical context) that could help identify, assess and mitigate cyber security incidents.

- Future CADOT capability enhancements should support integration with an asset management system for associating devices with cyber events and a case management system for event tracking. However, a decision to evolve CADOT into a full security information and event management (SIEM) tool should be balanced against the potential complexity and utility of leveraging existing tools in this space.

7.   Commercially-Available Technologies

The next step in the CADOT design process is to review available technologies and tools that can be leveraged to address the recommended CADOT requirements and design features. Figure 4 shows a mapping of an initial sampling of commercially-available operational technology cyber security products (namely, Claroty, CyberX, Cynalytica, Dragos, Perspecta Labs, Tenable, SRI International (TIGR) [12] and Siemplify/Anomali) to accommodate the nine CADOT requirements. The pie charts indicate the degrees to which the commercial tools provide full, partial and no (missing) coverage of the CADOT requirements.

The initial sampling of commercial products appears to address many of the CADOT requirements. However, two CADOT requirements are not supported adequately by the sampled products. The ability to provide relevant associated or environmental data along with anomaly alerts to enable investigators to understand possible causes, and even whether alerts should be a priority, are largely non-existent at this time. Another CADOT requirement that is not well covered by commercial offerings

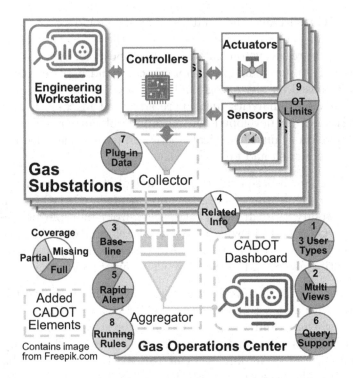

Figure 4. Mappings of cyber security technologies to meet CADOT needs.

is the ability to create user-defined running rules. This requirement is not well handled by the automated, historically-based-signature and pre-configured approaches of current products.

Additionally, while many cyber security products created for operational technology systems employ network-level monitoring, there is a growing, and currently unmet, need for operational technology devices, including programmable logic controllers, remote terminal units, bus devices, serial and analog devices, and other embedded electronic devices, that provide improved, built-in cyber awareness functionality. The needed vendor-provided device improvements include:

- Ability to continuously monitor the cyber security health of operational technology devices, especially internal memory and process control flow integrity.

- Ability to monitor network activities between system components.

- Ability to deflect or block adversarial attacks such as device memory injections, altered device control flows and unauthorized configuration modifications.

- Authentication framework for standardized, trusted and secure remediation and forensic analyses.

These improved devices and tools must be based on standardized protocols to ensure interoperability across vendors. They must also be compatible with commercially-available cyber security analytical tools and displays for effective and reliable integration in industrial control system environments. The new cyber-aware devices must operate under the unique environmental constraints imposed on operational technology devices, including small form factors, low power requirements, intermittent or limited communications bandwidth, and remote operation with limited physical monitoring and maintenance.

While operational technology vendors have attempted to address the need for cyber-aware and cyber-secure operational technology systems and devices, there is more to be done. The capability requirements discussed in this chapter represent the most important gaps that should be addressed to provide adequate awareness of the cyber security states of operational technology systems. Future work will continue the evaluation of cyber security products for addressing the requirements. The consortium of natural gas distribution utilities will work with vendors to define needed cyber security enhancements, collaborate on their development and provide independent testing and validation. These are the important next steps to provide operational technology asset owners and operators with the means to identify cyber security issues in a timely manner and address them before the physical assets they monitor and control are damaged.

8. Conclusions

Operational technology systems that manage and control critical infrastructure assets are vulnerable to cyber attacks. It is necessary to establish and maintain reliable monitoring of the cyber security health of these systems and continually provide operators with awareness of the true states of their systems. There is growing, but limited, availability of technologies and tools that provide the needed cyber security awareness.

This chapter has summarized collaboration efforts with members of the natural gas distribution sector on developing a set of recommended functional requirements for operational technology-based cyber security health monitoring and awareness systems. The design-driven process is reviewed and the nine key recommendations for securing operational technology systems are discussed.

An initial review of commercially-available products suggests that they address many of the recommended requirements. However, while the operational technology community has invested considerable effort in developing cyber-aware and cyber-secure systems and devices, much more remains to be done. Future work will continue the collaboration with the natural gas distribution sector and the operational technology community to continue to advance the state of the art in this domain that is vital to critical infrastructure protection.

Any opinions, findings, conclusions or recommendations expressed in this chapter are those of the authors and do not necessarily reflect the views of the U.S. Department of Homeland Security, Gas Technology Institute or individual utilities, and should not be interpreted as necessarily representing the official policies or endorsements, either expressed or implied, of the U.S. Department of Homeland Security, U.S. Government, Gas Technology Institute or individual utilities.

Acknowledgements

This research was sponsored by the U.S. Department of Homeland Security Science and Technology Directorate (DHS S&T) under Contract No. HSHQDC-16-C-00034. The authors thank DHS S&T Program Manager, Mr. Gregory Wigton, for his guidance and support. The authors also thank Dr. Tony Tang from the University of Toronto for his assistance in coordinating and facilitating the CADOT ideation workshop. Additionally, the authors thank Mr. Matthew Manning from the Gas Technology Institute and the utility representatives who completed the CADOT survey and/or participated in the CADOT ideation workshop.

References

[1] Cybersecurity and Infrastructure Security Agency, Alert (AA20-205A) NSA and CISA recommended immediate actions to reduce exposure across operational technologies and control systems, Arlington, Virginia (www.us-cert.cisa.gov/ncas/alerts/aa20-205a), October 24, 2020.

[2] Cybersecurity and Infrastructure Security Agency, Securing Industrial Control Systems: A Unified Initiative, FY2019–2023, Arlington, Virginia (www.cisa.gov/sites/default/files/publications/Securing_Industrial_Control_Systems_S508C.pdf), 2020.

[3] Cybersecurity and Infrastructure Security Agency, Assessments, Arlington, Virginia (`us-cert.cisa.gov/ics/Assessments`), 2021.

[4] Cybersecurity and Infrastructure Security Agency, Downloading and installing Cyber Security Evaluation Tool (CSET), Arlington, Virginia (`us-cert.cisa.gov/ics/Downloading-and-Installing-CSET`), 2021.

[5] K. Davis, Texas A&M: CYPRES, Cybersecurity for Energy Delivery Systems Peer Review, Texas A&M Engineering Experiment Station, College Station, Texas (`www.energy.gov/ceser/cybersecurity-energy-delivery-systems-2020-peer-review-presentations`), October 6-7, 2020.

[6] Dragos, Dragos: Neighborhood Keeper, Cybersecurity for Energy Delivery Systems Peer Review, Hanover, Maryland (`www.energy.gov/ceser/cybersecurity-energy-delivery-systems-2020-peer-review-presentations`), 2020.

[7] D. Gammel, Schweitzer Engineering Laboratories: Ambassador, Cybersecurity for Energy Delivery Systems Peer Review, Schweitzer Engineering Laboratories, Pullman, Washington (`www.energy.gov/ceser/cybersecurity-energy-delivery-systems-2020-peer-review-presentations`), 2020.

[8] Gas Technology Institute, Identifying and Addressing High-Priority Cybersecurity Issues, Des Plaines, Illinois (`www.gti.energy/identifying-and-addressing-high-priority-cybersecurity-issues`), 2021.

[9] Hasso Plattner Institute of Design, Getting Started with Design Thinking, Stanford University, Stanford, California (`www.dschool.stanford.edu/resources/getting-started-with-design-thinking`), 2021.

[10] C. Hurd and M. McCarty, A Survey of Security Tools for the Industrial Control System Environment, INL/EXT-17-42229 Revision 1, Idaho National Laboratory, Idaho Falls, Idaho, 2017.

[11] M. Locasto and D. Balenson, A comparative analysis approach for deriving failure scenarios in the natural gas distribution infrastructure, in *Critical Infrastructure Protection XIII*, J. Staggs and S. Shenoi (Eds.), Springer, Cham, Switzerland, pp. 19–50, 2019.

[12] M. Locasto and D. Balenson, Threat intelligence for grid recovery, presented at the *More Situational Awareness for Industrial Control Systems (MOSAICS) Industry Day* (`www.rdp21.org/wp-content/uploads/2020/11/MOSAICS-Industry-Day-SRI-TIGR-v3-1.pdf`), 2020.

[13] J. McCarthy, O. Alexander, S. Edwards, D. Faatz, C. Peloquin, S. Symington, A. Thibault, J. Wiltberger and K. Viani, Situational Awareness for Electric Utilities, NIST Special Publication 1800-7, National Institute of Standards and Technology, Gaithersburg, Maryland, 2019.

[14] M. Nielsen, General Electric: Natural Gas Compression, Cybersecurity for Energy Delivery Systems Peer Review, GE Research, Niskayuna, New York (www.energy.gov/ceser/cyber security-energy-delivery-systems-2020-peer-review-prese ntations), 2020.

[15] Office of Cybersecurity, Energy Security and Emergency Response, 2020 Cybersecurity for Energy Delivery Systems Peer Review, U.S. Department of Energy, Washington, DC (www. energy.gov/ceser/articles/2020-cybersecurity-energy-del ivery-systems-peer-review), 2020.

[16] Office of Cybersecurity, Energy Security and Emergency Response, Cybersecurity for Energy Delivery Systems 2020 Peer Review Presentations, U.S. Department of Energy, Washington, DC (www.energy.gov/ceser/cybersecurity-energy-del ivery-systems-2020-peer-review-presentations), 2020.

[17] Office of Cybersecurity, Energy Security and Emergency Response, Cybersecurity Research, Development and Demonstration (RD&D) for Energy Delivery Systems, U.S. Department of Energy, Washington, DC (www.energy.gov/ceser/activities/ cybersecurity-critical-energy-infrastructure/cybersecur ity-research-development-and), 2020.

[18] Office of Electricity, Liberty Eclipse Energy Cyber Incident Exercise, Exercise Summary Report, U.S. Department of Energy, Washington, DC (www.energy.gov/sites/default/files/ 2017/05/f34/LE%20FINAL%20Exercise%201May2017_ Public%20Doc.pdf), 2017.

[19] Transportation Security Administration, Pipeline Security Guidelines, Springfield, Virginia (www.tsa.gov/sites/default/files/ pipeline_security_guidelines.pdf), 2021.

Chapter 3

ANALYZING ADVANCED PERSISTENT THREATS USING GAME THEORY: A CRITICAL LITERATURE REVIEW

Rajesh Kumar, Siddhant Singh and Rohan Kela

Abstract   Advanced persistent threats present significant security challenges due to their customized, stealthy and adaptive nature. Since no generic solution exists to combat advanced persistent threats, the recommended option is to employ information security best practices. While practitioner-oriented security guidelines have been published by the International Organization for Standardization and the U.S. National Institute of Standards and Technology, they cannot be employed in rigorous quantitative analyses required for objective decision making such as choosing countermeasures that balance security, cost and usability. In contrast, game-theoretic approaches, which express the behavior of rational agents that maximize their utility, provide appropriate models for objective decision making.

This chapter conducts a critical analysis of several game-theoretic approaches for analyzing advanced persistent threats. Eleven highly-cited, peer-reviewed articles from the research literature are examined in terms of their objectives, features, game models and solutions. The models provide valuable insights into advanced persistent threat behavior, support resource-optimal decision making and can be mapped to the various risk management stages. However, they have some delicate modeling and analysis limitations. The critical analysis exposes the omissions in the literature and points to future research focused on integrating practitioner perspectives in game-theoretic approaches to advance information security risk management.

Keywords: Advanced persistent threats, game theory, literature review

1.   Introduction

Critical infrastructure assets utilize advanced automation, computation and communications technologies to provide vital goods and ser-

© IFIP International Federation for Information Processing 2022
Published by Springer Nature Switzerland AG 2022
J. Staggs and S. Shenoi (Eds.): Critical Infrastructure Protection XV, IFIP AICT 636, pp. 45–69, 2022.
https://doi.org/10.1007/978-3-030-93511-5_3

vices [39]. However, these assets, which were historically isolated from the outside world, now connect directly or indirectly to the Internet. The increased connectivity exposes the assets to cyber attacks that exploit vulnerabilities arising from connecting multiple heterogeneous components.

Advanced persistent threats are a sophisticated and dreaded class of attacks that have received much attention in the context of industrial control systems used across the critical infrastructure sectors [6]. These threats, which are manifested by expert and well-resourced adversaries, are customized, stealthy and adaptive in nature. As a result, they can cause significant harm to critical infrastructure assets. An example is the notorious Stuxnet virus that reportedly damaged nearly a thousand uranium hexafluoride centrifuges in Iran's Natanz facility [23].

Advanced persistent threats are difficult to combat because they are highly sophisticated and customized. In fact, accurate detection and prevention of advanced persistent threats are considered to be impractical [41]. Therefore, the best option is to plan ahead of the attackers by instituting pervasive information security hygiene that adopts security best practices, customizes security needs based on the perceived threats, patches vulnerabilities, devises back-up plans for emergencies and compromises, institutes security awareness and training, etc. While numerous security guidelines have been published by entities such as the International Organization for Standardization [19] and the National Institute of Standards and Technology [40], they cannot be engaged in rigorous quantitative analysis models required for objective decision making such as selecting countermeasures that balance security, cost and usability.

Game-theoretic approaches, which express the behavior of rational agents that maximize their utility, are well-suited for objective decision making. This chapter conducts a critical analysis of game-theoretic approaches for analyzing advanced persistent threats. Eleven highly-cited, peer-reviewed articles from the research literature are examined in terms of their objectives, features, game models and solutions. The models provide valuable insights into advanced persistent threat behavior, support resource-optimal decision making and can be mapped to the various risk management stages. However, they have some delicate modeling and analysis limitations. The critical analysis also exposes the omissions in the literature and points to future research focused on integrating practitioner perspectives in game-theoretic approaches to advance information security risk management.

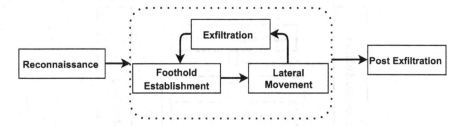

Figure 1. Advanced persistent threat attack stages.

2. Preliminaries

This section briefly discusses advanced persistent threats, information security risk management and game theory.

2.1 Advanced Persistent Threats

An advanced persistent threat is an adversary with sophisticated expertise and significant resources that enable it to create opportunities to achieve its objectives by leveraging multiple attack vectors [20]. An advanced persistent threat attack is sophisticated and customized to the vulnerabilities of the targeted entity.

Figure 1 shows the typical stages in an advanced persistent threat attack. The attack involves five stages:

- **Reconnaissance:** The attacker scans and monitors the targeted entity, understands the landscape and hunts the network for potential entry points. After an entry point is identified, the attacker harvests information from websites, social media and other available resources to bootstrap an attack.

- **Foothold Establishment:** The attacker identifies vulnerabilities to exploit and/or employs social engineering techniques in order to infiltrate the targeted system.

- **Lateral Movement:** Upon gaining a foothold, the attacker scans the internal network environment and searches for vulnerabilities that may not be visible from outside the network. The attacker exploits the identified vulnerabilities, creates multiple covert communications channels and moves within the network, all the while attempting to escalate its privileges and move to its goal.

- **Exfiltration:** Having gained access to sensitive information in the network, the attacker exfiltrates the information using its covert

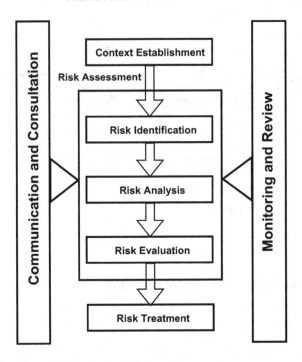

Figure 2. Information security risk management stages.

communications channels. Depending on the motive, the attacker may vitiate and/or impair hardware and software systems in the compromised network.

- **Post Exfiltration:** Upon attaining its objective, the attacker removes all traces of its presence and may leave backdoors to target the entity in the future.

2.2   Information Security Risk Management

Information security risk is the potential that a threat will exploit the vulnerabilities of an asset or group of assets belonging to an entity and cause harm [40]. Information security risk management involves the continuous identification, review, treatment and monitoring of information security risks to achieve risk acceptance [47].

Figure 2 shows the information security risk management stages based on the ISO 31000 guidelines [19]. The five information security risk management stages are:

- **Context Establishment:** The entity establishes the scope and boundaries of risk management. To set the criteria against which risk will be assessed, the context must align with the objectives of the entity. A study is conducted to understand the landscape of the entity and determine the internal and external parameters for managing risk.

- **Risk Identification** The events that hinder, alter or delay the achievement of the entity's objective are identified and elucidated. This includes a complete decomposition of the entity's assets, associated vulnerabilities and potential threats. Risks that are not identified during this stage are not revisited in the ensuing stages. Therefore, comprehensive risk identification is essential.

- **Risk Analysis:** An understanding of the risk is developed. For each scenario, the consequences of the risk and its likelihood of occurrence are evaluated against the baseline security measures. The results help identify the risk treatment options.

- **Risk Evaluation:** The outcomes of risk analysis are classified and ranked. This enables security practitioners to allocate resources for mitigation actions.

- **Risk Treatment:** A range of controls are considered to mitigate the risk. The efficacy of each option is assessed and a decisive plan is executed to implement the selected controls.

2.3   Game Theory

Game theory is the study of mathematical models of conflict and cooperation between intelligent and rational decision makers [32]. It provides an elegant framework to reason about advanced persistent threat attributes such as stealth and uncertainty. Consequently, game theory is a natural choice for formally reasoning about strategic interactions and capturing constraints on attacker incentives, defense resource allocations and attack impacts.

Game theory has been applied to a variety of important information security and decision-theoretic problems. Applications of game theory include intrusion detection [22], network security [26], cyber insurance [43] and smart grids [48]. Interested readers are referred to [14, 16, 25, 46] for additional details about game theory.

3.   Literature Review

This chapter critically analyzes the highly-cited literature on game-theoretic approaches for advanced persistent threat analysis. Unlike seminal surveys of advanced persistent threats that enumerate historical advanced persistent threats [2, 21] or identify the characteristics or stages of advanced persistent threats [3, 6], this work focuses on advanced persistent threats from the information security risk management perspective. Information security risk management refers to the techniques and tools used to predict and prioritize risks, and identify and deploy the most appropriate countermeasures that minimize the residual risk. This perspective provides a wide lens to analyze advanced persistent threats focused on critical infrastructure assets and target their entire lifecycles via prevention, monitoring, assessment and response.

Following the systematic literature review process of Luh et al. [27], eleven articles were curated for the survey. The articles were selected using keyphrase searches at three popular academic research websites, Google Scholar [15], Microsoft Academic [30] and ScienceDirect [10]. Three sets of keyphrases were used: (i) advanced persistent threat + game theory, (ii) APT + game theory and (iii) Stuxnet + game theory.

The search results were reviewed manually. Articles not in English, articles published before 2010 and survey papers, magazine articles, workshop reports and commercial reports were excluded. The search results were filtered according to the number of citations on Google Scholar as of December 15, 2020. An initial suitability review was conducted by judging the title, abstract and conclusions. The primary focus during article curation was to cover the breadth of techniques and applications.

The next step was to select articles that present a framework, model or method focused on targeted attacks, multistage attacks and other attacks with characteristics of advanced persistent threats. Additionally, the selected articles had to focus on representing, detecting and/or preventing advanced persistent threat attacks. Also, the articles had to adopt holistic perspectives of advanced persistent threat attacks instead of merely focusing on specific security mechanisms.

The literature on game-theoretic approaches for advanced persistent threats is sparse, with most works published between 1995 and 2019. Although the final selection of eleven articles may seem low, steps were taken during the curation to ensure that the articles adequately covered game models, solutions and application areas. The articles are classified into two broad categories, application areas discussed in Section 4 and metrics discussed in Section 5.

4. Application-Area-Based Classification

This section discusses the surveyed game-theoretic approaches used for advanced persistent threat analysis. The surveyed articles are placed in four classes based on their application areas: (i) resource allocation, (ii) cyber deception, (iii) information leakage and (iv) optimal design. The goal of the classification is to organize the diverse approaches for clarity. Tables 1 and 2 summarize the surveyed articles, including their objectives, features, game models and solutions.

4.1 Resource Allocation

Resource allocation is the optimal distribution of resources to minimize the likelihood of an attack and its potential damage by prioritizing the order of protection of critical assets. Three articles are placed in the resource allocation class.

The article by Huang and Zhu [18] models attacker and defender interactions as a multistage dynamic game. The model assumes that the defender has already deployed some countermeasures at each stage that can thwart the attacker. The model comprises k stages, where each stage corresponds to a sub-game. At the end of each stage, the two players obtain payoffs based on their interactions. The attacker has two payoff configurations labeled adversarial and legitimate. The defender has two payoff configurations labeled sophisticated and primitive.

The players receive rewards and penalties based on their interactions. Each player seeks to maximize the expected cumulative utility. At each stage, a player performs an action based on available information and forms a belief about the other player. At the end of a stage, the beliefs are updated using a Bayesian rule with Markov approximations. The solution obtained using an iterative dynamic programming algorithm is a perfect Bayesian Nash equilibrium. The article demonstrates the utility of the approach using a hypothetical case study involving the compromise of a SCADA system that manages the well-known Tennessee Eastman process in which an attacker seeks to reduce the operational efficiency.

The article by Rass and Zhu [37] models attacker and defender interactions as a multistage dynamic game. Defensive strategies are designed to prevent the attacker from reaching a central asset. The model input is a system that is segmented into layers according to their distances from the central asset. The game model is a sequence of nested games, where the attacker seeks to reach the target from the outermost layer. During the game, the attacker may be detected via random inspection by the defender. Upon succeeding with a certain likelihood at a given

Table 1. Summary of the game-theoretic advanced persistent threat approaches.

Article (Year, Citations)	Objective	Features	Game Model	Solution
Huang and Zhu [18] (2020, 32)	Defense in depth	Multistage game, Dynamic programming algorithm	Dynamic nonzero-sum game with incomplete information	Perfect Bayesian Nash equilibrium (PBNE) (mixed strategy), β−PBNE
Rass and Zhu [37] (2016, 38)	Defense in depth	Multistage game, Sequential finite recursive game, Complete information	Two-player zero-sum game	Saddle-point equilibrium
Hu et al. [17] (2015, 110)	Model of a malicious insider	Continuous time, Imperfect information, Static and dynamic attack rates/recapture rates	Two-player differential game	Nash equilibrium
Min et al. [31] (2018, 39)	Optimal CPU allocation	Colonel Blotto game, Complete information, Reinforcement learning, Cloud security	Two-player zero-sum game	Nash equilibrium (mixed strategy)
Xiao et al. [49] (2017, 77)	Attack deterrence via optimal scanning of storage devices	Prospect theory, Cloud storage, Bounded rationality, Q-learning, Asymmetric information	Two-player static and dynamic game	Nash equilibrium (pure strategy; mixed strategy)
Yang et al. [50] (2018, 38)	Optimal repair	Repair strategies, Epidemic modeling, Dynamic game	Two-player differential game	Nash equilibrium

Table 2. Summary of the game-theoretic advanced persistent threat approaches (continued).

Article (Year, Citations)	Objective	Features	Game Model	Solution
Tian et al. [42] (2019, 7)	Optimal honeypot allocation strategy	Incomplete information, Honeypot, Resource constraints, One-shot game	Bayesian game	Bayesian Nash equilibrium
Zhu and Basar [51] (2013, 118)	Dynamic reconfiguration of attack surface under minimum cost	Multistage game, Online learning, Continuous time, Complete/incomplete information	Two-player zero-sum game	Saddle-point equilibrium (mixed strategy)
van Dijk et al. [44] (2012, 233)	Control of a shared resource with minimum cost	Infinite game, adaptive/non-adaptive strategies, Complete information, Continuous time	Two player multistage game	Nash equilibrium
Pawlick et al. [35] (2015, 78)	Trust in the cloud	Signaling game, FlipIt game, Continuous time, Periodic strategy, Incomplete information	Dynamic Bayesian game plus two-player multistage game	Gestalt equilibrium
Rass et al. [36] (2017, 69)	Multi-criteria decision making	Complete information, Loss distribution, Fictitious play algorithm, Asymmetric information, Qualitative data, Uncertain payoff	Two-player zero-sum game	Saddle-point equilibrium

stage, the attacker chooses to enter the next stage or remain at the same
stage. The attacker incurs a cost during a move. The defender deploys
preventive and detective measures with a randomized inspection strategy to maximize the cost to the attacker. Each sub-game is a finite
zero-sum game in which the strategic attacker-defender interactions determine the structure of the sub-game in the next stage. The article
presents a closed-form recursive approach to obtain a saddle-point equilibrium. Toy examples are used to demonstrate the applicability of the
approach. However, the article does not describe any tool support for
the approach.

The article by Rass et al. [36] models attacker and defender interactions as a two-player zero-sum game. Several attacker attributes typical
of advanced persistent threat scenarios, such as attacker moves, data uncertainty and attacker payoff uncertainty, are considered. The attributes
are quantified using continuous, totally-ordered distributions as payoffs.
The distributions are constructed based on qualitative data provided by
experts. The input to the model is a set of attack paths obtained using
topological vulnerability analysis and a set of countermeasures. The set
of attack paths comprises all the advanced persistent threat scenarios.
A saddle-point equilibrium solution is obtained. Several toy examples
and simulations are provided to demonstrate the utility of the approach.

4.2   Cyber Deception

Cyber deception tricks attackers and defenders by propagating false
beliefs and behaving against their vested interests [34]. Two articles
are placed in this class due to their use of cyber deception techniques,
namely, honeypots and moving target defenses.

The article by Tian et al. [42] models the interactions between an
advanced persistent threat attacker and resource-constrained honeypot
defender as an incomplete static game. The defender can employ two
types of honeypots, high interaction and low interaction honeypots. A
high interaction honeypot emulates a real server and provides adequate
information about attacker malicious behavior, but its maintenance requires considerable human effort. A low interaction honeypot provides
limited functionality and is less expensive to maintain. Two types of
attacks are considered, strong access and weak access, based on attack
costs. The resource constraints for a defender are personnel costs for
analyzing honeypot data and operating system costs. The asymmetric
information game model assumes that the defender's actions are observable. A Bayesian Nash equilibrium solution is obtained. Numerical
simulations are provided to demonstrate the approach.

The article by Zhu and Basar [51] models the strategic interactions between an attacker and defender as a two-player zero-sum game. The input is a multilayered system in which an attacker seeks to launch a multistage attack, conducting intrusions and compromising the assets in each layer. The defender deploys a moving target defense as a proactive measure by varying the system configurations across the layers to manipulate the attack surface dynamically and minimize the damage. Increased security using moving target defense contributes to an increased usability cost. An optimal configuration policy is sought that minimizes the damage inflicted by the attacker. A saddle-point equilibrium solution under a mixed strategy is obtained after repeated plays. Numerical simulations of toy examples are provided to demonstrate the utility of the approach.

4.3   Information Leakage

Information leakage is the intentional or inadvertent disclosure of sensitive information [1]. Two articles are placed in this class, one involving malicious insiders and the other involving information leakage from the cloud.

The article by Hu et al. [17] investigates the interactions between an advanced persistent threat attacker who works with malicious insiders to trade information in lieu of benefits against a defender. A two-layer game model is employed, where the first layer models the strategic interactions between the attacker and defender, and the second layer models the interactions between the attacker and malicious insiders. The inputs are the system model, one advanced persistent threat attacker, one defender and a certain number of insiders. The state of the system evolves with time with the attacker capturing the resources at some rate and defender recapturing the compromised resources at some rate. The actions of the attacker and defender result in instantaneous costs based on the state evolution at any time instant, capture and recapture rates, required resources and risk appetites of the players. The defender seeks to minimize the damage while the attacker seeks to minimize the attack cost. The insiders seek to maximize their individual profits over the long term. The system state is modeled as a differential equation. Two settings are considered, static and dynamic. In the static case, the attacker cannot adapt to the system state (i.e., the capture and recapture rates are set). In the dynamic case, the players can choose their optimal actions according to the system state. In both cases, the optimal solutions are Nash equilibria. An iterative numerical solution employing the steepest descent method is obtained for the dynamic case. Numerical simulations of toy examples are used to demonstrate the approach.

The article by Pawlick et al. [35] studies interactions between three players, an advanced persistent threat attacker, cloud device and remote cloud-controlled device. The cloud can be compromised by the attacker without being detected. The device can follow its onboard autonomous operation system if it believes a message it receives is from the compromised cloud. The problem is modeled as two coupled games, a signaling game between the device and possibly compromised cloud, and a repeated game similar to a FlipIt game [44] between the attacker and cloud defender. The solution is a Gestalt equilibrium, an equilibrium where a perfect Bayesian equilibrium in the signaling game and Nash equilibrium in the FlipIt game are satisfied simultaneously. A case study involving a cloud-controlled vehicle is used to illustrate the approach.

4.4   Optimal Design

Optimal design is concerned with establishing a desirable equilibrium by varying the design parameters. The objective is to obtain the highest return by balancing security against usability, budget, etc. [5]. Four articles are placed in the optimal design class. The articles deal with the optimal number of scanning devices in cloud storage to ensure minimum information leakage, optimal scan interval for a defender, optimal repair strategy and cost-optimal strategy for controlling shared resources.

The article by Min et al. [31] focuses on the optimal allocation of central processing units (CPUs) to storage devices under resource constraints. The defender uses the CPUs to scan the storage devices to detect and minimize information leakage whereas the attacker uses the CPUs to steal data while remaining stealthy. The CPU allocation problem is modeled as a Colonel Blotto game, a type of two-player zero-sum game. The solution is a Nash equilibrium under a mixed strategy. Each player randomizes its actions to deceive the opponent. The attacker seeks to steal as much data as possible from the storage devices using a subset of the CPUs while remaining undetected. The defender seeks to scan the storage devices using a subset of CPUs to detect the advanced persistent threat and minimize damage. The attacker and defender can use a time-division technique to scan the storage devices using a single CPU in a time slot. If the number of CPUs used by the attacker is greater than the number of CPUs used by the defender at any time, the data is considered to be at risk. The utility to the attacker or defender depends on the data that is safe and the amount of data in the storage devices at a given time due to defender intervention. The CPU allocation problem is modeled as a Markov decision process, where the defender observes the CPU allocation in the previous attack and the current data storage distribution. Improved policy learning algorithms, specifically, the host booting policy hill climbing and deep-Q network algorithms, are used to accelerate learning in the Markov decision process. Numerical results are used to showcase the utility of the approach.

The article by Xiao et al. [49] studies the influence of subjective attacker decisions against a defender. Both the agents attempt to control storage devices. The model inputs are the number of storage devices that can be scanned by an advanced persistent threat attacker upon choosing an attack interval/action and a defender who chooses a scan interval to recapture the compromised storage devices. The attacker bears the attack cost and the defender is rewarded with a gain for detection. The game model seeks to derive the optimal defender strategy for controlling the resources. The subjectivity involved in attacker decisions is modeled using prospect theory and Prelec weighting functions. The game is formulated in two ways, one is a static game with complete information and the other is a dynamic game used when the attacker model is not known; both the variations use pure and mixed strategies. The dynamic game employs a Markov decision process and Q-learning to obtain the optimal action policy. The game solution is a Nash equilibrium. Numerical examples are used to demonstrate how subjective attacker strategies impact the utility to the defender.

The article by Yang et al. [50] investigates optimal repair strategies for compromised hosts under the manpower and cost constraints. The model input is a system comprising a storage device and a number of hosts, each of which is in the on or off state. A host in the on (active) state can communicate with a storage server as well as other hosts that are in the on state; hosts in the off state are inactive. The hosts move between the on and off states depending on their required activity. Active hosts can be in the secure or insecure mode; they move from one mode to another based on the advanced persistent threat attack, lateral movement and repair policy. Cost functions are used to quantify the attacker reward based on the worst-case loss of sensitive information. Similarly, the defender pays a penalty for information leakage. The continuous-time dynamic system state evolution is modeled using a differential equation. The game solution is a Nash equilibrium. Numerical examples with toy examples and small case studies are used to demonstrate the utility of the approach.

The article by van Dijk et al. [44] considers an advanced persistent threat attacker that competes with a defender to control a shared resource. Each player can take an action to control the resource, which generates a payoff to the owner. The attacker seeks to learn the system configuration incrementally, remaining stealthy while minimizing the cost of movement. The defender seeks to control the shared resource using the minimum number of moves because each movement inflicts a cost. Each player can make a move at any point in time. If the players make a move at the same time, then the control of the resource is unchanged. The players are unaware of each other's moves and the controller of the shared resource, which is only revealed after they make their moves. Several types of feedback that players receive after their moves are considered, ranging from non-adaptive (renewal, periodic and exponential) to adaptive (full history and last move). In addition to player strategies, additional information is also considered when the game starts (no information, rate of play and knowledge of strategy). Numerical examples and simulations are provided to showcase the applicability of the approach.

5.   Metric-Based Classification

Most of the surveyed game-theoretic approaches focus on the equilibrium strategies of attackers and defenders, which depend on the types of game models used to represent the strategic situations. Therefore, the first classification of the surveyed articles (following the approach of Do et al. [9]) is based on game model types and solutions. Note that Tables 1 and 2 summarize the eleven surveyed articles based on objectives, features, game models and solutions.

The previous section classifies the articles based on their application areas. This section classifies the articles based on their mappings to the risk management process. To accomplish this, several metrics are specified in this section.

5.1   Mitigation Measures

Mitigation measures are broadly classified as proactive measures and reactive measures [2]:

- **Proactive Measures (PRO):** Proactive mitigation keeps a defender ahead of an attacker by deploying controls that dynamically change the attack surface. Proactive measures include moving target defense [24], randomization and honeypots [7].

- **Reactive Measures (REA):** In reactive mitigation, a defender follows the steps taken by an attacker all the while attempting to prevent its advances, limit its spread and reduce the damage.

Reactive measures are applied in the prevent, detect and respond phases:

- **Prevent (P):** Prevent measures seek to restrict the movements of attackers. An attack is slowed or mitigated based on attacker capabilities and ability to subvert defenses. For example, access control mechanisms can block attacker progress until the mechanisms are subverted by the attacker.

- **Detect (D):** Detect measures seek to identify attacks. An example is signature-based intrusion detection. Note that detect measures are distinct from prevent measures in that they do not hinder the attacker.

- **Respond (R):** Respond measures seek to contain attacks in a timely manner. An example is the installation of a software patch to address a vulnerability. Respond measures can be viewed in a broader context to include measures that ensure continuity of service, for example, by rebooting, repairing and reallocating more resources. Also, respond measures can reduce the damage due to attacks, for example, by using a risk transfer technique such as cyber insurance.

The second column in Table 3 shows the classification of articles based on mitigation measures. Analysis of the eleven articles reveals that the majority of the models adopt reactive measures. Only three articles, by Huang and Zhu [18], Tian et al. [42] and Zhu and Basar [51], leverage proactive mitigation strategies. The articles dealing with reactive measures mainly focus on the prevent and respond phases. Only the article by Rass and Zhu [37] focuses on the detect phase.

5.2 Risk Management Stages

Risk management stages adhering to the ISO 31000 guidelines [19] are considered in this work. The five risk management stages are: (i) context establishment (CE), (ii) risk identification (RI), (iii) risk analysis (RA), (iv) risk evaluation (RE) and (v) risk treatment (RT).

The third column in Table 3 shows the classification of articles based on their coverage of the risk management stages. All the reviewed articles deal with risk analysis while only a few deal with risk treatment. The risk identification and risk evaluation stages are not emphasized in any of the surveyed articles. Additionally, most of the articles do not focus on context establishment. This is because context establishment is an informal process that is not amenable to formal analysis using a game-theoretic model.

Table 3. Metric-based classification of the game-theoretic advanced persistent threat approaches.

Article	Mitigation Measures (Phases)	Risk Management Stages	APT Stages	Validation Methods	Model Assumptions	Tool Support
Huang and Zhu [18]	REA (P, R), PRO	RA, RT	All	THE, HYP	IND, STA, RAT	None
Rass and Zhu [37]	REA (P, D)	RA	All	HYP, THE	RAT, STA, IND	None
Hu et al. [17]	REA (R)	RA	All	HYP, THE	RAT	None
Min et al. [31]	REA (R)	RA, RT	Ex	HYP, THE	RAT, IND	None
Xiao et al. [49]	REA (R)	RA	Ex	HYP, THE	IND	None
Yang et al. [50]	REA (R)	RT	PEx	HYP, THE, SIM	RAT	None
Tian et al. [42]	PRO	RA	RE	THE, HYP	STA, RAT	None
Zhu and Basar [51]	PRO	RA	All	HYP, THE	RAT, IND	None
van Dijk et al. [44]	REA (P, R)	RA, RT	All	THE, HYP	RAT, IND	None
Pawlick et al. [35]	REA (P)	RA	Ex	THE, HYP	STA, RAT	None
Rass et al. [36]	REA (P)	RA	All	THE, HYP	RAT, STA, IND	None

5.3 Advanced Persistent Threat Stages

The five advanced persistent threat stages considered in this work are:
(i) reconnaissance (RE), (ii) foothold establishment (FE), (iii) lateral
movement (LM), (iv) exfiltration (Ex) and (v) post exfiltration (PEx).

The fourth column in Table 3 shows the classification of articles based
on their coverage of the advanced persistent threat stages. Most of
the reviewed articles cover the spectrum of advanced persistent threat
stages. However, the articles by Tian et al. [42] and Yang et al. [50]
focus exclusively on reconnaissance and post exfiltration, respectively;
the approaches are not relevant to any of the other stages.

5.4 Validation Methods

The validation methods considered in this work are drawn from Verendel [45]. The four types of validation methods are:

- **Empirical (EMP):** Empirical methods involve systematic experimental gathering of data from operational settings.

- **Hypothetical (HYP):** Hypothetical methods employ hypothetical (conceptual as opposed to realistic) examples that may not be
  closely related to actual phenomena and have limited degrees of
  realism.

- **Simulation (SIM):** Simulation methods rely on simulations.

- **Theoretical (THE):** Theoretical methods engage formal or precise theoretical arguments to support the results.

The fifth column in Table 3 shows the classification of articles based
on validation methods. The surveyed articles primarily employ hypothetical and theoretical validation methods. This is a drawback because
no comments can be made about model scalability and practical applications.

5.5 Model Assumptions

The model assumptions used to evaluate the surveyed game-theoretic
approaches are inspired by Verendel [45]. However, compositionality is
not considered because it not deeply rooted in game theory. The three
model assumptions are:

- **Rationality (RAT):** Most game-theoretic models are based on
  expected utility theory, which assumes rational player behavior.
  Given several actions, a player always chooses the action that yields

the highest utility. This assumption may not always hold in information security settings. As a result, several game-theoretic models do not use expected utility theory and instead employ, for example, prospect theory [29].

- **Stationarity (STA):** Stationarity implies that the model parameters are invariant with time. This is an important metric, because in real scenarios, player actions are continuous over time. Many game-theoretic model assume stationarity to simplify computations.

- **Independence (IND):** Many models, especially stochastic models, consider random events to be independent (e.g., exponential distribution). This assumption may not be realistic, but it simplifies model computations.

The sixth column in Table 3 shows the classification of articles based on model assumptions. Note that the vast majority of surveyed articles assume rational player behavior, which may not hold in practice.

5.6   Tool Support

The tool support metric considers if a model is supported by a practitioner-usable tool. The seventh column in Table 3 shows the classification of articles based on tool support. Unfortunately, none of the surveyed articles explicitly mention a commercial tool or prototype that could support its game-theoretic approach.

6.   Critical Analysis

Advanced persistent threat attacks are sophisticated. Addressing them is challenging due to the uncertainty about attacker moves and the fact that customized instead of generic defensive solutions are needed. At best, an entity can attempt to keep ahead of the unknown adversary by patching known vulnerabilities, closing potential backdoors and adopting risk management best practices. Even if a defender is constantly alert to attacks, it cannot be sure of the presence of the invisible adversary, let alone its actions and incentives.

Game theory is a promising paradigm for tackling the uncertainty inherent in advanced persistent threats. Its mathematical rigor empowers security practitioners with techniques and tools to make informed, objective and transparent decisions. The growing popularity of game-theoretic models is evidenced by the rich set of articles on the subject that target diverse application areas.

This chapter has explored game-theoretic models designed at different abstractions, each with varying assumptions about the available information, agent incentives, moves, resource constraints, etc. The strategic situations vary from modeling a single application domain such as cloud security to supporting a multilayered approach such as defense in depth. A few articles consider malicious insiders during the important reconnaissance stage of advanced persistent threats. Other articles provide different mitigation solutions, target different advanced persistent threat stages and lay the foundation for security by design. Some articles consider the use of proactive defenses with adaptive strategies, such as honeypots and moving target defense mechanisms, to detect and block attackers at an early stage. The game-theoretic models are diverse – games with incomplete information, stochastic games, extensive form games, Bayesian games, inspection games and multi-player games with complete/incomplete information.

While game-theoretic models can help understand attacker behaviors and incentives, they are founded on certain assumptions, such as unbounded rationality on the part of players, which may not be realistic. This is a limitation in many of the surveyed articles. However, there are articles in which such constraints are relaxed. For example, Xiao et al. [49] employ prospect theory and Prelec weighting functions to model bounded rational behavior.

Certain challenges must be surmounted before game theory can be incorporated in practical information security risk management tools. The two challenges, unrealistic model assumptions and limited input data, are discussed below.

Model Assumptions. Game-theoretic models are mathematical abstractions. Kiennert et al. [22] note that the models rely on subtle and implicit assumptions that limit their practical applications in security scenarios.

The game-theoretic models in most of the surveyed articles assume a limited action set comprising an attacker and a defender. In real scenarios, the situation is more complex. Often, the environments in which players make their moves are noisy with dynamic system updates, reconfigurations, repairs and scheduled maintenance. Additionally, there may be other players in addition to attackers and defenders. For example, Hu et al. [17] consider malicious insiders as the third type of player. While modeling real scenarios as two-player games can be helpful, such treatments are overly simplified. In other cases, for example, in the articles by Rass and Zhu [37] and van Dijk et al. [44], complete information about attacker payoffs is assumed, which is unrealistic and impractical.

Some of the game-theoretic models analyzed in this chapter are overly simplified whereas others are complex. The most representative models, such as those with continuous-time, multistage and two-sided incomplete information attributes, are closer to real advanced persistent threat scenarios. However, they quickly become impractical (e.g., complex algorithms, no closed-form solutions and difficult-to-achieve equilibria).

For example, a stochastic game is an appropriate choice for a multistage advanced persistent threat scenario. However, it is marred by assumptions about payoffs (analysis is restricted to zero-sum stochastic games because a general resolution algorithm is known only for zero-sum games) and states (most models are restricted to completely-observable states). Overly simple two-player zero-sum games do not adequately model advanced persistent threat scenarios where, due to asymmetric information, player incentives are unknown. Similarly, models based on repeated plays of a game assume that the same game is played over time. However, in multistage advanced persistent threat scenarios, a game is not actually repeated because it may not be reset to the original configuration before a repetition [44]. In such scenarios, stochastic models with adaptive learning and evolutionary strategies hold promise [28].

A more compelling question is how to obtain the right game-theoretic model. Many of the authors of the surveyed articles have used intuition to produce stylistic models that are rarely based on historical data, log data or testbed data. Most of the surveyed articles rely on simulations of inferences to demonstrate player utilities at equilibrium, which are prone to parameter perturbations. Among all the surveyed articles, only the article by Huang and Zhu [18] handles parameter perturbations using sensitivity analysis. Finally, none of the surveyed articles describe a testbed or empirical validation of the results using red-blue team penetration testing.

Input Data. Game-theoretic models are data intensive. The equilibrium strategies are based on the player utilities that are usually expressed using real-valued data. Although the availability of precise information about payoffs constrains game-theoretic models, most of the models work well with ordered data. This raises the issue of how ordered data can be obtained. Rass et al. [36] note that, most of the time, limited historical data is available and it is mostly based on practitioner experience about asset value and damage.

Game-theoretic models rely on quantitative data. Extending a model with qualitative data is a potential research area [36]. Another approach is to base a model on noisy payoffs as in [18]. Other approaches that draw on Dempster-Shafer evidence theory [8] and fuzzy logic [11] can support quantitative analyses using qualitative data with degrees of uncertainty.

Looking Forward. From a practitioner's point of view, game-theoretic approaches are cumbersome when working directly with the mathematical models. To render a rigorous game-theoretic approach amenable for use by the security community, it is prudent to create a practitioner tool that wraps the mathematical engine within a graphical user interface. Additionally, instead of using toy examples, case studies involving real scenarios should be employed to demonstrate the applicability and scalability of game-theoretic approaches. Unfortunately, the survey results are disappointing on both these fronts. No reviewed article mentions tool support and very few articles provide real case studies.

7. Conclusions

Game-theoretic approaches, which express the behavior of rational agents and maximize their utility, hold promise for making objective decisions about countermeasures against advanced persistent threats that balance security, cost and usability. The critical analysis of game-theoretic approaches for analyzing advanced persistent threats presented in this chapter examines the approaches in terms of their objectives, features, game models and solutions. Additionally, the game-theoretic approaches are classified according to their applications areas as well as their mappings to the ISO 31000 information security risk management stages. The critical analysis exposes the delicate modeling and analysis limitations of the game-theoretic approaches and their omissions. The analysis also points to future research focused on integrating practitioner perspectives in game-theoretic approaches to advance information security risk management.

References

[1] M. Ahmadian and D. Marinescu, Information leakage in cloud data warehouses, *IEEE Transactions on Sustainable Computing*, vol. 5(2), pp. 192–203, 2020.

[2] A. Alshamrani, S. Myneni, A. Chowdhary and D. Huang, A survey of advanced persistent threats: Techniques, solutions, challenges and research opportunities, *IEEE Communications Surveys and Tutorials*, vol. 21(2), pp. 1852–1877, 2019.

[3] R. Brewer, Advanced persistent threats: Minimizing the damage, *Network Security*, vol. 2014(4), pp. 5–9, 2014.

[4] L. Busoniu, R. Babuska and B. De Schutter, A comprehensive survey of multiagent reinforcement learning, *IEEE Transactions on Systems, Man and Cybernetics, Part C (Applications and Reviews)*, vol. 38(2), pp. 156–172, 2008.

[5] H. Cavusoglu, S. Raghunathan and B. Mishra, Optimal design of information technology security architectures, *Proceedings of the International Conference on Information Systems*, pp. 749–756, 2002.

[6] P. Chen, L. Desmet and C. Huygens, A study on advanced persistent threats, in *Communications and Multimedia Security*, B. De Decker and A. Zuquete (Eds.), Springer, Berlin Heidelberg, Germany, pp. 63–72, 2014.

[7] F. Cohen, The use of deception techniques: Honeypots and decoys, in *Handbook of Information Security, Volume 3*, H. Bidgoli (Ed.), John Wiley, Chichester, United Kingdom, pp. 646–655, 2006.

[8] X. Deng, X. Zheng, X. Su, F. Chan, Y. Hu, R. Sadiq and Y. Deng, An evidential game theory framework for a multi-criteria decision making process, *Applied Mathematics and Computation*, vol. 244, pp. 783–793, 2014.

[9] T. Do, N. Tran, C. Hong, C. Kamhoua, K. Kwiat, E. Blasch, S. Ren, N. Pissinou and S. Iyengar, Game theory for cyber security and privacy, *ACM Computing Surveys*, vol. 50(2), article no. 30, 2017.

[10] Elsevier, ScienceDirect, Amsterdam, The Netherlands (`www.sci encedirect.com`), 2020.

[11] C. Esposito, M. Ficco, F. Palmieri and A. Castiglione, Smart cloud storage service selection based on fuzzy logic: Theory of evidence and game theory, *IEEE Transactions on Computers*, vol. 65(8), pp. 2348–2362, 2016.

[12] J. Filar and B. Tolwinski, On the algorithm of Pollatschek and Avi-Itzhak, in *Stochastic Games and Related Topics*, T. Raghavan, T. Ferguson, T. Parthasarathy and O. Vrieze (Eds.), Springer, Dordrecht, The Netherlands, pp. 59–70, 1991.

[13] A. Fink, Equilibrium in a stochastic n-person game, *Journal of Sciences of the Hiroshima University, Series A-I (Mathematics)*, vol. 28(1), pp. 89–93, 1964.

[14] D. Fudenberg and J. Tirole, *Game Theory*, MIT Press, Cambridge, Massachusetts, 2000.

[15] Google, Google Scholar, Mountain View, California (`scholar.google.com`), 2020.

[16] J. Harrington, *Games, Strategies and Decision Making*, Worth Publishers, New York, 2009.

[17] P. Hu, H. Li, H. Fu, D. Cansever and P. Mohapatra, Dynamic defense strategy against advanced persistent threat with insiders, *Proceedings of the IEEE Conference on Computer Communications*, pp. 747–755, 2015.

[18] L. Huang and Q. Zhu, A dynamic games approach to proactive defense strategies against advanced persistent threats in cyber-physical systems, *Computers and Security*, vol. 89, article no. 101660, 2020.

[19] International Organization for Standardization, ISO 31000:2018 Risk Management – Guidelines, Geneva, Switzerland, 2018.

[20] Joint Task Force Transformation Initiative, Managing Information Security Risk: Organization, Mission and Information System View, NIST Special Publication 800-39, National Institute of Standards and Technology, Gaithersburg, Maryland, 2011.

[21] N. Kaloudi and J. Li, The AI-based cyber threat landscape: A survey, *ACM Computing Surveys*, vol. 53(1), article no. 20, 2020.

[22] C. Kiennert, Z. Ismail, H. Debar and J. Leneutre, A survey of game-theoretic approaches for intrusion detection and response optimization, *ACM Computing Surveys*, vol. 51(5), article no. 90, 2018.

[23] D. Kushner, The real story of Stuxnet, *IEEE Spectrum*, vol. 50(3), pp. 48–53, 2013.

[24] C. Lei, H. Zhang, J. Tan, Y. Zhang and X. Liu, Moving target defense techniques: A survey, *Security and Communication Networks*, vol. 2018, article no. 3759626, 2018.

[25] K. Leyton-Brown and Y. Shoham, *Essentials of Game Theory: A Concise Multidisciplinary Introduction*, Morgan and Claypool Publishers, San Rafael, California, 2008.

[26] X. Liang and Y. Xiao, Game theory for network security, *IEEE Communications Surveys and Tutorials*, vol. 15(1), pp. 472–486, 2013.

[27] R. Luh, S. Marschalek, M. Kaiser, H. Janicke and S. Schrittwieser, Semantics-aware detection of targeted attacks: A survey, *Journal of Computer Virology and Hacking Techniques*, vol. 13(1), pp. 47–85, 2017.

[28] J. Marden and J. Shamma, Game theory and distributed control, in *Handbook of Game Theory with Economic Applications, Volume 4*, H. Young and S. Zamir (Eds.), Elsevier, Amsterdam, The Netherlands, pp. 861–899, 2015.

[29] R. McDermott, *Risk-Taking in International Politics*, University of Michigan Press, Ann Arbor, Michigan, 2001.

[30] Microsoft, Microsoft Academic, Redmond, Washington (`academic.microsoft.com/home`), 2020.

[31] M. Min, L. Xiao, C. Xie, M. Hajimirsadeghi and N. Mandayam, Defense against advanced persistent threats in dynamic cloud storage: A Colonel Blotto game approach, *IEEE Internet of Things Journal*, vol. 5(6), pp. 4250–4261, 2018.

[32] R. Myerson, *Game Theory: Analysis of Conflict*, Harvard University Press, Cambridge, Massachusetts, 1991.

[33] J. Osborne and A. Rubinstein, *A Course in Game Theory*, MIT Press, Cambridge, Massachusetts, 1994.

[34] J. Pawlick, E. Colbert and Q. Zhu, A game-theoretic taxonomy and survey of defensive deception for cyber security and privacy, *ACM Computing Surveys*, vol. 52(4), article no. 82, 2019.

[35] J. Pawlick, S. Farhang and Q. Zhu, Flip the cloud: Cyber-physical signaling games in the presence of advanced persistent threats, in *Decision and Game Theory for Security*, M. Khouzani, E. Panaousis and G. Theodorakopoulos (Eds.), Springer, Cham, Switzerland, pp. 289–308, 2015.

[36] S. Rass, S. Konig and S. Schauer, Defending against advanced persistent threats using game theory, *PLOS ONE*, vol. 12(1), article no. e0168675, 2017.

[37] S. Rass and Q. Zhu, GADAPT: A sequential game-theoretic framework for designing defense-in-depth strategies against advanced persistent threats, in *Decision and Game Theory for Security*, Q. Zhu, T. Alpcan, E. Panaousis, M. Tambe and W. Casey (Eds.), Springer, Cham, Switzerland, pp. 314–326, 2016.

[38] L. Shapley, Stochastic games, *Proceedings of the National Academy of Sciences*, vol. 39(10), pp. 1095–1100, 1953.

[39] J. Stankovic, J. Sturges and J. Eisenberg, A 21st century cyber-physical systems education, *IEEE Computer*, vol. 50(12), pp. 82–85, 2017.

[40] G. Stoneburner, A. Goguen and A. Feringa, Risk Management Guide for Information Technology Systems, NIST Special Publication 800-30, National Institute of Standards and Technology, Gaithersburg, Maryland, 2002.

[41] B. Tarzey, The trouble heading for your business in 2013, *Computer Weekly*, March 1, 2013.

[42] W. Tian, X. Ji, W. Liu, J. Zhai, G. Liu, Y. Dai and S. Huang, Honeypot game-theoretical model for defending against APT attacks with limited resources in cyber-physical systems, *Electronics and Telecommunications Research Institute Journal*, vol. 41(5), pp. 585–598, 2019.

[43] D. Tosh, I. Vakilinia, S. Shetty, S. Sengupta, C. Kamhoua, L. Njilla and K. Kwiat, Three-layer game theoretic decision framework for cyber investment and cyber insurance, in *Decision and Game Theory for Security*, S. Rass, B. An, C. Kiekintveld, F. Fang and S. Schauer (Eds.), Springer, Cham, Switzerland, pp. 519–532, 2017.

[44] M. van Dijk, A. Juels, A. Oprea and R. Rivest, FlipIt: The game of "stealthy takeover," *Journal of Cryptology*, vol. 26(4), pp. 655–713, 2013.

[45] V. Verendel, Quantified security is a weak hypothesis: A critical survey of results and assumptions, *Proceedings of the New Security Paradigms Workshop*, pp. 37–50, 2009.

[46] K. Wang, M. Du, D. Yang, C. Zhu, J. Shen and Y. Zhang, Game-theory-based active defense for intrusion detection in cyber-physical embedded systems, *ACM Transactions on Embedded Computing Systems*, vol. 16(1), article no. 18, 2016.

[47] G. Wangen, C. Hallstensen and E. Snekkenes, A framework for estimating information security risk assessment method completeness, *International Journal of Information Security*, vol. 17(6), pp. 681–699, 2018.

[48] H. Wu and W. Wang, A game theory based collaborative security detection method for Internet of Things systems, *IEEE Transactions on Information Forensics and Security*, vol. 13(6), pp. 1432–1445, 2018.

[49] L. Xiao, D. Xu, C. Xie, N. Mandayam and H. Poor, Cloud storage defense against advanced persistent threats: A prospect-theoretic study, *IEEE Journal on Selected Areas in Communications*, vol. 35(3), pp. 534–544, 2017.

[50] L. Yang, P. Li, Y. Zhang, X. Yang, Y. Xiang and W. Zhou, Effective repair strategy against advanced persistent threats: A differential game approach, *IEEE Transactions on Information Forensics and Security*, vol. 14(7), pp. 1713–1728, 2019.

[51] Q. Zhu and T. Basar, Game-theoretic approach to feedback-driven multistage moving target defense, in *Decision and Game Theory for Security*, S. Das, C. Nita-Rotaru and M. Kantarcioglu (Eds.), Springer, Cham, Switzerland, pp. 246–263, 2013.

II

INDUSTRIAL CONTROL SYSTEMS SECURITY

Chapter 4

ATTACKING THE IEC 61131 LOGIC ENGINE IN PROGRAMMABLE LOGIC CONTROLLERS

Syed Ali Qasim, Adeen Ayub, Jordan Johnson and Irfan Ahmed

Abstract   Programmable logic controllers monitor and control physical processes in critical infrastructure assets, including nuclear power plants, gas pipelines and water treatment plants. They are equipped with control logic written in IEC 61131 languages such as ladder diagrams and structured text that define how the physical processes are monitored and controlled. Cyber attacks that seek to sabotage physical processes typically target the control logic of programmable logic controllers.

Most of the attacks described in the literature inject malicious control logic into programmable logic controllers. This chapter presents a new type of attack that targets the control logic engine that is responsible for executing the control logic. It demonstrates that a control logic engine can be disabled by exploiting inherent features such as the program mode and starting/stopping the engine. Case studies involving control logic engine attacks on real programmable logic controllers are presented. The case studies present internal details of the logic engine attacks to enable industry and the research community to understand the control logic engine attack vector. Additionally, control engine attacks on power substation, conveyor belt and elevator testbeds are presented to demonstrate their impacts on physical systems.

Keywords: Programmable logic controllers, IEC 61131 logic engine, attacks

1.   Introduction

Industrial control systems monitor and control infrastructure assets such as electric power grids, nuclear plants, water treatment facilities and gas pipelines [2, 3, 14]. An industrial control system environment comprises a control center and field sites. The control center houses human-machine interfaces (HMIs) and engineering workstations, and

© IFIP International Federation for Information Processing 2022
Published by Springer Nature Switzerland AG 2022
J. Staggs and S. Shenoi (Eds.): Critical Infrastructure Protection XV, IFIP AICT 636, pp. 73–95, 2022.
https://doi.org/10.1007/978-3-030-93511-5_4

the field sites house the actual industrial (physical) processes that are monitored and controlled via sensors, actuators and programmable logic controllers (PLCs). Programmable logic controllers are embedded devices that monitor and control industrial processes [5]. They incorporate control logic programs written in IEC 61131 languages such as ladder diagrams, structured text and instruction lists that define how physical processes are to be monitored and controlled.

The control logic of a programmable logic controller is typically targeted by a cyber attack to sabotage a physical process [6]. Most control logic attacks described in the literature inject malicious control logic into programmable logic controllers over networks [4, 7, 13, 18, 19, 21, 25, 27, 28]. For example, the Stuxnet malware targeted Iran's uranium-235 processing facility by injecting control logic into Siemens Step 7 engineering software and S7-300 programmable logic controllers [9].

This chapter presents a new type of control logic attack that targets the control logic engine of a programmable logic controller, which executes the control logic. It demonstrates that the control logic engine can be disabled by exploiting inherent features such as the program mode and starting/stopping the engine. Two case studies drawing on attacks listed in the MITRE ATT&CK knowledge base [16], such as man-in-the-middle, unauthorized command message, loss of availability, denial of control and manipulation of control, are presented.

The first case study involves the Schweitzer Engineering Laboratory SEL-3505 Real-Time Automation Controller (RTAC) that is equipped with security features such as device access control and traffic encryption. The second case study involves three traditional programmable logic controllers with no security features, Schneider Electric Modicon M221, Allen-Bradley MicroLogix 1100 and 1400 programmable logic controllers.

The two case studies present internal details of the logic engine attacks, including proprietary programmable logic controller communications protocols to enable industry and the research community to understand the control logic engine attack vectors. Additionally, control engine attacks on power substation, conveyor belt and elevator testbeds are presented to demonstrate their impacts on physical systems.

2.   Background and Related Work

This section provides an overview of industrial control systems and discusses related research efforts.

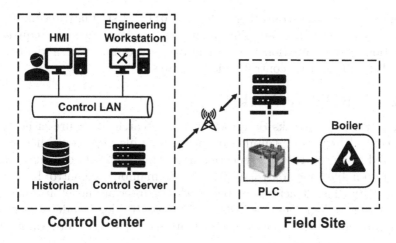

Figure 1. Industrial control system.

2.1 Industrial Control Systems

Figure 1 shows an industrial control system that operates a steam generation system. The industrial control system has a field site that houses the physical steam generation process system and a control center that operates the physical system in a safe and efficient manner. The physical process is monitored and controlled using sensors, actuators and a programmable logic controller. Water entering the boiler is converted to steam, which is transported via a pipeline. The programmable logic controller receives sensor data about parameters such as water level, pressure and temperature in the boiler. It processes the sensor data using control logic to adjust the parameter values by operating valves. The programmable logic controller also sends process state data to the control center over a network.

The control center has a human-machine interface, historian, control server and engineering workstation. The human-machine interface shows operators the current state of the physical process. The historian logs programmable controller inputs (sensor data) and outputs (control actions) for analytic and forensic purposes. The control server communicates with the field site over a network. The engineering workstation runs engineering software provided by the programmable logic controller vendor to program, configure and maintain the programmable logic controller remotely. A control engineer can create a control logic program using the engineering software and proceed to download (write) it to the programmable logic controller or upload (read) the code running on the programmable logic controller. The IEC 61131-3 standard recommends five control logic programming languages, ladder diagrams, sequential function charts, function block diagrams, structured text and instruction lists, for writing control logic programs.

2.2   Related Work

Control logic attacks described in the research literature either target control logic code running on programmable logic controllers (also referred to as control logic injection attacks) [12, 22, 26] or compromise programmable logic controller firmware to manipulate control logic execution [10]. The attacks described in this chapter are novel in that they target control logic engines instead of the control logic code in targeted programmable logic controllers without modifying the programmable logic controller firmware.

Senthival et al. [25] have presented three types of denial of engineering operations attacks. In the first type of attack, an attacker intercepts network traffic between an engineering workstation and targeted programmable logic controller and replaces the original ladder diagram with an infected diagram or vice versa when it is downloaded or uploaded, respectively. In the second type of attack, an attacker with man-in-the-middle access replaces part of the original ladder diagram with noise when it is uploaded, causing the engineering software to crash. The third type of attack, which also crashes the engineering software, only requires the attacker to remotely download infected control logic to the targeted programmable logic controller.

Kalle et al. [13] have presented a control logic injection attack that involves four phases. The attack first compromises a programmable logic controller and steals its control logic. The stolen binary is decompiled, following which malicious logic is injected and the modified code is compiled and transferred to the programmable logic controller. The malicious logic is hidden from the engineering software by employing a virtual programmable logic controller that captures network traffic corresponding to the original logic and sends it to the engineering software when it attempts to read the modified control logic in the programmable logic controller.

McLaughlin and McDaniel [15] have presented a similar control logic injection attack. The control logic bytecode of a targeted programmable logic controller is downloaded and decompiled into a logical model in order to find mappings between the devices connected to the programmable logic controller and the variables in the control logic. The attack changes the mappings arbitrarily and downloads the control logic to the programmable logic controller to cause harm. This attack requires knowledge about industrial control system operations.

Yoo and Ahmed [27] have presented two control logic injection attacks, data execution, and fragmentation and noise padding. The data execution attack exploits the fact that a programmable logic controller does not enforce data execution prevention and transfers malicious control logic to its data blocks. The attack then changes the control flow of the programmable logic controller to execute the logic in its data blocks. In contrast, the fragmentation and noise padding attack subverts deep packet inspection by sending write requests using malicious control logic. Each write request packet contains one byte of the control logic and the rest of the packet contains noise. Every subsequent write request attempts to overwrite the memory region of the programmable logic controller that was written with noise by the previous request.

Govil et al. [11] incorporated malware in a ladder logic bomb that is inserted into the control logic of a programmable logic controller. Such a logic bomb is difficult to detect by manually validating the control logic in a programmable logic controller. The logic bomb is activated by a trigger signal or it can execute autonomously to disrupt or damage the physical system over time.

Garcia et al. [10] have developed a model-aware rootkit that was incorporated in programmable logic controller firmware using JTAG (Joint Test Action Group) ports [20]. The rootkit generates fake, but seemingly authentic, inputs from legitimate inputs. The programmable logic controller processes the authentic inputs according to its control logic and generates output commands to actuators. However, the rootkit blocks the outputs of the programmable logic controller at the firmware level and instead sends malicious outputs generated from the fake inputs to the sensors. This deceives a control engineer who monitors the physical process via the human-machine interface.

Schuett et al. [22] have evaluated the possibility of modifying programmable logic controller firmware to execute remotely-triggered attacks. They reverse engineered programmable logic controller firmware, introduced malicious modifications and repackaged and installed the modified firmware in the programmable logic controller. The compromised firmware enabled time-based and remotely-triggered denial-of-service attacks on the programmable logic controller.

3.   Attacking Control Logic Engines

This section describes the adversarial model and the attacks used in the programmable logic controller case studies.

Table 1. Attacks executed in the case studies.

Programmable Logic Controller	MITRE ATT&CK Knowledge Base Attacks
SEL-3505 RTAC	Network sniffing, man-in-the-middle, manipulation of control
Modicon M221	Network sniffing, unauthorized command message, loss of availability, denial of control, manipulation of control
MicroLogix 1100	Network sniffing, unauthorized command message, denial of control, manipulation of control, man-in-the-middle, denial of view
MicroLogix 1400	Network sniffing, unauthorized command message, denial of control, manipulation of control, man-in-the-middle, denial of view

The adversarial model assumes that the attacker is in the industrial control network and can communicate with the targeted programmable logic controller to launch a control logic engine attack. The attacker may use a common information technology system attack such as an infected USB drive or vulnerable webserver to infiltrate the industrial control network and proceed to execute the control logic attack on the targeted programmable logic controller. The attacker has the following capabilities in the industrial control network:

- Reading communications between the targeted programmable logic controller and engineering workstation.

- Initiating connections with the targeted programmable logic controller to send malicious messages remotely.

- Dropping or modifying messages in communications by assuming a man-in-the-middle position.

The two case studies demonstrate IEC 61131 control logic engine attacks on four programmable logic controllers. A control logic engine attack is defined as an attack that disrupts or impairs the normal functioning of a control logic engine. The case studies focus on attacks that stop control logic engines from executing control logic. Various subsets of attacks listed in the MITRE ATT&CK knowledge base [16] are employed on the programmable logic controllers (Table 1). The attacks, their MITRE ATT&CK knowledge base identifiers and descriptions are as follows:

- **Network Sniffing (T0842):** The attack sniffs network traffic to gain information about the physical process and its control strategy.

- **Man-in-the-Middle (T0830):** The attack intercepts, modifies and/or drops packets transmitted between the engineering workstation and programmable logic controller.

- **Unauthorized Command Message (T0855):** The attack sends an unauthorized command message to an industrial control system device to make it function incorrectly.

- **Loss of Availability (T0826):** The attack disrupts an industrial control system device to prevent the delivery of products and/or services.

- **Denial of Control (T0813):** The attack temporarily prevents the control of the physical process.

- **Manipulation of Control (T0831):** The attack manipulates the control of the physical process.

- **Denial of View (T0815):** The attacker disrupts or prevents an operator from viewing the status of the physical process.

4.   Case Study 1: SEL-3505 RTAC

The first case study focuses on a Schweitzer Engineering Laboratories SEL-3505 Real-Time Automation Controller (RTAC) with security features such as encrypted traffic and device-level access control. The SEL-3505 RTAC incorporates a logic engine that executes its control logic. The attack, which is launched from a man-in-the-middle position between the engineering software and programmable logic controller, prevents the controller from executing the control logic in one of two ways – by modifying the packet that starts the logic engine or by dropping the packet entirely. Note that the initial communications with the controller are encrypted using transport layer security (TLS). Unencrypted communications begin only after a legitimate user has logged in, which prevents a man-in-the-middle attack.

4.1   Controller Details

The SEL-3505 RTAC is equipped with an IEC 61131 control logic engine. It has a web interface for monitoring and configuring the network interface, system logs, user accounts and security settings. A control engineer can write the control logic, configure communications protocols,

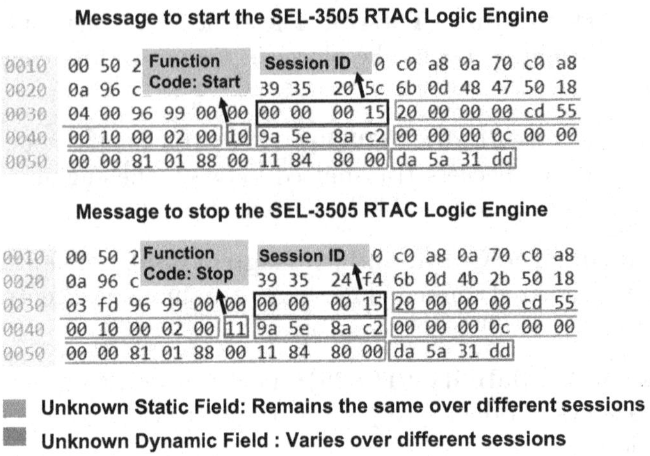

Message to start the SEL-3505 RTAC Logic Engine

Message to stop the SEL-3505 RTAC Logic Engine

Unknown Static Field: Remains the same over different sessions

Unknown Dynamic Field : Varies over different sessions

Figure 2. Messages sent to the SEL-3505 RTAC to start and stop its logic engine.

read/write projects, and start or stop the logic engine using the SEL-5033 AcSELerator RTAC software [23].

The SEL-3505 RTAC uses the ex-GUARD [17] system to control task execution. All tasks that are not approved by the whitelist are blocked [23]. The device communicates with the AcSELerator software on port 5432. Most communications, including session establishment, user authentication and reading/writing projects from/to the device, are encrypted using TLS encryption. However, after a user logs in, the SEL-3505 RTAC opens port 1217 and starts a second communications channel for sharing its state in real time. Surprisingly, the communications on port 1217 are unencrypted.

4.2   Vulnerabilities and Attacks

Exploration of the SEL-3505 RTAC communications internals revealed that it receives unencrypted commands on port 1217 to start and stop the logic engine. Additionally, the packets carrying the commands could be identified. Reverse engineering the commands enabled the understanding of function codes and other fields such as session IDs.

Figure 2 shows the two request packets sent by the AcSELerator software to the SEL-3505 RTAC to start and stop its logic engine. The session ID is incremented by three in each new session and the function codes for starting and stopping the logic engine are 0x10 and 0x11, respectively. The other messages remain the same in different sessions

---

Input: TCP Packet
1. if (packet_src == AcSELerator & packet_dst == RTAC & packet_port == 1217)
    2. if (packet_payload_contains (static_fields))
        3. Modify/Drop

Figure 3. Pseudocode for the Ettercap filters.

(identified as unknown static fields) and their semantics are not required to launch attacks.

The following attacks listed in the MITRE ATT&CK knowledge base were launched in the case study:

- **Network Sniffing (T0842):** Network sniffing is the first step in finding vulnerabilities to launch subsequent attacks. Since the sniffer is in the same network as the engineering workstation and programmable logic controller, network traffic can be captured and subsequently analyzed to gain information needed to launch attacks. The information includes the port on which unencrypted communications are sent as well as specific message fields that are used to design Ettercap filters [8].

- **Man-in-the-Middle (T0830):** After sniffing the network traffic and identifying the packets responsible for starting/stopping the logic engine, Ettercap filters are used to poison the ARP caches of the target machines and assume a man-in-the-middle position between the AcSELerator software and SEL-3505 RTAC. The contents of packets sent by the engineering software to the device are then modified or the packets are simply dropped.

- **Manipulation of Control (T0831):** The man-in-the-middle position is leveraged to stop the control logic engine of the SEL-3505 RTAC from executing its control logic, which impacts the control of the physical process.

The information obtained via network sniffing was leveraged to create two Ettercap filters (DropFilter and Start-StopFilter) that identify messages containing the logic engine start and stop commands. The commands in the packets sent to the SEL-3505 RTAC can be modified (i.e., by converting start to stop and vice versa) and the packets transmitted or the packets could be simply dropped to stop the logic engine or prevent a control engineer from accessing the logic engine. Figure 3 shows pseudocode corresponding to the Ettercap filters.

The filters first identify messages sent between the AcSELerator software and SEL-3505 RTAC using their IP address and port 1217, respectively. As shown in Figure 2, large numbers of packets containing the start and stop commands are the same in different sessions (termed as unknown static fields). The filters search these static bytes in the TCP payloads of the messages to identify the right messages. After correctly identifying a message, DropFilter uses the `drop()` command to drop the message. Similarly, Start-StopFilter changes the function code located at index 15 in the TCP payload from start (`0x10`) to stop (`0x11`) and vice versa.

4.3   Experimental Evaluation

The control logic engine attack was evaluated on a power substation testbed comprising an SEL-3505 RTAC connected to an engineering workstation, circuit breaker and emulated voltage measurement device designed to behave as a voltmeter. The SEL-3505 RTAC was configured to open the circuit breaker when the voltmeter reports a voltage level higher than a specified threshold. Expensive power equipment could be damaged or destroyed if the circuit breaker does not open when the voltage rises beyond the threshold.

The system is monitored from a human-machine interface as shown in Figure 4(a). Note that vRTAC shows the ground truth of the system even when the SEL-3505 RTAC has failed. Specifically, it shows the inconsistency between the true state and the state reported by the device during the attack.

When the SEL-3505 RTAC starts up, it automatically enables the logic engine, so the first step is to stop the logic engine. This is a typical operation when system maintenance or reprogramming is performed. At this point, ARP spoofing attacks are launched against the SEL-3505 RTAC and engineering workstation using the Ettercap packet filters. When an operator sends the command to start the logic engine, it is intercepted and the function code is modified or the packet is dropped before it reaches the SEL-3505 RTAC.

Since the logic engine fails to start even after the operator sends multiple start commands, the device is unable to control or monitor the power system. During this time, if the voltmeter detects a high voltage, such as from a short circuit in the system, a controller is not in place to open the circuit breaker. Therefore, power is allowed to flow and reach critical transformers, potentially damaging or destroying them and causing a power outage. This state is shown in Figure 4(b). Specifically, the

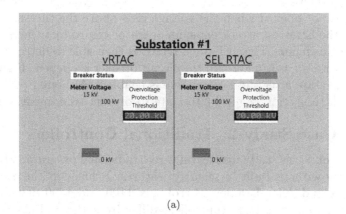

(a)

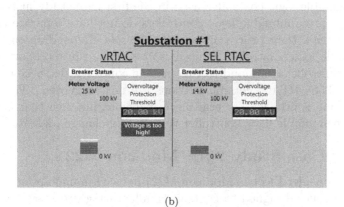

(b)

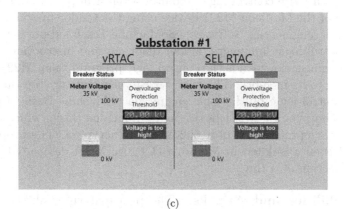

(c)

Figure 4. Impact of the SEL-3505 RTAC control engine attack.

SEL-3505 RTAC no longer reports an up-to-date voltage value and the breaker is not opened when the voltage rises above the threshold.

After the Ettercap attack ends, an operator can restart the SEL-3505 RTAC logic engine. The SEL-3505 RTAC is then able to detect the high voltage from the voltmeter and the circuit breaker is opened. Figure 4(c) shows the state after the logic engine is enabled. Although the breaker is opened, the action would be too late to prevent equipment damage.

5.   Case Study 2: Traditional Controllers

The second case study focuses on three traditional programmable logic controllers without built-in security features: Schneider Electric Modicon M221 and Allen-Bradley MicroLogix 1100 and 1400 devices. The three programmable logic controllers differ from the SEL-3505 RTAC programmable logic controller used in the first case study in two ways. First, the programmable logic controllers do not have separate logic engines; instead, their processors assume the role. Depending on the programmable logic controller, it needs to be in the run mode or be given a start controller command to execute the control logic. Second, unlike the SEL-3505 RTAC, communications are not encrypted. The control logic engine is attacked by crafting a malicious message that is sent to the programmable logic controller to remotely change its state.

5.1   Case Study 2(a): Modicon M221

The Schneider Electric Modicon M221 device is a nano programmable logic controller designed to control manufacturing processes. A control engineer can write control logic, monitor a physical process and control the state of the Modicon M221 device using the vendor-provided SoMachine Basic engineering software. SoMachine Basic supports two IEC 61131 control logic languages, ladder diagrams and instruction lists. A control engineer downloads the control logic program to an M221 device by writing to its memory. The engineer can also start or stop the execution of control logic by the logic engine via SoMachine Basic. Communications between an M221 device and SoMachine Basic, which employ a proprietary protocol on port 502, are not encrypted. The proprietary protocol is encapsulated in Modbus/TCP. An M221 device only allows one connection at a time.

Vulnerabilities and Attacks. The principal vulnerability is that communications between an M221 device and its engineering software are not encrypted. Two other vulnerabilities are that the M221 device states that execute and disable the execution of the control logic program can be changed remotely via the engineering software and an M221 device can only have a single connection to the engineering software at a time.

The following attacks listed in the MITRE ATT&CK knowledge base were launched in the case study:

- **Network Sniffing (T0842):** Network sniffing enables the communications between the SoMachine Basic engineering software and M221 device to be captured. Protocol information obtained by analyzing the captured traffic can be leveraged in subsequent attacks.

- **Unauthorized Command Message (T0855):** Protocol information obtained by analyzing the captured network traffic is used to create a message that stops an M221 device from executing its control logic program. Since the communications are not encrypted, any crafted message can be sent to an M221 device remotely.

- **Loss of Availability (T0826):** An M221 device allows only a single connection at a time. Therefore, an attack that does not close the session that was established to send the crafted message, could prevent a control engineer from connecting to and communicating with the targeted M221 device.

- **Denial of Control (T0813):** An M221 device allows only a single connection at a time. Therefore, an attack that does not close the session that was established to send the crafted message, could prevent a control engineer from using the targeted M221 device to control the physical process.

- **Manipulation of Control (T0831):** Stopping the control logic engine of an M221 device from executing its control logic impacts the control of the physical process.

Differential analysis as well as manual analysis were employed to reverse engineer the proprietary M221 device protocol and identify the packets sent by the SoMachine Basic software to start and stop the logic engine of an M221 device. Figures 5(a) and 5(b) show the packets. The function codes 0x40 and 0x41 are used to start and stop an M221 logic engine, respectively. As shown in Figure 5(c), an M221 device sends a success message to the SoMachine Basic software to acknowledge its change of state. This information was leveraged to write a Python script that establishes a session with an M221 device and sends crafted messages to start and stop the execution of its control logic.

```
0000   00 80 f4 0e 5b 39 00 Modbus 27 Session  Start
0010         05 8c 40 00 80 Function 00 ID      Controller
0020   Address  5 46 01 f6 6a Code    b 4e d0 1   6b 50 18
0030   03 6d 95 df 00 00 13 58  00 00 00 06    5a 8b 40
0040   ff 00
```

(a) Request message to start the Modicon M221 device.

```
0000   00 80 f4 0e 5b 39 00 Modbus 27 Session  Stop
0010         05 46 40 00 80 Function 00 ID      Controller
0020   Address  5 46 01 f6 6a Code    3 4e d0 15  7 50 18
0030   03 65 95 df 00 00 13 21  00 00 00 06    5a 8b 41
0040   ff 00
```

(b) Request message to stop the Modicon M221 device.

```
0000   00 50 56 27 24 f7 00 Modbus 3e Session
0010   00 32 08 5f 00 00 40 Function ae ID       Success
0020   0a 67 01 f6 c5 46 4e Code    5b 6a b5 81  7 50 18
0030   11 1c 47 54 00 00 13 58  00 00 00 04    5a 8b fe
```

(c) Response message with success function code.

Figure 5.   Messages sent to start and stop the Modicon M221 device.

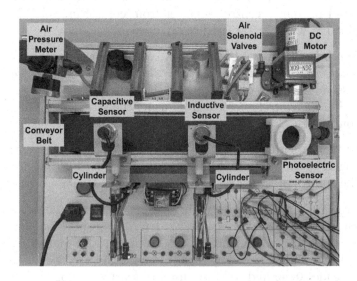

Figure 6.   Top view of the conveyor belt testbed.

Experimental Evaluation.   The control logic engine attack was evaluated using the conveyor belt testbed shown in Figure 6. The conveyor

belt, which sorts different types of objects with the help of sensors and actuators, is controlled by an M221 device. The SoMachine Basic software runs on a Windows 7 virtual machine while the attack scripts run on an Ubuntu 16.04 virtual machine.

It is assumed that the attacker has infiltrated the network containing the M221 device and engineering workstation. The attacker uses network scanning to identify the IP address of the M221 device. Next, the attacker initiates a Modbus protocol session with the M221 device and sends it a stop controller request. Upon receiving the request, the M221 device stops executing its control logic, which halts the conveyor belt. However, the attacker does not terminate the Modbus session. Because the M221 device can only have one session at a time, a control engineer is unable to communicate with the M221 device and issue a start controller request to get the conveyor belt operational.

5.2   Case Study 2(b): MicroLogix 1100 and 1400

The Allen-Bradley MicroLogix 1100 and 1400 programmable logic controllers belong to same family and have many similarities. Both the devices are monitored and controlled via the RSLogix 500 engineering software and use the unencrypted PCCC protocol encapsulated in EtherNet/IP to communicate with the RSLogix 500 software [24]. The RSLogix 500 software supports ladder diagrams for writing control logic. Upon connecting with a MicroLogix device, a control engineer can upload the control logic (read the control logic on the device) or download new control logic (write to device memory). The two MicroLogix devices have three modes of operation, Run, Program and Remote, that are set and changed using a command line interface. In the Run mode, a device executes the control logic and controls a physical process. To access or change the control logic, a control engineer places the device in the Program mode, which also pauses the logic engine. For operational ease, the device is often placed in the Remote mode, which enables a control engineer to change the mode from Run to Program and vice versa remotely using the engineering software.

Vulnerabilities and Attacks.   The ability to change the operational modes of MicroLogix 1100 and 1400 devices is exploited. Specifically, changing the mode to Program pauses control logic execution and the device waits for an operator to update its control logic and configuration.

The following attacks listed in the MITRE ATT&CK knowledge base were launched in the case study:

- **Network Sniffing (T0842):** Network sniffing provides valuable information about the communications protocol used by the MicroLogix devices and RSLogix 500 engineering software. Analysis of the captured traffic helps identify the packets responsible for changing the device state to the Program mode, which pauses control logic execution.

- **Unauthorized Command Message (T0855):** The information obtained by network sniffing is leveraged to craft a message that remotely changes the MicroLogix device state from the Run mode to the Program mode.

- **Denial of Control (T0813):** Pausing the control logic program prevents a control engineer from controlling the physical process.

- **Manipulation of Control (TO831):** Pausing the control logic program impacts the control of the physical process.

- **Man-in-the-Middle (TO830):** The change to the MicroLogix device state is hidden from the control engineer by poisoning the ARP caches of the engineering software and MicroLogix device to achieve a man-in-the-middle position, following which the MicroLogix device state is modified from Program to Run whenever the engineering software requests the device state.

- **Denial of View (T0815):** The man-in-the-middle attack deceives the control engineer who assumes that the MicroLogix device is still in the Run mode and is controlling the physical process.

Manual reverse engineering was employed to identify the request messages sent by the RSLogix 500 software to change the device mode to Remote-Run or Remote-Program. Figures 7(a) and 7(b) show the messages sent to place MicroLogix devices in the Remote-Run and Remote-Program modes. The function code 0x80 changes the mode, following which the function codes 0x01 or 0x06 place the devices in the Remote-Run or Remote-Program modes, respectively.

It was also determined that RSLogix 500 software periodically requests the device status. Figure 8(a) shows that the function code (FC) 0x03 is used to request device status. Differential analysis of the response messages for the Remote-Run and Remote-Program modes revealed that a function code of 0x21 is used for the Remote-Run mode

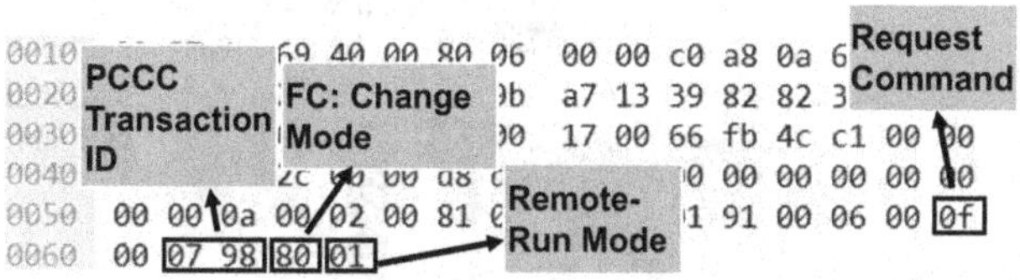

(a) Request message to set device to the Remote-Run mode.

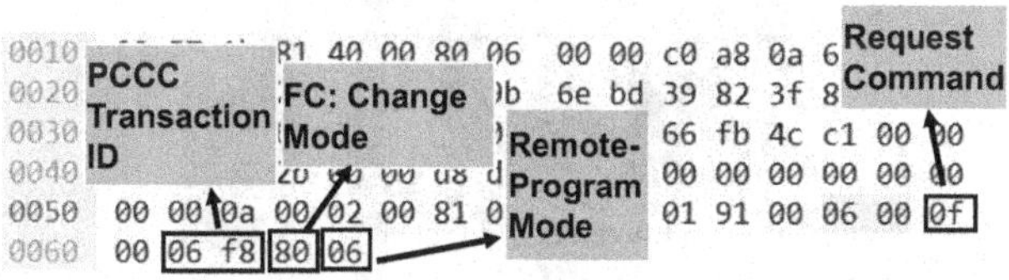

(b) Request message to set device to the Remote-Program mode.

Figure 7. Messages sent to change the mode of the MicroLogix devices.

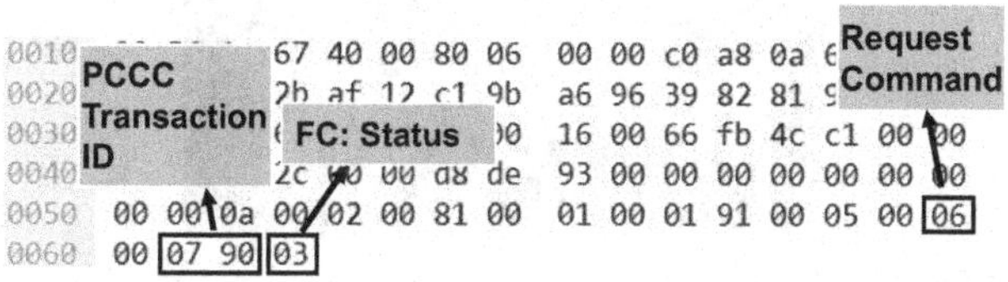

(a) Request message to device for current status.

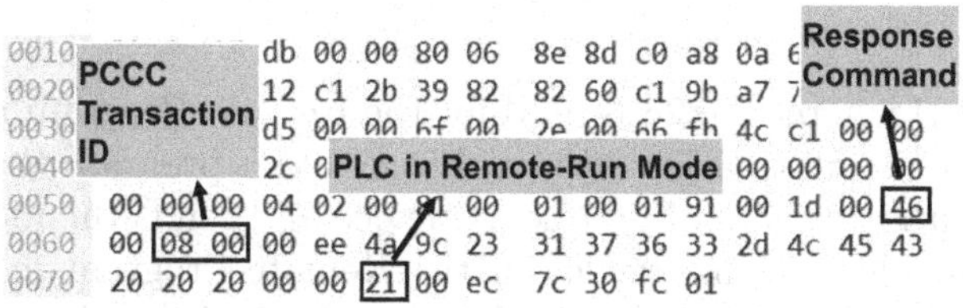

(b) Response message from device in the Remote-Run mode.

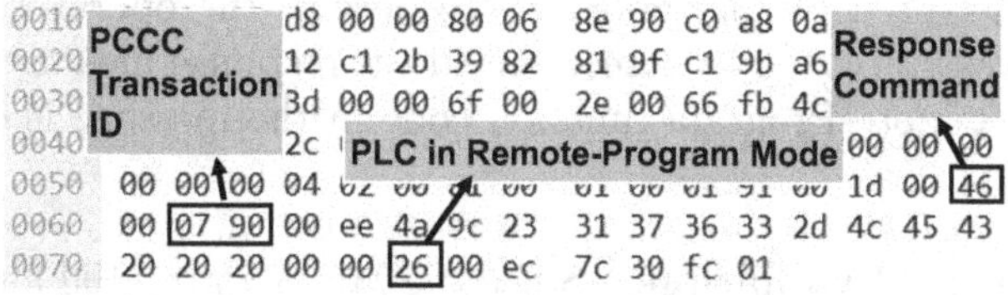

(c) Response message from device in the Remote-Program mode.

Figure 8. Status request to and response messages from the MicroLogix devices.

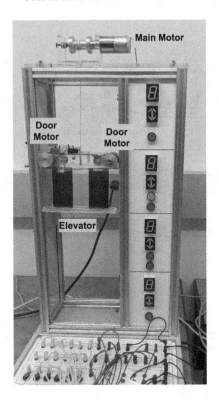

Figure 9.   Front view of the elevator testbed.

(Figure 8(b)) whereas 0x26 is used for the Remote-Program mode (Figure 8(c)). This information was used to create a program that initiates a session with a targeted MicroLogix device and sends the mode change messages to place in the device in the Remote-Program mode, which pauses the execution of its control logic. Since the RSLogix 500 software periodically requests device status, the change in the device mode would be detected by an operator. To deceive the operator, an Ettercap filter was employed to detect the status response message, following which the Remote-Program function code in the message is changed to Remote-Run.

Experimental Evaluation.   Since the MicroLogix 1100 and 1400 devices use the same communications protocol and function codes, the logic engine attack was only executed on a MicroLogix 1400 device. Figure 9 shows the elevator testbed used in the evaluation. The elevator has four floors. An elevator user can select a floor from inside or outside the elevator that is input to the MicroLogix 1400 device, which moves the elevator to the selected floor. RSLogix 500 software running on a Windows 7 virtual machine (engineering workstation) communicates with the MicroLogix 1400 device. Attacks are launched from an Ubuntu 18.04.3 LTS machine. As in the other case studies, the MicroLogix 1400 programmable logic controller, engineering workstation and attacker machine are in the same network.

The first attack step is to assume a man-in-the-middle position using ARP poisoning. Following this, a session is established with the MicroLogix 1400 device that controls the elevator. Next, a request message is send to the MicroLogix 1400 device to change its mode to Remote-Program, which causes the device to stop executing its control logic, thereby halting elevator operation. An Ettercap filter is used to detect a status response message sent by an elevator control operator and change the Remote-Program function code in the message to Remote-Run. Thus, the operator is unaware that the attack has rendered the elevator non-operational.

6. Mitigation

The principal problem is the lack of encrypted communications. The Modicon M221 and MicroLogix 1100 and 1400 programmable logic controllers do not have encryption. Although the SEL-3505 RTAC employs TLS encryption for most of its communications, the communications that occur on port 1217 are not encrypted. This makes it easier for an attacker to reverse engineer the protocol and launch a number of attacks.

The Modicon M221 and MicroLogix 1400 devices implement password authentication to prevent the control logic from being read and, in some cases, written by unauthorized users. However, an attacker can change the device state to prevent the control logic from running without any authentication. Therefore, it is important to also use password protection when issuing commands to change the device state.

The Modicon M221 device also has a default feature that enables users to connect to it without any authentication. It allows a connection to one user at a time, exposing itself to attacks that only require a successful connection to the device. Specifically, the attacker connects with the device, pauses the execution of its control logic and keeps the session active to prevent a legitimate user from accessing the device. Such attacks can be defeated by requiring a password to establish a connection with the device.

Man-in-the-middle attacks on all the programmable logic controllers considered in the case studies can be prevented using DHCP snooping and ARP inspection [1].

7.   Conclusions

Most of the attacks described in the literature inject malicious control logic into programmable logic controllers. In contrast, this chapter has presented a novel type of attack that targets the control logic engine that is responsible for running the control logic. These attacks disable control logic engines by exploiting inherent features such as starting and stopping the engines, and changing the operating modes of the programmable logic controllers. Case studies involving control engine attacks on programmable logic controllers that manage power substation, conveyor belt and elevator testbeds demonstrate the significance of the control logic engine attack vector as well as the impacts of control engine attacks on physical systems.

Acknowledgements

This chapter has been authored by UT-Battelle LLC under Contract DE-AC05-00OR22725 with the US Department of Energy (DOE). The research was partially supported by the Virginia Commonwealth Cyber Initiative.

References

[1] H. Adjei, T. Shunhua, G. Agordzo, Y. Li, G. Peprah and E. Gyarteng, SSL stripping technique (DHCP snooping and ARP spoofing inspection), *Proceedings of the Twenty-Third International Conference on Advanced Communications Technology*, pp. 187–193, 2021.

[2] I. Ahmed, S. Obermeier, M. Naedele and G. Richard III, SCADA systems: Challenges for forensic investigators, *IEEE Computer*, vol. 45(12), pp. 44–51, 2012.

[3] I. Ahmed, S. Obermeier, S. Sudhakaran and V. Roussev, Programmable logic controller forensics, *IEEE Security and Privacy*, vol. 15(6), pp. 18–24, 2017.

[4] I. Ahmed, V. Roussev, W. Johnson, S. Senthivel and S. Sudhakaran, A SCADA system testbed for cybersecurity and forensic research and pedagogy, *Proceedings of the Second Annual Industrial Control System Security Workshop*, pp. 1–9, 2016.

[5] A. Ayub, H. Yoo and I. Ahmed, Empirical study of PLC authentication protocols in industrial control systems, *Proceedings of the IEEE Security and Privacy Workshops*, pp. 383–397, 2021.

[6] S. Bhatia, S. Behal and I. Ahmed, Distributed denial-of-service attacks and defense mechanisms: Current landscape and future directions, in *Versatile Cybersecurity*, M. Conti, G. Somani and R. Poovendran (Eds.), Springer, Cham, Switzerland, pp. 55–97, 2018.

[7] T. Chen and S. Abu-Nimeh, Lessons from Stuxnet, *IEEE Computer*, vol. 44(4), pp. 91–93, 2011.

[8] Ettercap Project, Ettercap (`www.ettercap-project.org`), 2021.

[9] N. Falliere, L. O'Murchu and E. Chien, W32.Stuxnet Dossier, Version 1.4, Symantec, Mountain View, California, 2011.

[10] L. Garcia, F. Brasser, M. Cintuglu, A. Sadeghi, O. Mohammed and S. Zonouz, Hey, my malware knows physics! Attacking PLCs with a physical-model-aware rootkit, *Proceedings of the Twenty-Fourth Annual Network and Distributed System Security Symposium*, 2017.

[11] N. Govil, A. Agrawai and N. Tippenhauer, On ladder logic bombs in industrial control systems, in *Computer Security*, S. Katsikas, F. Cuppens, N. Cuppens, C. Lambrinoudakis, C. Kalloniatis, J. Mylopoulos, A. Anton and S. Gritzalis (Eds.), Springer, Cham, Switzerland, pp. 110–126, 2018.

[12] R. Johnson, Survey of SCADA security challenges and potential attack vectors, *Proceedings of the International Conference on Internet Technology and Secured Transactions*, 2010.

[13] S. Kalle, N. Ameen, H. Yoo and I. Ahmed, CLIK on PLCs! Attacking control logic with decompilation and virtual PLCs, *Proceedings of the Network and Distributed System Security Symposium Workshop on Binary Analysis Research*, 2019.

[14] N. Kush, E. Foo, E. Ahmed, I. Ahmed and A. Clark, Gap analysis of intrusion detection in smart grids, *Proceedings of the Second International Cyber Resilience Conference*, pp. 38–46, 2011.

[15] S. McLaughlin and P. McDaniel, SABOT: Specification-based payload generation for programmable logic controllers, *Proceedings of the ACM Conference on Computer and Communications Security*, pp. 439–449, 2012.

[16] MITRE Corporation, ATT&CK for Industrial Control Systems, Bedford, Massachusetts (`collaborate.mitre.org/attackics/ind ex.php/Main_Page`), 2021.

[17] Office of Electricity Delivery and Energy Reliability, exe-GUARD, DOE/OE-0009, U.S. Department of Energy, Washington, DC (`www.energy.gov/sites/prod/files/2017/04/f34/SEL_Exe-guard_FactSheet.pdf`), 2012.

[18] S. Qasim, J. Lopez and I. Ahmed, Automated reconstruction of control logic for programmable logic controller forensics, in *Information Security*, Z. Lin, C. Papamanthou and M. Polychronakis (Eds.), Springer, Cham, Switzerland, pp. 402–422, 2019.

[19] S. Qasim, J. Smith and I. Ahmed, Control logic forensics framework using a built-in decompiler of engineering software in industrial control systems, *Forensic Science International: Digital Investigation*, vol. 33(S), article no. 301013, 2020.

[20] M. Rais, R. Awad, J. Lopez and I. Ahmed, JTAG-based PLC memory acquisition framework for industrial control systems, *Forensic Science International: Digital Investigation*, vol. 37(S), article no. 301196, 2021.

[21] M. Rais, Y. Li and I. Ahmed, Spatiotemporal G-code modeling for secure FDM-based 3D printing, *Proceedings of the Twelfth ACM/IEEE International Conference on Cyber-Physical Systems*, pp. 177–186, 2021.

[22] C. Schuett, J. Butts and S. Dunlap, An evaluation of modification attacks on programmable logic controllers, *International Journal of Critical Infrastructure Protection*, vol. 7(1), pp. 61–68, 2014.

[23] Schweitzer Engineering Laboratories, SEL-3505/SEL-3505-3 Real-Time Automation Controller (RTAC), Pullman, Washington (`selinc.com/products/3505`), 2021.

[24] S. Senthivel, I. Ahmed and V. Roussev, SCADA network forensics of the PCCC protocol, *Digital Investigation*, vol. 22(S), pp. S57–S65, 2017.

[25] S. Senthivel, S. Dhungana, H. Yoo, I. Ahmed and V. Roussev, Denial of engineering operations attacks on industrial control systems, *Proceedings of the Eighth ACM Conference on Data and Application Security and Privacy*, pp. 319–329, 2018.

[26] R. Sun, A. Mera, L. Lu and D. Choffnes, SoK: Attacks on Industrial Control Logic and Formal Verification-Based Defenses, arXiv: 2006.04806 (`arxiv.org/abs/2006.04806`), 2020.

[27] H. Yoo and I. Ahmed, Control logic injection attacks on industrial control systems, in *ICT Systems Security and Privacy Protection*, G. Dhillon, F. Karlsson, K. Hedstrom and A. Zuquete (Eds.), Springer, Cham, Switzerland, pp. 33–48, 2019.

[28] H. Yoo, S. Kalle, J. Smith and I. Ahmed, Overshadow PLC to detect remote control logic injection attacks, in *Detection of Intrusions and Malware, and Vulnerability Assessment*, R. Perdisci, C. Maurice, G. Giacinto and M. Almgren (Eds.), Springer, Cham, Switzerland, pp. 109–132, 2019.

Chapter 5

ANOMALY DETECTION IN AUTOMATION CONTROLLERS

Robert Mellish, Scott Graham, Stephen Dunlap and Patrick Sweeney

Abstract   Cyber-physical systems incorporate powerful devices that are used to monitor and control physical processes. These devices along with collectable statistics can be leveraged as sensors for network-based and host-based anomaly detection. Host-based anomaly detection can be used in a defense-in-depth strategy to complement traditional network-based anomaly detection systems as well in systems for which network-based options are infeasible due to their operating environments.

This chapter discusses the development of an anomaly detection system for a SEL-3505 RTAC programmable logic controller using the recommended IEC 61131 programming tools. The required device statistics are harvested by creating a Modbus server on the test system and polling the server to retrieve data. The collected data is used to create a representative fingerprint for the associated task. When the measured behavior differs from the fingerprint, an anomaly is detected and an alarm is raised. This approach is flexible and easily implemented in existing installations. The performance of the anomaly detection system is evaluated against several network-based attacks across multiple firmware revisions and project types. Recommendations are made to improve anomaly detection performance.

Keywords: Anomaly detection, automation controllers

1.   Introduction

The risks to industrial control systems have increased as their networks have become more interconnected with corporate networks and the open Internet. While advances have been made to secure industrial control networks by adapting traditional information technology network security solutions and developing specialized solutions such as

Published by Springer Nature Switzerland AG 2022
J. Staggs and S. Shenoi (Eds.): Critical Infrastructure Protection XV, IFIP AICT 636, pp. 97–118, 2022.
https://doi.org/10.1007/978-3-030-93511-5_5

process-aware detection methods, much more needs to be done to bolster the resilience and security of these vital assets.

This research explores the utilization of end devices such as programmable logic controllers as sensors for network intrusion detection in addition to their traditional process monitoring and control roles. Specifically, it examines the effects of network intrusions on the task execution time of a SEL-3505 real-time automation controller (RTAC) and the potential efficacy of an anomaly detection system (ADS) that engages the task execution time as its data feature.

The research has three contributions. The first is the analysis of the limitations of a real-time automation controller implementation that allow for network intrusions. The second is strong experimental evidence of the ability to detect network anomalies by tracking task times. The third is a data collection framework that evaluates discrimination strategies with multiple data features for the real-time automation controller.

2.   SEL-3505 RTAC Device

The SEL-3505 RTAC used in this research is produced by Schweitzer Engineering Laboratories, a U.S. manufacturer of power protection and automation equipment. Schweitzer Engineering Laboratories does not provide information about the numbers of devices it has sold and installed. However, success stories posted on the company website [19] reveal that its devices protect power systems in the countries of Georgia and Grand Cayman, control microgrids in several U.S. universities, mitigate arc flashes at North American mining companies and manage power in refineries. A recent study of the worldwide protective relay market ranks Schweitzer Engineering Laboratories as the number one relay manufacturer in North America [18]. Although the exact numbers are elusive, it is clear that Schweitzer Engineering Laboratories devices are used throughout the global critical infrastructure.

The SEL-3505 RTAC is marketed as an electric substation controller. It combines physical input/output (I/O) with flexible IEC 61331 control logic and provides several serial ports and dual Ethernet ports. Schweitzer Engineering Laboratories provides communications libraries that enable SEL-3505 RTAC devices to interact with numerous other devices. A SEL-3505 RTAC can also be used as a data concentrator, communicating with multiple legacy devices over serial protocols and converting the data streams to Ethernet-based communications. These features render SEL-3505 RTAC devices popular for use in industrial control systems as well as attractive targets for attackers.

A SEL-3505 RTAC incorporates an embedded Linux host with applications that provide programmable logic controller functionality. A web server is provided for configuration and management. User accounts can be created and diagnostics executed from a password-protected web page. The diagnostics include checking the control logic status and performing factory resets if necessary. The web interface uses a PostgreSQL back-end that supports functions such as downloading new project files and making changes to the device firewall. Project files are created using proprietary Windows-based AcSELerator RTAC engineering software. The AcSELerator software, which is undocumented, creates a compiled binary that is executed by the widely-used CODESYS programmable logic controller framework [14]. The CODESYS runtime IEC 61131 logic engine enables the Linux host to act as a generic programmable logic controller. Understanding these interfaces is crucial to securing the devices and the networks in which they reside. Detecting anomalies in their operation can help recognize potential intrusions as they are taking place.

A SEL-3505 RTAC has several security features. These include application whitelisting that protects against rootkits, built-in denial-of-service detection, system priority readjustment and functionality that enables all configured sequence of events data tags to be available in a syslog client [8, 20]. Whitelisting prevents the execution of unauthorized processes and denial-of-service detection supports responses to brute force attacks on the network stack. However, the SEL-3505 RTAC does not provide detection functionality for identifying misuse or subtle exploitation of authorized applications.

To address this limitation, this research proposes the addition of an anomaly detection system to identify network intrusions. If the intrusion detection system is implemented in IEC 61131 function blocks, it could be generalized across other programmable logic controllers, providing end-device protection in any number of industrial control networks.

3.   Anomaly Detection System

At an abstract level, a host-based anomaly detection system can be distilled into a workload, system outputs, system parameters and decision algorithm that work in concert with a data collector at the heart of the anomaly detection system. Figure 1 shows an anomaly detection system comprising these components.

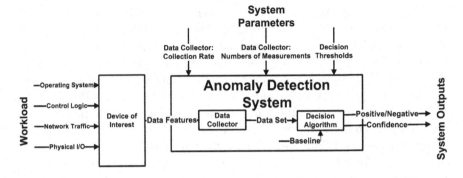

Figure 1. Anomaly detection system.

3.1   Workload

The workload encompasses actions that the hardware must complete on a continual basis. When completing these actions, the hardware produces measurable responses that can be leveraged in anomaly detection. Some actions are mandated by the manufacturer and are immutable and transparent to end users. Other actions are created by end users to fulfill their process requirements. The final category of workload includes the burden imposed on the hardware by the physical process it monitors and controls, and the network traffic it receives.

The workload is created by the following components:

- **Operating System:** While programmable logic controllers and other industrial devices may be portrayed as user logic running on bare metal, in practice there is firmware that handles the network stack and communications needed to program the devices. These firmware functions compete for resources and can slow down process control tasks even if they still meet the real-time requirements. Popular operating systems include OS-9, VxWorks and Linux. Modifications to an operating system, whether malicious or manufacturer mandated, can cause changes to the workload. Some workload changes have been shown to be detectible by current anomaly detection methods [4, 6].

- **Control Logic:** The control logic is implemented by user-created functions that a programmable logic controller continuously executes to monitor and control its assigned physical process. The control logic for a complex process often constitutes the bulk of the workload. The detection of malicious control logic modifications has been the subject of considerable research [4, 6].

- **Network Traffic:** The packets sent and received by a device impose a workload on the device. Some devices act as communications gateways that connect to numerous devices with a single upstream device. Others simply translate physical process information to a digital representation that is displayed on a human-machine interface. Engineering functions such as programming, performing diagnostics and retrieving system logs impose additional workload. The effects of the workload can be seen in the task times of devices that are under duress from network scans [13].

  Network intrusions are anomalous actions that are the focus of anomaly detection. An intrusion places additional burden on a device by creating network traffic, executing additional processes on the operating system and/or exfiltrating data. An anomaly detection system must discern between the normal workload and the burden imposed by intrusions through careful selection of features and analysis tools.

- **Physical Input/Output:** Programmable logic controllers are responsible for monitoring and controlling physical processes using specialized sensors and actuators. In some programmable logic controllers, input/output data processing has been shown to cause no increases in task times [4] because inputs vary in frequency. This may indicate that input/output is being handled by a scheduled task or by a secondary processor. A SEL-3505 RTAC has a field programmable gate array (FPGA) that conditions binary and analog input and output data, offloading the task from the processor. However, due to the limitations of monitoring field programmable gate arrays, the effects of physical input/output variations on task times are not explored in this research.

3.2   System Outputs

The outputs of an anomaly detection system are the algorithm decision and the confidence level associated with the decision. A common set of performance metrics is required to compare different anomaly detection systems. Historically, the following metrics have been used to compare the performance of anomaly detection systems [4, 11]:

- **True Positive Rate (TPR):** The true positive rate is the rate at which an anomaly detection system correctly identifies an anomaly.

- **True Negative Rate (TNR):** The true negative rate is the rate at which an anomaly detection system correctly identifies a normally-behaving system.

- **False Positive Rate (FPR):** The false positive rate is the rate at which an anomaly detection system incorrectly identifies a normally-behaving system as an anomaly.

- **False Negative Rate (FNR):** The false negative rate is the rate at which an anomaly detection system fails to identify an anomaly.

The false positive rate is the type I error of an anomaly detection system. If the rate is too high, alarms become a nuisance and may be disregarded when true anomalies occur. The false negative rate expresses the frequency at which anomalies go undetected. Keeping this rate low is the principal objective when designing an anomaly detection system.

In addition to the error rates, the following factors must be considered when designing an anomaly detection system:

- **Detection Latency:** Although it may not be used frequently, detection latency is an important metric for anomaly detection systems. The detection latency is the length of time required to detect an anomaly. Its infrequent use may be attributed to the need for a more mature anomaly detection system than those typically discussed in the literature.

- **System Overhead:** Industrial control devices have limited computational and storage resources, and must meet strict real-time operational constraints. Therefore, a deployed anomaly detection system must be as lightweight as possible to eliminate negative impacts on the controlled physical process. System overhead may be measured as an increase in task time or processor burden percentage.

3.3   Tuning Parameters

Tuning parameters are properties of an anomaly detection system that can be changed to increase its overall performance. The tuning parameters are:

- **System Features:** Depending on the privileges provided to an anomaly detection system, there are variety of features to consider. These include statistics such as task time, CPU burden, numbers of network packets sent and received, system RAM in use, and more. Certain features may lend themselves better to detecting specific attacks and an anomaly detection system designer must carefully identify, justify and defend the chosen features. Previous research efforts have used task time as a feature [4, 6]. This research seeks to understand the intrusions that can be discerned using the previously-employed features.

- **Data Collection Rate:** The data collection rate can directly affect the sensitivity of an anomaly detection system. If attacks are ephemeral, a slow polling rate could miss anomalies. If data polling is too frequent, the burden on the device becomes significant and the real-time operational requirements will not be met.

- **Number of Data Points:** The number of consecutive data points needed to make a decision and the data collection rate directly correlate with detection latency. Depending on the time complexity of the decision algorithm, an increase in the number of data points could have an undesirable increase in detection latency.

3.4   Decision Algorithm

A decision algorithm is central to an anomaly detection system and is paramount to its overall success. A decision algorithm uses the collected data to make an assessment about the operation of the device of interest. Several methods have been employed to detect anomalies. Depending on the data features collected, different decision algorithms have been adopted. Vargas et al. [23] have monitored RAM usage using simple moving averages. Formby and Beyah [6] have used a cumulative sum algorithm on task time to detect modifications to control logic. Dunlap et al. [4] have also considered task time, but they selected a permutation test to discern changes. Alves et al. [1] have leveraged an embedded machine learning intrusion detection system in conjunction with OpenPLC to detect network anomalies by inspecting TCP headers. To facilitate a portable solution that could be implemented using IEC 61131 control logic, this research engages statistical methods instead of machine learning approaches.

4.   Experimental Design

This section describes the experimental design, including the experimental factors, data collection, discriminator selection and system evaluation.

4.1   Experimental Factors

The proposed anomaly detection system employs functions native to the SEL-3505 RTAC as well as supplementary functions written in Python that could be integrated by the manufacturer into a future SEL-3505 RTAC firmware release or they could be programmed in the con-

Table 1. Experimental factors.

Firmware Revision	Project File Type	Network Intrusion
R145	Low task time	Baseline
R146	High task time	ARP spoofing
R147		PostgreSQL queries
		CODESYS connection

trol logic engine by a control engineer. In this research, an experimental treatment comprises a firmware revision, control logic project file type and network intrusion.

Table 1 shows the experimental factors. Selecting one factor from each column yielded 24 (= 3 × 2 × 4) combinations. These variations were intended to capture the effectiveness of an anomaly detection system across various workloads and intrusions. Ten trials were conducted for each experimental treatment, leading to 240 total trials. The order in which trials were conducted was determined by creating a list of all the trials and randomizing their order.

Firmware Revisions. Previous research has shown that monitoring task times in programmable logic controllers can identify firmware modifications [4, 6]. To verify that this research could be generalized to the SEL-3505 RTAC, three firmware revisions released by Schweitzer Engineering Laboratories were considered, R145, R146 and R147.

SEL-3505 RTAC Project File Types. Two project files were considered, one a low task time project and the other a high task time project. Project 1 was a limited-functionality project with an average task time of approximately 1,300 μs. It contained only the control logic needed for SEL-3505 RTAC operation along with a single Modbus server for data collection. Such a project would be unlikely to be deployed in an operational environment, because even a data concentrator would have additional network connections and data mapping logic. Nevertheless, the project realized the lowest possible task time while still providing the data needed for anomaly detection.

Project 2 was much more complex with an average task time of approximately 9,000 μs. The long task time was realized by performing numerous complex mathematical operations that used pseudorandom inputs provided by SEL-3505 RTAC's SELRand library and time-varying inputs such as the numbers of bytes sent and received by the Ethernet ports.

The two projects represent the extremes in task times. Future research will examine the use of branching projects whose complexity varies based on the current states of the processes being monitored.

Network Intrusions. In order to assess the viability of using task time as a data feature for intrusion detection, a number of feasible network intrusions or attacks had to be devised against the SEL-3505 RTAC. Therefore, the implementation details of the SEL-3505 RTAC were carefully explored to understand features that attackers could exploit. Successful exploits result in potentially-detectible footholds; identifying the exploits and mechanisms that enable them is the purpose of an anomaly detection system.

The following intrusion mechanisms were employed in the experiments for their demonstrated viability as attack vectors or as manifestations of established footholds:

- **Baseline:** The baseline treatment used the network traffic necessary to harvest anomaly detection system data. This provided an experimental backdrop for detecting network intrusions. Repeated baseline trials were evaluated against each other to determine the false positive rate for each algorithm.

- **ARP Spoofing:** ARP spoofing is a standard mechanism for performing man-in-the-middle attacks that are often used to demonstrate the vulnerabilities of industrial control devices and networks [5, 15, 16, 22]. The exploit leverages the lack of authentication in the address resolution protocol (ARP) to send unsolicited resolution responses containing false information about the network topology. The false link layer information causes network traffic to be misdirected to a network attacker.

  Although the use of encrypted traffic would severely limit an attacker's ability to collect information or inject packets, common industrial control protocols still rely on legacy implementations and their communications are largely in plaintext. This lack of security enables a variety of modification attacks against common protocols such as Modbus [15] and DNP3 [5]. The lack of encryption in the configuration protocols of devices also poses security risks to industrial control networks with regard to ARP spoofing [10, 21].

  Improper configuration of a SEL-3505 RTAC can pose additional risks. The device generates a self-signed certificate upon installing a new firmware revision. The certificate is used to encrypt the HTTPS connection for initial configuration as well as PostgreSQL traffic. If the certificate is not replaced, an adversary could perform a man-in-the-middle attack and impersonate the SEL-3505 RTAC using a previously-compromised certificate from another SEL-3505 RTAC. This would enable an attacker to harvest credentials from the supposed secure connection and inject arbitrary modifications into the system configuration or programming traffic.

- **PostgreSQL Queries:** A SEL-3505 RTAC uses a PostgreSQL database to manage the control logic on the device and to interface with the operating system. Engineering functions are programmed as SQL queries that are callable from the web interface. These functions include changing the IP address, testing network connectivity by pinging other devices and reading system diagnostic information. As an open-source database, PostgreSQL vulnerabilities are typically discovered and patched relatively quickly compared with programmable logic controller patching by manufacturers. However, a burden is placed on manufacturers to incorporate the most up-to-date database versions in their device firmware and for end users to patch their own devices.

  If the PostgreSQL database is exploited or database credentials are compromised, an attacker can launch denial-of-service attacks because a SEL-3505 RTAC can be restarted by a database query. A system restart is an easily-detectible anomaly but subtler attacks are also possible. The PostgreSQL queries employed for foothold emulation during the experiments included reads of the control logic project from the SEL-3505 RTAC. The exfiltration of the control logic is a major reconnaissance activity by an attacker as it provides in-depth knowledge of the physical process controlled by the SEL-3505 RTAC as well as the devices that communicate with the SEL-3505 RTAC.

- **CODESYS Connection:** The CODESYS runtime application executing on a SEL-3505 RTAC is responsible for industrial control protocol communications and control logic operation. It uses the standard port 1217 for engineering functions. The functions include uploading and downloading control logic programs, monitoring real-time control logic values, forcing control logic values for debugging purposes, and stopping and starting control logic execution. If enabled, the connection also allows access to the SEL-3505 RTAC filesystem.

  Vulnerabilities related to the use of CODESYS as a programmable logic controller framework have been documented [14] and exploited to decompile the control logic [7]. While CODESYS has

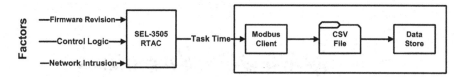

Figure 2. Experimental data collection system.

recently implemented an authentication mechanism to establish connections, this feature is not activated in a SEL-3505 RTAC and credentials are not required on port 1217 itself. Instead, TCP connections to port 1217 are blocked by default and the port can be opened and closed by accessing the PostgreSQL database.

SEL-3505 RTAC filesystem access is a concern because it uses TLS 1.1 for PostgreSQL traffic and web server configuration. The private server key used for encryption can be exfiltrated from a SEL-3505 RTAC using a CODESYS connection and then used to decrypt any communication and extract information such as a username and password. Additionally, an attacker could insert or modify SEL-3505 RTAC files that may enable further exploitation.

In order to emulate this network intrusion, a passive CODESYS connection was kept active during data collection. The passive connection had the minimum workload generated by a CODESYS connection with no files being read from the SEL-3505 RTAC and no process values changed from the engineering workstation.

4.2 Data Collection

A total of 30,000 task time samples were collected for each trial. The data was collected by creating a Modbus server on the SEL-3505 RTAC and polling the server via a Modbus client implemented in Python using the pymodbus module. After receiving a response from the server, the client waited 1 ms before polling again. Task time was used as the data feature due to its ability to detect logic and firmware modifications, as well as its sensitivity to changes in network traffic as described in previous research [4, 6, 13].

Each dataset was saved as a CSV file for future analysis using the selected decision algorithms. Future research will focus on real-time detection using a continual data collection technique and eventually employ a SEL-3505 RTAC function block that goes beyond Modbus data collection. Figure 2 shows a notional data collection process and the experimental factors.

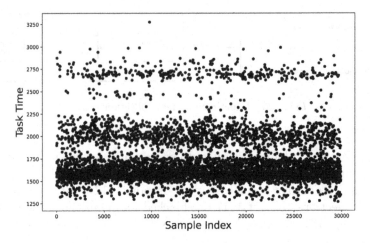

Figure 3.   Scatter plot of task time distribution.

4.3   Discriminator Selection

Pilot studies confirmed previous research results that task times do not have normal distributions [4, 13]. Figure 3 shows a scatter plot of the sampled task times from a pilot study with no network intrusions. Three distinct clusters are discernible and no apparent correlation exists between when a sample was taken and its associated task time. The three clusters are seen in more detail in the kernel density estimation plot in Figure 4.

Because the task time population does not have a normal distribution, the following three non-parametric statistical tests were selected as discriminators to evaluate the efficacy at detecting network intrusions using task time:

- **Permutation Test:** This re-sampling test investigates the probability that two sample populations are from the same distribution. The test can be performed without making any assumptions about the sample distributions [25]. It has been used to detect control logic and firmware modifications [4]. The `mlxtend` Python module was used to perform this test [17].

- **Mann-Whitney U Test:** This non-parametric test explores the null hypothesis that one population is stochastically larger than the other [3, 9]. While it is commonly used in the behavioral sciences, the test has been employed to evaluate statistical differences in sampled and forecasted network traffic [2, 12]. The test was con-

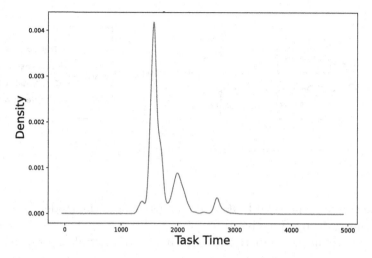

Figure 4. Kernel density estimation of task time.

ducted on task time data using the `scipy.stats.mannwhitneyu`
Python function [24].

- **Kolmogorov-Smirnov Test:** This non-parametric goodness-of-
  fit test probes the hypothesis that two independent samples are
  drawn from the same distribution. The test has the advantage of
  considering the entirety of a distribution function instead of just
  the difference in a test statistic. For the test to be valid, the task
  time distribution is assumed to be continuous. The Kolmogorov-
  Smirnov test statistic is the maximum absolute difference between
  two distribution functions [3] and has been used to detect control logic modifications [6]. The test was conducted using the
  `scipy.stats.kstest` Python function [24].

4.4   System Evaluation

To test each discriminator, the datasets must be separated by firmware
revision and project type. This reduces the buoying effect that inflates
the true positive rate when testing a low task time dataset against a high
task time dataset. Next, each intrusion-free dataset is tested against all
the other datasets in its (firmware revision, project type) subset.

Figure 5 shows the experimental analysis process. The results of the
tests are used to compute the true positive and false positive rates for
each decision algorithm. The process is repeated, varying the decision
threshold to generate a receiver operating characteristic (ROC) curve

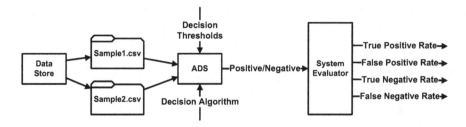

Figure 5.   Experimental analysis process.

for each algorithm. The ROC curve helps explore the trade-off between the true and false positive rates [4]. Additionally, the area under the curve metric helps compare the performance of multiple algorithms [26].

5.   Experimental Results

This section presents the anomaly detection results and discusses strategies for improving the anomaly detection rates.

5.1   Anomaly Detection Rates

The compiled results from the 240 experimental trials are presented. Figure 6 shows the ROC curves for the three decision algorithms. The area under the curve (AUC) is also displayed for each algorithm. An ideal classifier would have an area under the curve of 1.0. The Mann-Whitney U test has the highest area under the curve of 0.89. The Kolmogorov-Smirnov test has a slightly lower value of 0.88. The permutation test has a value of 0.80. The ROC curves were employed to select decision thresholds for the algorithms to showcase their representative performance.

Tables 2, 3 and 4 show the results of the permutation test, Mann-Whitney U test and Kolmogorov-Smirnov test, respectively. Values shown in bold do not meet the performance thresholds of less than 0.1 for the false positive rate or greater than 0.9 for the combined true positive rate. These performance thresholds are based on previous research in anomaly detection systems [4]. Each (firmware revision, project type) pair is shown to highlight when an algorithm performed poorly overall or if a specific test case was more difficult to detect.

The permutation test failed to meet the false positive rate threshold, but it performed well in detecting network intrusions, with two (firmware revision, project type) pairs just missing the 0.9 cutoff. The Mann-Whitney U test performed well with regard to the overall false positive

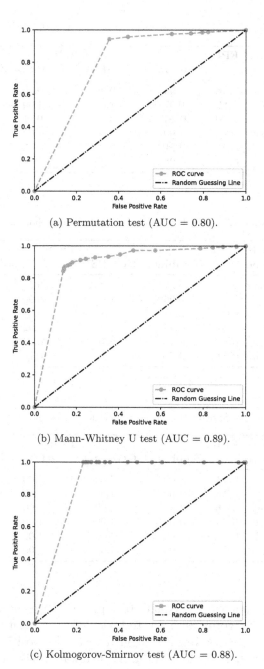

(a) Permutation test (AUC = 0.80).

(b) Mann-Whitney U test (AUC = 0.89).

(c) Kolmogorov-Smirnov test (AUC = 0.88).

Figure 6. ROC curves.

Table 2. Permutation test results (decision threshold = 0.0001).

Firmware Revision	Task Time	FPR	TPR			
			Combined	CODESYS	ARP Spoof	PostgreSQL
R145	Low	**0.46**	0.94	0.96	0.86	0.99
R146	Low	**0.22**	0.97	1.00	1.00	0.92
R147	Low	**0.40**	**0.87**	0.81	0.91	0.90
R145	High	**0.20**	1.00	1.00	1.00	1.00
R146	High	**0.69**	**0.90**	0.92	0.92	0.85
R147	High	**0.17**	0.98	0.98	1.00	0.95

Table 3. Mann-Whitney U test results (decision threshold = 1×10^{-14}).

Firmware Revision	Task Time	FPR	TPR			
			Combined	CODESYS	ARP Spoof	PostgreSQL
R145	Low	0.09	0.96	0.99	0.97	0.91
R146	Low	0.00	0.96	1.00	0.90	0.99
R147	Low	0.09	**0.81**	0.81	0.81	0.81
R145	High	0.00	0.97	1.00	0.92	1.00
R146	High	**0.67**	**0.70**	0.70	0.73	0.67
R147	High	0.00	**0.78**	0.74	0.75	0.86

Table 4. Kolmogorov-Smirnov test results (decision threshold = 1×10^{-17}).

Firmware Revision	Task Time	FPR	TPR			
			Combined	CODESYS	ARP Spoof	PostgreSQL
R145	Low	**0.11**	1.00	1.00	1.00	1.00
R146	Low	0.00	1.00	1.00	1.00	1.00
R147	Low	**0.16**	1.00	1.00	1.00	1.00
R145	High	**0.22**	1.00	1.00	1.00	1.00
R146	High	**0.91**	1.00	1.00	1.00	1.00
R147	High	0.00	1.00	1.00	1.00	1.00

rate, but it did not yield adequate true positive rates in half of the test cases. The Kolmogorov-Smirnov test yielded true positive rates of 1.0 across all the test cases, but it struggled with false positive rates, failing to meet the threshold for four of the six (firmware revision, project type) pairs.

A potential outlier in the data is firmware revision R146 with a high project task time. All the tests have markedly different false positive rates for this test case. This could be due to some unknown behavior in the firmware revision or automated conversion process that renders an RTAC AcSELerator project compatible with a new firmware revision.

Figure 7 shows the ROC curves for the three tests without the R146 outlier. The area under the curve values for the Mann-Whitney U test and Kolmogorov-Smirnov test are boosted to 0.94 and 0.97, respectively. However, the permutation test has a modest improvement to just 0.83.

5.2   Improving Detection Rates

The results presented above were collected using all 30,000 samples in each dataset without performing any pre-test data treatments. Future research will explore the effect of sample size on the performance of each algorithm. Additionally, data conditioning methods such as removing outliers or only using specific percentiles of sorted data for detection will be employed. With a compiled dataset and data collection framework in place, further discrimination strategies may be employed, including multiple data features such as tracking memory use in addition to task time. Since multi-dimensionality increases the computational complexity, it should be balanced against the performance gain.

Candidate algorithms that are vetted should be implemented in the CODESYS environment for deployment in a real-time SEL-3505 RTAC. By offloading detection from a central system to the real-time automation controller itself, the burden of network traffic would be removed and the potential for malicious tampering of data in transit would be reduced. This would also enable integration with pre-existing capabilities such as syslog to enable a single point of security auditing for the SEL-3505 RTAC. With multiple detection tests implemented in discrete function blocks, voting schemes could be used and tuned. Additionally, a wider array of attack types could be evaluated to demonstrate the robustness of the anomaly detection solution and provide detailed comparisons with anomaly detection strategies described in the literature.

6.   Conclusions

This research has focused on the development of an anomaly detection system for a SEL-3505 RTAC using task time as the data feature. The ability to detect network intrusions using task time data was evaluated using three statistical tests. While the permutation test has been used previously to detect control logic and firmware modifications, the experiments demonstrated that it was unable to discriminate between normal variations in device behavior and the burden created by network intrusions; specifically, the overall false positive rate was unacceptably

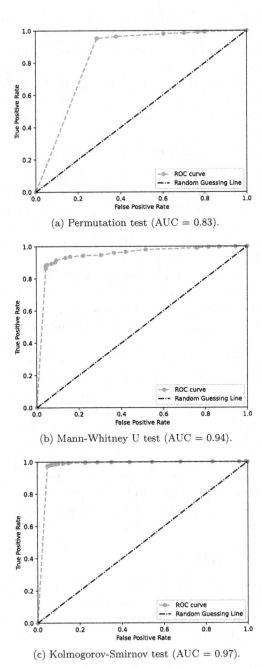

(a) Permutation test (AUC = 0.83).

(b) Mann-Whitney U test (AUC = 0.94).

(c) Kolmogorov-Smirnov test (AUC = 0.97).

Figure 7.   ROC curves without R146 data.

high. In contrast, the Mann-Whitney U and Kolmogorov-Smirnov tests yielded good anomaly detection results, failing to meet the performance thresholds for only a few experimental treatments. The Kolmogorov-Smirnov test was able to detect network intrusions in all the trials and, when the performance associated with the outlier (firmware revision R146 and high task time) was discounted, the test yielded only 44 false positives out of 450 baseline-to-baseline comparisons, a strong showing for a proof-of-concept test.

Future work will focus on improving anomaly detection performance using data conditioning and exploring the effects of sample size. The data collection framework also provides the flexibility to test future strategies against many data features and project types.

The SEL-3505 RTAC has several security features, but it is not designed to detect the network intrusions tested in this research. ARP spoofing in the absence of a network-based intrusion detection system goes undetected, exposing the industrial control system and the physical system it monitors and controls to disruption or damage. While anomaly detection is not the only alternative, task time is a promising data feature for detecting network intrusions. Moreover, anomaly detection can be implemented in existing installations without adding new devices by deploying the detection functionality in programmable logic controller function blocks. Future research will focus on identifying vulnerabilities and mitigations for the SEL-3505 RTAC as well as other Schweitzer Engineering Laboratories equipment.

The views expressed in this chapter are those of the authors, and do not reflect the official policy or position of the U.S. Air Force, U.S. Department of Defense or U.S. Government. This document has been approved for public release, distribution unlimited (Case #88ABW-2020-3828).

References

[1] T. Alves, R. Das and T. Morris, Embedding encryption and machine learning intrusion prevention systems in programmable logic controllers, *IEEE Embedded Systems Letters*, vol. 10(3), pp. 99–102, 2018.

[2] J. Bernacki and G. Kolaczek, Anomaly detection in network traffic using selected methods of time series analysis, *International Journal of Computer Network and Information Security*, vol. 7(9), pp. 10–18, 2015.

[3] Y. Dodge, *The Concise Encyclopedia of Statistics*, Springer, New York, 2008.

[4] S. Dunlap, J. Butts, J. Lopez, M. Rice and B. Mullins, Using timing-based side channels for anomaly detection in industrial control systems, *International Journal of Critical Infrastructure Protection*, vol. 15, pp. 12–26, 2016.

[5] S. East, J. Butts, M. Papa and S. Shenoi, A taxonomy of attacks on the DNP3 protocol, in *Critical Infrastructure Protection III*, C. Palmer and S. Shenoi (Eds.), Springer, Berlin Heidelberg, Germany, pp. 67–81, 2009.

[6] D. Formby and R. Beyah, Temporal execution behavior for host anomaly detection in programmable logic controllers, *IEEE Transactions on Information Forensics and Security*, vol. 15, pp. 1455–1469, 2020.

[7] A. Keliris and M. Maniatakos, ICSREF: A framework for automated reverse engineering of industrial control system binaries, *Proceedings of the Twenty-Sixth Annual Network and Distributed System Security Symposium*, 2019.

[8] D. Kite, Leveraging Security-Using the SEL RTAC's Built-In Security Features, SEL White Paper LWP0018-01, Schweitzer Engineering Laboratories, Pullman, Washington, 2016.

[9] H. Mann and D. Whitney, On a test of whether one of two random variables is stochastically larger than the other, *The Annals of Mathematical Statistics*, vol. 18(1), pp. 50–60, 1947.

[10] L. Martin-Liras, M. Prada, J. Fuertes, A. Moran, S. Alonso and M. Dominguez, Comparative analysis of the security of configuration protocols for industrial control devices, *International Journal of Critical Infrastructure Protection*, vol. 19, pp. 4–15, 2017.

[11] R. Mitchell and I. Chen, A survey of intrusion detection techniques for cyber-physical systems, *ACM Computing Surveys*, vol. 46(4), article no. 55, 2014.

[12] N. Nachar, The Mann-Whitney U: A test for assessing whether two independent samples come from the same distribution, *Tutorials in Quantitative Methods for Psychology*, vol. 4(1), pp. 13–20, 2008.

[13] M. Niedermaier, J. Malchow, F. Fischer, D. Marzin, D. Merli, V. Roth and A. von Bodisco, You snooze, you lose: Measuring PLC cycle times under attacks, *Proceedings of the Twelfth USENIX Workshop on Offensive Technologies*, 2018.

[14] A. Nochvay, Security Research: CODESYS Runtime, A PLC Control Framework, Version 1.0, Kaspersky, Woburn, Massachusetts (`ics-cert.kaspersky.com/media/KICS-CERT-Codesys-En.pdf`), 2019.

[15] C. Parian, T. Guldimann and S. Bhatia, Fooling the master: Exploiting weaknesses in the Modbus protocol, *Procedia Computer Science*, vol. 171, pp. 2453–2458, 2020.

[16] D. Pliatsios, P. Sarigiannidis, T. Lagkas and A. Sarigiannidis, A survey of SCADA systems: Secure protocols, incidents, threats and tactics, *IEEE Communications Surveys and Tutorials*, vol. 22(3), pp. 1942–1976, 2020.

[17] S. Raschka, MLxtend: Providing machine learning and data science utilities and extensions to Python's scientific computing stack, *Journal of Open Source Software*, vol. 3(24), pp. 638–639, 2018.

[18] Schweitzer Engineering Laboratories, SEL ranked top protective relay manufacturer in industry survey, Pullman, Washington (www.selinc.com/company/news/126347), June 12, 2019.

[19] Schweitzer Engineering Laboratories, Customer Highlights, Pullman, Washington (www.selinc.com/solutions/success-stories), 2020.

[20] Schweitzer Engineering Laboratories, SEL-3505 SEL-3505-3 Real-Time Automation Controller Instruction Manual, Pullman, Washington, 2020.

[21] S. Senthivel, S. Dhungana, H. Yoo, I. Ahmed and V. Roussev, Denial of engineering operations attacks on industrial control systems, *Proceedings of the Eighth ACM Conference on Data and Application Security and Privacy*, pp. 319–329, 2018.

[22] J. Staggs, D. Ferlemann and S. Shenoi, Wind farm security: Attack surface, targets, scenarios and mitigation, *International Journal of Critical Infrastructure Protection*, vol. 17, pp. 3–14, 2017.

[23] C. Vargas Martinez and B. Vogel-Heuser, A host intrusion detection system architecture for embedded industrial devices, *Journal of the Franklin Institute*, vol. 358(1), pp. 210–236, 2021.

[24] P. Virtanen, R. Gommers, T. Oliphant, M. Haberland, T. Reddy, D. Cournapeau, E. Burovski, P. Peterson, W. Weckesser, J. Bright, S. van der Walt, M. Brett, J. Wilson, K. Millman, N. Mayorov, A. Nelson, E. Jones, R. Kern, E. Larson, C. Carey, I. Polat, Y. Feng, E. Moore, J. VanderPlas, D. Laxalde, J. Perktold, R. Cimrman, I. Henriksen, E. Quintero, C. Harris, A. Archibald, A. Ribeiro, F. Pedregosa, P. van Mulbregt and SciPy 1.0 Contributors, SciPy 1.0: Fundamental algorithms for scientific computing in Python, *Nature Methods*, vol. 17, pp. 261–272, 2020.

[25] R. Wilcox, *Applying Contemporary Statistical Techniques*, Academic Press, Burlington, Massachusetts, 2003.

[26] D. Zhu and Y. Cui, Understanding the random guessing line in a ROC curve, *Proceedings of the Second International Conference on Image, Vision and Computing*, pp. 1156–1159, 2017.

Chapter 6

DETECTING ANOMALOUS PROGRAMMABLE LOGIC CONTROLLER EVENTS USING PROCESS MINING

Ken Yau, Kam-Pui Chow and Siu-Ming Yiu

Abstract   Programmable logic controllers that monitor and control industrial processes are attractive targets for cyber attackers. Although techniques and tools have been developed for detecting anomalous programmable logic controller behavior, they rely heavily on knowledge of the complex programmable logic controller control programs that perform process monitoring and control. To address this limitation, this chapter describes an automated process mining methodology that relies on event logs comprising programmable logic controller inputs and outputs. The methodology discovers a process model of normal programmable logic controller behavior, which is used to detect anomalous behavior and support forensic investigations. Experiments involving a popular Siemens SIMATIC S7-1212C programmable logic controller and a simulated traffic light system demonstrate the utility and effectiveness of the methodology.

Keywords: Programmable logic controller, process mining, anomaly detection

1.   Introduction

Programmable logic controllers, which are widely used to monitor and control industrial processes, are computer systems that are designed to operate reliably under harsh industrial conditions such as extreme temperatures, vigorous vibrations, humidity and/or dusty conditions [21]. Historically, programmable logic controllers were proprietary systems that operated in isolation with no external network connections. However, modern programmable logic controllers use common embedded system platforms and commercial off-the-shelf software [3]. Addition-

© IFIP International Federation for Information Processing 2022
Published by Springer Nature Switzerland AG 2022
J. Staggs and S. Shenoi (Eds.): Critical Infrastructure Protection XV, IFIP AICT 636, pp. 119–133, 2022.
https://doi.org/10.1007/978-3-030-93511-5_6

ally, they are often networked using TCP/IP and wireless protocols and may connect to vendor networks, corporate networks and even the Internet [12]. The vital roles played by modern programmable logic controllers in critical infrastructure assets make them attractive targets for attackers. Their use of commodity hardware and software coupled with their network connectivity significantly increase their exposure to cyber threats. Securing programmable logic controllers from cyber attacks is a priority [13].

Programmable logic controllers exhibit anomalous behavior in attack scenarios as well as during malfunctions and error situations. Detecting anomalous behavior is an important first step in securing programmable logic controllers and mitigating the negative impacts on the industrial processes they operate. However, anomaly detection is a challenging problem because it demands detailed knowledge of the complex programmable logic controller control programs that monitor and control industrial processes. Additionally, due to their real-time operation of industrial processes, it is difficult to stop programmable logic controllers to investigate anomalies [19].

To address these limitations, this chapter presents an automated process mining methodology that relies on event logs comprising programmable logic controller inputs and outputs. The methodology discovers a process model of normal programmable logic controller behavior, which is used to detect anomalous behavior and support forensic investigations. Experiments involving a popular Siemens SIMATIC S7-1212C programmable logic controller and a simulated traffic light system demonstrate the utility and effectiveness of the automated process mining methodology.

2. Related Work

Process mining techniques enable analysts to extract insights about process operations from collections of event records or logs [1]. Process mining has traditionally been used to analyze business processes. However, process mining is increasingly being applied to anomaly detection.

Van der Aalst and de Medeiros [14] advocate the use of process mining to analyze audit trails for security violations. They demonstrate how process mining can support security efforts ranging from low-level intrusion detection to high-level fraud prevention. They also show how process mining can be used to identify anomalous behavior in an online shopping website.

Myers et al. [7] have investigated the application of process mining discovery algorithms on control device log data to detect cyber attacks on industrial control systems. Their research shows that inductive miner process discovery (without noise alteration) is most effective at discovering process models for detecting cyber attacks on industrial control systems.

Laftchiev et al. [6] have proposed an anomaly detection approach for discrete manufacturing systems. They focus on detecting incorrect event execution sequences in discrete manufacturing systems using output data from programmable logic controllers. They employ process mining to develop models of normal behavior and identify anomalous behavior as event sequences that deviate from the modeled normal behavior.

The methodology presented in this chapter differs from related work in that it attempts to detect anomalous behavior by monitoring and analyzing programmable logic controller inputs and outputs, eliminating the need to capture and engage detailed knowledge about the system being controlled. Additionally, the programmable logic controller event logs used for process mining can support post-incident forensic investigations.

The Stuxnet attacks [4] stimulated research efforts on discovering vulnerabilities in programmable logic controllers and addressing potential threats. Wu and Nurse [16] have shown that attacks on programmable logic controllers can be detected by monitoring the values of memory addresses in control programs. They identify the memory addresses used by control program code, and monitor and log the memory values to capture normal programmable logic controller behavior. The normal behavior serves as a reference to identify anomalous programmable logic controller behavior.

Yau et al. [17, 18, 20] have focused on forensic approaches for programmable logic controllers. One approach detects and records anomalous programmable logic controller events based on changes to the control program logic. Another approach captures the values of relevant memory addresses of a running control program and applies machine learning techniques to the captured data to create a model for recognizing anomalous programmable logic controller behavior.

Wu and Nurse [16] and Yau et al. [16–18, 20] have shown that anomalous programmable logic controller behavior can be detected by checking whether or not the control program logic has been changed. However, the methods require the collection and analysis of numerous memory values used by control programs. In contrast, the methodology described in this chapter detects anomalous programmable logic controller behavior simply by monitoring programmable logic controller input and output values.

3.   Process Mining

Process mining provides theoretical and practical foundations for discovering process models from various types of event data [10]. Many successful applications of process mining have been developed for business process management, but the adoption of process mining in other domains is limited.

Process mining seeks to discover, monitor and improve real processes by extracting knowledge from event logs. The techniques include process discovery, conformance checking and process enhancement [7]. This research employs process discovery to learn a Petri net model of a programmable logic controller as it controls a traffic light system. The Petri net model obtained by the process mining of event logs captures normal programmable logic controller behavior. Programmable logic controller behavior that does not match the expected behavior modeled by the Petri net is deemed to be anomalous.

Several types of process models can be constructed using process mining. The proposed methodology employs the Petri net formalism, which is widely used in computer science and systems engineering. Petri nets combine a mathematical theory with graphical representations of dynamic system behavior. The theory enables the precise modeling and analysis of system behavior; the graphical representation provides visualizations of modeled system states [15].

Definition. A Petri net is a five-tuple $PN = (P, T, I, O, M_0)$ where P is a finite set of places; T is a finite set of transitions where $P \cup T \neq \phi$ and $P \cap T = \phi$; $I : P \times T \to \mathbb{N}$ is an input function that defines directed arcs from places to transitions where $\mathbb{N}$ is a set of non-negative integers; $O : T \times P \to \mathbb{N}$ is an output function that defines directed arcs from transitions to places; and $M_0 : P \to \mathbb{N}$ is the initial Petri net marking.

A Petri net marking is an assignment of tokens to places. Tokens reside in places. The numbers and positions of tokens may change during Petri net execution. In fact, tokens are used to define Petri net execution.

The basic idea in Petri net modeling is to describe state changes in a system using transitions that symbolize actions. A Petri net contains places (circles) and transitions (boxes) that may be connected by directed arcs (Figure 1). Places symbolize states, conditions or resources that must be met or be available before an action can be carried out. Places may contain tokens that move to other places by executing (firing) actions. A token in a place means that the corresponding condition is fulfilled or that a resource is available. In the transition diagram in

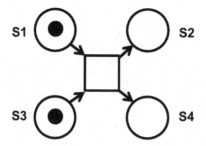

Figure 1. Petri net transition diagram.

Figure 1, the transition may fire when there are tokens in places S1 and S3. Firing removes the tokens in S1 and S3 and puts new tokens in S2 and S4.

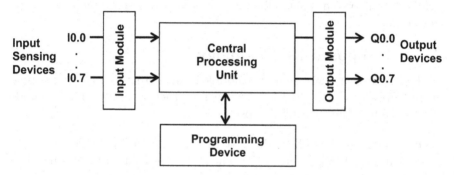

Figure 2. Programmable logic controller.

4. Overview

A programmable logic controller uses programmable memory to store instructions and implement functions such as logic, sequencing, timing, counting and arithmetic for its monitoring and control tasks [2]. Figure 2 shows a schematic diagram of a programmable logic controller.

A programmable logic controller executes a control program that changes the status of programmable logic controller outputs based on the status of its inputs. Each input and output is identified by its address. In the case of a Siemens SIMATIC S7-300 programming logic controller, the addresses of the inputs and outputs are expressed in terms of byte and bit numbers. For example, I0.1 is an input at bit 1 in byte 0 and Q0.2 is an output at bit 2 in byte 0.

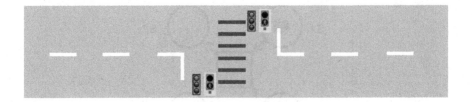

Figure 3. TLIGHT traffic light system.

The experiments employed a Siemens S7-1212C controller loaded with a TLIGHT traffic light simulation program to demonstrate the process-mining-based anomaly detection methodology. TLIGHT is a sample program that is provided with the Siemens SIMATIC S7-300 Programmable Controller Quick Start User Guide [11]. Figure 3 shows the TLIGHT traffic signal system controlling vehicle and pedestrian traffic at an intersection.

5.   Proposed Methodology

This section describes the methodology for detecting anomalous programmable logic controller behavior using process mining. The methodology involves the following steps:

- A simulated traffic light system is set up using a Siemens programmable logic controller. The system is isolated from other networks.

- Programmable logic controller activities (inputs and outputs) are recorded every second to create an activity log that represents normal programmable logic controller behavior.

- Process mining is used to create a Petri net model from the activity log.

- An invalid state transition detector is created to identify anomalous behavior based on the Petri net model.

- The traffic light system is connected to a network and anomalous traffic light system behavior is induced.

- The accuracy of the invalid state transition detector is evaluated based on its ability to identify anomalous programmable logic controller behavior.

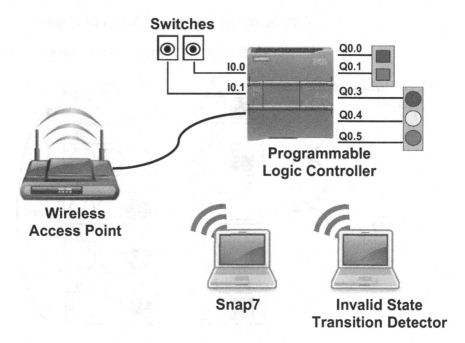

Figure 4. Experimental setup.

5.1 Traffic Light System

Figure 4 shows the experimental setup. A Siemens S7-1212C programmable logic controller running the TLIGHT traffic light program was employed. The simulated traffic light control system was created by establishing the input and output associations. Specifically, the programmable logic controller inputs I0.0 and I0.1 were connected to switches associated with the two green light request buttons for pedestrians. The programmable logic controller outputs were connected as follows: Q0.0 to the red light for pedestrians, Q0.1 to the green light for pedestrians, Q0.3 to the red light for vehicles, Q0.4 to the yellow light for vehicles and Q0.5 to the green light for vehicles.

The Ethernet port of the programmable logic controller was used to establish a network connection for communicating with two peripheral devices, Snap7 [8] and the invalid state transition detector. Snap7 is an open-source, 32/64 bit, multi-platform Ethernet communications suite for interfacing with Siemens S7 programmable logic controllers. In the experiments, Snap7 was used to induce anomalous traffic light behavior by altering certain memory values in the control program of the programmable logic controller. The invalid state transition detec-

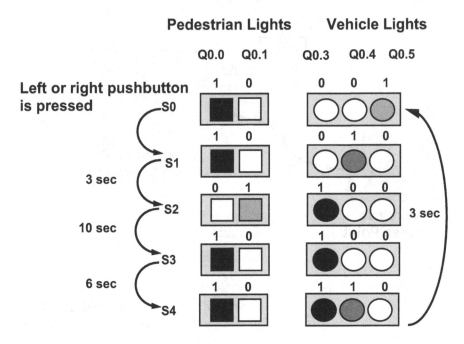

Figure 5.   Traffic light state sequences.

tor was employed to detect anomalous behavior and capture evidence for forensic purposes. The detector was developed using libnodave, an open-source communications library for SIMATIC S7 programmable logic controllers [5]

The TLIGHT traffic light program controls vehicle and pedestrian traffic at an intersection. Figure 5 shows the five traffic light states (S0, S1, S2, S3 and S4) and their sequences (with timings).

5.2   Programmable Logic Controller Behavior

The libnodave open-source library was also used to develop a logging program. The values used by TLIGHT were stored at input/output addresses I0.0, I0.1, Q0.0, Q0.1, Q0.3, Q0.4 and Q0.5. The logging program monitored these programmable logic controller addresses over the network and recorded the values along with their timestamps every second.

The programmable logic controller inputs and outputs were transformed to activities that manifested normal programmable logic controller behavior. The input activities were I-00 (I0.0=0 and I0.1=0), I-01, I-10 and I-11. The output activities corresponded to the traffic

Case number		Event ID	Activity	Input	Output	Date/Time
20	S0	103	Q-10001	00	10001	7/6/2019 7:24:10 PM
21		104	I-10	10	10010	7/6/2019 7:24:11 PM
21		105	Q-10010	10	10010	7/6/2019 7:24:11 PM
21	S1	106	Q-10010	00	10010	7/6/2019 7:24:12 PM
21		107	Q-10010	00	10010	7/6/2019 7:24:13 PM
21		108	Q-01100	00	01100	7/6/2019 7:24:14 PM
21		109	Q-01100	00	01100	7/6/2019 7:24:15 PM
21		110	Q-01100	00	01100	7/6/2019 7:24:16 PM
21		111	Q-01100	00	01100	7/6/2019 7:24:17 PM
21	S2	112	Q-01100	00	01100	7/6/2019 7:24:18 PM
21		113	Q-01100	00	01100	7/6/2019 7:24:19 PM
21		114	Q-01100	00	01100	7/6/2019 7:24:20 PM
21		115	Q-01100	00	01100	7/6/2019 7:24:21 PM
21		116	Q-01100	00	01100	7/6/2019 7:24:22 PM
21		117	Q-01100	00	01100	7/6/2019 7:24:23 PM
21		118	Q-10100	00	10100	7/6/2019 7:24:24 PM
21		119	Q-10100	00	10100	7/6/2019 7:24:25 PM
21	S3	120	Q-10100	00	10100	7/6/2019 7:24:26 PM
21		121	Q-10100	00	10100	7/6/2019 7:24:27 PM
21		122	Q-10100	00	10100	7/6/2019 7:24:28 PM
21		123	Q-10100	00	10100	7/6/2019 7:24:29 PM
21		124	Q-10110	00	10110	7/6/2019 7:24:30 PM
21	S4	125	Q-10110	00	10110	7/6/2019 7:24:31 PM
21		126	Q-10110	00	10110	7/6/2019 7:24:32 PM
22		127	I-00	00	10001	7/6/2019 7:24:33 PM

Figure 6. Programmable logic controller activity log.

light states: Q-10001 (S0), Q-10010 (S1), Q-01100 (S2), Q-10100 (S3) and Q-10110 (S4). Figure 6 shows a portion of the programmable logic controller activity log for normal traffic light operations.

Process mining requires data pertaining to a process, cases, events and attributes. A process comprises cases. A case comprises events (activities) where each event is related to precisely one case. Events within a case are ordered. An event may have attributes such as resource and timestamp.

The experimental data comprised one process, 7,832 cases and 34,956 events (activities). A case corresponded to a complete execution of the TLIGHT traffic light system.

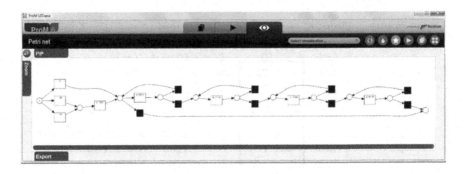

Figure 7.   Petri net model.

5.3   Petri Net Model

The ProM 6.6 process mining framework [9] was used to discover a process model. This extensible framework supports a variety of process mining techniques in the form of plug-ins. The function mine Petri net with the inductive miner was applied to the dataset containing traffic light activities over a four-hour period. Figure 7 shows the discovered Petri net model.

To improve the Petri net model, the programmable logic controller activity log was aggregated to obtain the duration of each state and this data was added to the process model. Next, the Petri net model was transformed to a finite state machine. A finite state machine is very similar to a Petri net. In the case of the traffic light system, the transformation rendered the state transitions more clear and understandable. Figure 8 shows the final finite state model that represents normal TLIGHT operations (i.e., programmable logic controller behavior).

5.4   Invalid State Transition Detector

The invalid state transition detector, which was also developed using libnodave, identifies anomalous programmable logic controller behavior. Specifically, it used the finite state machine shown in Figure 8 to detect two types of anomalous behavior:

- Invalid states, i.e., states other than S0, S1, S2, S3 and S4.

- Invalid time intervals between two consecutive states.

Instances of anomalous behavior raised alerts and the related evidence was recorded for a forensic investigation.

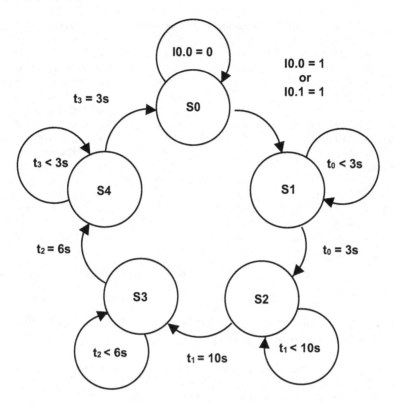

Figure 8. Finite state machine.

5.5 Anomalous Traffic Light Operations

Anomalous traffic light operations were induced using the Snap7 Ethernet communications suite. Specifically, Snap7 induced anomalous traffic light operations by flipping some memory values in the programmable logic controller control program between 0 and 1 intermittently.

5.6 Anomalous Behavior Detection

The invalid state transition detector monitored the programmable logic controller inputs and outputs as the S7 suite intermittently induced anom- alous traffic light operations. The detector created a log file of timestamped anomalous behavior transaction records containing programmable logic controller input values, previous state, current state and time intervals of state transitions.

Figure 9 shows a traffic light activity log with invalid states that start at 4:48:21 PM on 7/7/2019. The state 10000 corresponds to a situation

Date/Time	Input	Prevous State	Current State	Remarks
7/7/2019 4:48:21 PM	00	10000	10000	State 10000 is not valid
7/7/2019 4:48:22 PM	00	10000	10000	State 10000 is not valid
7/7/2019 4:48:23 PM	00	10000	10000	State 10000 is not valid
7/7/2019 4:48:24 PM	00	10000	10000	State 10000 is not valid
7/7/2019 4:48:25 PM	00	10000	10000	State 10000 is not valid
7/7/2019 4:48:26 PM	00	10000	10000	State 10000 is not valid
7/7/2019 4:48:27 PM	00	10000	10000	State 10000 is not valid
7/7/2019 4:48:28 PM	00	10000	10000	State 10000 is not valid
7/7/2019 4:48:29 PM	00	10000	10000	State 10000 is not valid
7/7/2019 4:48:30 PM	00	10000	10000	State 10000 is not valid
7/7/2019 4:48:31 PM	00	10000	10000	State 10000 is not valid
7/7/2019 4:48:32 PM	00	10000	10000	State 10000 is not valid
7/7/2019 4:48:34 PM	00	10000	10000	State 10000 is not valid
7/7/2019 4:48:35 PM	00	10000	10000	State 10000 is not valid
7/7/2019 4:48:36 PM	00	10000	10000	State 10000 is not valid

Figure 9. Traffic light log with invalid states.

where only one pedestrian red light is on and all the other traffic lights are off. Clearly, this is anomalous.

Date/Time	Input	Prevous State	Current State	Remarks
7/14/2019 9:44:08 AM	10	01100	01100	S2
7/14/2019 9:44:09 AM	10	01100	01100	S2
7/14/2019 9:44:10 AM	10	01100	01100	S2
7/14/2019 9:44:11 AM	10	01100	01100	S2
7/14/2019 9:44:12 AM	10	01100	01100	S2
7/14/2019 9:44:13 AM	10	01100	10100	Error :invalid time for transition S2 -> S3
7/14/2019 9:44:14 AM	10	10100	10100	S3
7/14/2019 9:44:15 AM	10	10100	10100	S3
7/14/2019 9:44:16 AM	10	10100	10100	S3
7/14/2019 9:44:17 AM	10	10100	10100	S3
7/14/2019 9:44:18 AM	10	10100	10100	S3
7/14/2019 9:44:19 AM	10	10100	10110	Error :invalid time for transition S3 -> S4
7/14/2019 9:44:20 AM	10	10110	10110	S4
7/14/2019 9:44:21 AM	10	10110	10110	S4

Figure 10. Traffic light log with invalid time interval between consecutive states.

Figure 10 shows a traffic light activity log with an invalid time interval between consecutive states. The anomalous behavior was induced by Snap7. In the log file, an invalid time interval exists between state S2 and S3 at 9:44:13 AM on 7/14/2019. The programmable logic controller inputs, outputs and traffic light system state transitions recorded with timestamps in the log file constitute evidence of anomalies. However, the log file alone may not be adequate in a forensic investigation because it does not have information about how the anomalies were induced, including if they were caused by attacks or malfunctions. On the other hand, an invalid state transition detection log raises alerts and provides information that would initiate a forensic investigation. In a forensic investigation, it would also be necessary to obtain and analyze supplementary log files such as network logs and the system logs of the device used to program the programmable logic controller. The time-stamps recorded by the invalid state transition detector would enable investigators to filter relevant data from the supplementary log files and narrow the scope of the forensic investigation.

The decision to focus on a Siemens SIMATIC S7 programmable logic controller was motivated by its widespread use and the fact that it was targeted by the Stuxnet malware [4]. However, the proposed methodology can be applied to other programmable logic controllers and other control applications because the solution approach is not tied to specific hardware, software and operating systems. Rather, it only considers programmable logic controller inputs and outputs.

6. Conclusions

The automated process mining methodology presented in this chapter produces a Petri net model from event logs comprising programmable logic controller inputs and outputs. The Petri net model, which expresses normal programmable logic controller behavior, serves as a reference to detect anomalous behavior. The event logs with timestamped input and output values are also useful in forensic investigations.

Experiments involving a popular Siemens SIMATIC S7-1212C programmable logic controller and a simulated traffic light system yielded high accuracy. All the anomalies were detected because the simulated traffic light system is simple and involves limited programmable logic controller inputs/outputs, states and state transitions. The accuracy would likely be lower for a physical system with large numbers of inputs, outputs, states and state transitions. Nevertheless, the methodology holds promise because it can detect anomalous behavior without relying on detailed system knowledge and a complicated control program. Additionally, the methodology differs from other approaches because it can detect anomalous programmable logic controller events simply by monitoring programmable logic controller inputs and outputs instead of monitoring numerous memory addresses.

This research is an initial step in developing protection and forensic capabilities for programmable logic controllers based on process mining techniques. Future work will attempt to apply process mining techniques to various industrial control system applications to support anomalous behavior detection and forensic investigations in industrial control systems and civilian applications.

References

[1] A. Augusto, R. Conforti, M. Dumas, M. La Rosa, F. Maria Maggi, A. Marrella, M. Mecella and A. Soo, Automated Discovery of Process Models from Event Logs: Review and Benchmark, *IEEE Transactions on Knowledge and Data Engineering*, vol. 31(4), pp. 686–705, 2019.

[2] W. Bolton, *Programmable Logic Controllers*, Newnes, Burlington, Massachusetts, 2009.

[3] European Union Agency for Network and Information Security, Critical Infrastructures and Services, Heraklion, Greece (enisa.europa.eu/topics/critical-information-infrastruc infrastructures-and-services), 2017.

[4] N. Falliere, L. O'Murchu and E. Chien, W32.Stuxnet Dossier, Version 1.4, Symantec, Mountain View, California, 2011.

[5] T. Hergenhahn, libnodave (sourceforge.net/projects/libno dave), 2014.

[6] E. Laftchiev, X. Sun, H. Dau and D. Nikovski, Anomaly detection in discrete manufacturing systems using event relationship tables, *Proceedings of the International Workshop on Principles of Diagnosis*, 2018.

[7] D. Myers, K. Radke, S. Suriadi and E. Foo, Process discovery for industrial control system cyber attack detection, in *ICT Systems Security and Privacy Protection*, S. De Capitani di Vimercati and F. Martinelli (Eds.), Springer, Cham, Switzerland, pp. 61–75, 2017.

[8] D. Nardella, Step 7 Open Source Ethernet Communications Suite, Bari, Italy (snap7.sourceforge.net), 2016.

[9] RapidProM Team, ProM Tools, Eindhoven University of Technology, Eindhoven, The Netherlands (promtools.org/doku.php), 2019.

[10] V. Rubin, A. Mitsyuk, I. Lomazova and W. van der Aalst, Process mining can be applied to software too! *Proceedings of the Eighth ACM/IEEE International Symposium on Empirical Software Engineering and Measurement*, article no. 57, 2014.

[11] Siemens, SIMATIC S7-300 Programmable Controller Quick Start, Primer, Preface, C79000-G7076-C500-01, Nuremberg, Germany, 1996.

[12] T. Spyridopoulos, T. Tryfonas and J. May, Incident analysis and digital forensics in SCADA and industrial control systems, *Proceedings of the Eighth IET International System Safety Conference Incorporating the Cyber Security Conference*, 2013.

[13] K. Stouffer, V. Pillitteri, S. Lightman, M. Abrams and A. Hahn, Guide to Industrial Control Systems (ICS) Security, NIST Special Publication 800-82, Revision 2, National Institute of Standards and Technology, Gaithersburg, Maryland, 2015.

[14] W. van der Aalst and A. de Medeiros, Process mining and security: Detecting anomalous process execution and checking process conformance, *Electronic Notes in Theoretical Computer Science*, vol. 121, pp. 3–21, 2005.

[15] J. Wang, Petri nets for dynamic event-driven system modeling, in *Handbook of Dynamic System Modeling*, P. Fishwick (Ed.), Chapman and Hall/CRC, Boca Raton, Florida, pp. 24-1–24-17, 2007.

[16] T. Wu and J. Nurse, Exploring the use of PLC debugging tools for digital forensic investigations of SCADA systems, *Journal of Digital Forensics, Security and Law*, vol. 10(4), pp. 79–96, 2015.

[17] K. Yau and K. Chow, PLC forensics based on control program logic change detection, *Journal of Digital Forensics, Security and Law*, vol. 10(4), pp. 59–68, 2015.

[18] K. Yau and K. Chow, Detecting anomalous programmable logic controller events using machine learning, in *Advances in Digital Forensics XIII*, G. Peterson and S. Shenoi (Eds.), Springer, Cham, Switzerland, pp. 81–94, 2017.

[19] K. Yau, K. Chow and S. Yiu, A forensic logging system for Siemens programmable logic controllers, in *Advances in Digital Forensics XIV*, G. Peterson and S. Shenoi (Eds.), Springer, Cham, Switzerland, pp. 331–349, 2018.

[20] K. Yau, K. Chow, S. Yiu and C. Chan, Detecting anomalous behavior of a PLC using semi-supervised machine learning, *Proceedings of the IEEE Conference on Communications and Network Security*, pp. 580–585, 2017.

[21] W. Yew, PLC Device Security – Tailoring Needs, White Paper, SANS Institute, Bethesda, Maryland (sansorg.egnyte.com/dl/aN9oVirLPG), 2021.

Chapter 7

SIMULATING MEASUREMENT ATTACKS IN A SCADA SYSTEM TESTBED

Brandt Reutimann and Indrakshi Ray

Abstract   Industrial control systems are target-rich environments for cyber crim-
inals, terrorists and advanced persistent threats. Researchers have investigated various types of industrial control systems in smart grids, gas
pipelines and manufacturing facilities to understand how they can be
compromised by cyber threats. However, the manner in which industrial control systems are attacked is domain-dependent. Testbeds are a
necessary tool to model specific domains and understand potential attacks. This chapter discusses the development of a virtual supervisory
control and data acquisition system testbed for gas systems and how it
is used to simulate the impacts of measurement attacks. The testbed
provides opportunities for researchers and domain experts to model,
simulate and understand the behavior of a real-world gas system and
respond to cyber attacks.

Keywords: Natural gas system, SCADA system, testbed, measurement attacks

1.   Introduction

Industrial control systems are target-rich environments for cyber crim-
inals, terrorists and advanced persistent threats. Control technologies
have become more connected to internal corporate networks as well as
the Internet. As a result, industrial control systems have become more
accessible to malicious actors. Securing industrial control systems and,
by extension, the critical infrastructure assets they manage, are a priority.

Most work in industrial control system security has focused on supervisory control and data acquisition (SCADA) systems. SCADA systems
are sophisticated from the engineering and information technology perspectives. They comprise large networks of interconnected sensors, actuators and controllers, along with human-machine interfaces, engineering

© IFIP International Federation for Information Processing 2022
Published by Springer Nature Switzerland AG 2022
J. Staggs and S. Shenoi (Eds.): Critical Infrastructure Protection XV, IFIP AICT 636, pp. 135–153, 2022.
https://doi.org/10.1007/978-3-030-93511-5_7

workstations and historians. Often SCADA systems are connected to corporate networks where typical information technology security can become just as much of a concern as SCADA system security.

The architecture, interconnectivity and scale of SCADA systems lead to large attack surfaces. Controllers in SCADA systems tend to be heterogeneous because it is infeasible to replace or update large numbers of devices at the same time. The modification and replacement costs are high because availability is a priority and industrial processes cannot simply be shut down. Isolating SCADA networks from the outside world is a good security strategy, but it is not impervious. Attackers can find ways to tunnel into air-gapped SCADA networks from corporate networks, the Internet or merely by using a thumb drive as in the case of Stuxnet [9]. An Idaho National Laboratory report describes 22 high significance attacks on SCADA systems between 2000 and 2018 [7].

Experimenting with SCADA systems to enhance their security is difficult and potentially dangerous. Information about most SCADA systems and the assets they control is proprietary. Studying live systems can cause safety hazards and place physical assets at risk. The solution is to develop and engage a high-fidelity simulation of a SCADA system that enables accurate experimentation without the downsides of interacting with a real system.

This chapter describes experiments with a testbed comprising a simulated SCADA system that operates a modeled gas system. The main problem is to understand what happens when the control layer sends incorrect information to a SCADA system about the state of a physical system, a scenario referred to as a measurement attack [2]. Two experiments involving measurement attacks are considered. The first is a single point of failure experiment that explores the impact of compromising a single controller in a large gas system. The second experiment explores the impact of manipulating several controllers using advanced knowledge of the gas system.

2.   Related Work

In order to enhance the security of SCADA systems, it is important to anticipate and defend against possible attacks. The best approach is to probe the systems for flaws and vulnerabilities. Unfortunately, this is a complex and possibly dangerous task. In one instance, ping sweeps caused a robotic arm to swing wildly on a factory floor and in another instance they caused a system failure that resulted in significant equipment damage [5].

A promising approach is to conduct security testing of simulated SCADA systems and environments. Researchers from Mississippi State University have created a testbed comprising several physical systems, including a water tank, water tower, small gas pipeline, factory conveyor belt and smart grid [14]. They also created virtual models of their water tank and gas pipeline systems, which were validated against the physical implementations of the systems [15]. Although the simulation models have actual physical implementations, the physical testbeds are extremely simple. The models have single feedback loops and simple control sequences that do not accurately reflect the real-world systems. As a result, the models support security testing involving attacks on the network and physical components of the testbed, not attacks on the control algorithms.

Researchers have demonstrated various network-based attacks on virtual SCADA system testbeds [2]. Other researchers have conducted attacks on virtual systems that model the large-scale behavior of SCADA systems from the testbed or network-based perspectives [6, 11]. However, these research efforts are limited because they only model the network behavior of SCADA systems or employ small-scale physical testbeds.

Many testbeds that employ physical implementations do not incorporate many of the components in real systems due to resource constraints. Some researchers attempt to address this problem using hybrid models with hardware-in-the-loop simulations [18]. However, these solutions are not as cost effective as software models and virtualized systems. Previous work on SCADA system simulation has focused mainly on single facilities or models of electrical systems [12]. Scalability, accuracy and fidelity are key requirements for designing system simulations from an engineering standpoint. Simulations of full-scale SCADA systems should also be considered when designing and evaluating the security of large-scale assets such as gas pipelines and electrical grids.

In addition to studying SCADA system simulation in general, the interactions between gas and electrical systems is a popular area of study. Gas systems can induce failures in electrical systems and vice versa. Researchers have modeled and analyzed the interdependencies between the systems [4, 10]. Other researchers have created and worked with models that simulate system interactions. The simulated systems have shown that failures of a few gas lines can lead to cascading failures in an interconnected electrical system [3]. However, the models only consider limited sets of variables as opposed to the high-fidelity model described in this chapter.

Despite the body of research in the area of SCADA system simulation, the work described in this chapter addresses some novel issues. Little, if any, work on SCADA system simulation focuses on gas systems or their effects on electrical systems, especially with regard to cyber vulnerabilities and attacks. Although this work does not cover the interactions between electrical and gas systems in detail, it explores vulnerabilities in a simulated gas system that has the potential to harm a hypothetical electrical system. The work also explores measurement attacks on a large-scale gas pipeline model. Additionally, it presents a simple SCADA system simulation architecture that can be used to create modular simulations of a variety of cyber-physical systems. Indeed, previous research has mostly created simulations of specific types of (mainly electrical) systems instead of presenting methods for creating more expansive simulation models.

3.   Gas System Model and Experimental Setup

This section describes the design and simulation of the gas system model used in the experiments, along with the experimental setup, including the experimental gas system scenario and data collection.

3.1   Gas System Model

The gas system model used in the experiments was designed to capture gas pipeline assets in the state of Colorado. The main objective was to make the model realistic enough that the system would fail due to cyber attacks and not because the engineering concepts underlying the model are weak. To accomplish the task, the model development team consulted with engineers at the Colorado Powerhouse and other gas system experts to define appropriate model constraints. The principal concern was to obtain data that would provide scale to the model. However, the process of acquiring accurate data on control systems was very challenging.

Data from several sources was collected and gas dynamics principles were employed to determine appropriate measurements. A Kinder Morgan system map provided the general locations of gas pipelines, compressors and power plants in the state of Colorado [19]. The map was augmented with large cities at their rough distances from gas pipelines and other assets. Moderate-sized power plants near medium-sized cities in Colorado and a large power plant in Denver were also included in the map. Distribution loads were sprinkled on the map to add complexity to the gas pipeline system. Having determined the placement of power plants, compressors and distribution loads, Xcel Energy resources were used to discover the peak load capacities (in MW) for power plants around the state [17]. The peak capacities (in MW) were converted to the required gas mass flow rates (in kg/s) using gas heating values.

The peak mass flow gas loads for each power plant (in kg/s) were used to determine the gas pipe diameters that would meet the demand at a nominal pressure of 800 psi using Bernoulli's equation (ignoring gravity and height differences). As the gas loads in the designed system and in the real world are very high, the gas pipelines had to be large enough to distribute the required gas. Gas pipe typically comes in nominal sizes that do not exceed 36 inches in diameter and, when more gas has to be distributed, additional pipes are laid in parallel. However, the system does not consider this situation and uses a single large pipe. This leads to adverse effects on some of the gas properties. For example, there is more friction when using several small pipes than when using a single large pipe. Additionally, gas flow rates are higher in smaller pipes, which means that temperature changes can be more dramatic.

Having determined the gas model structure and worked out the basic numerical constraints, the gas model was simulated using a SCADA system simulation tool. The SCADA system simulation tool developed by the research team comprises a controller and software simulator that interfaces with MATLAB Simulink to integrate virtual programmable logic controllers and hardware-in-the-loop devices. These virtual and real devices communicate using Modbus, their native SCADA protocol. This provides a window into the Simulink simulations using traditional controllers and control system software. The design considerations and development of the SCADA system simulation tool are outside the scope of this research and are not described in this chapter.

3.2 Experimental Setup

Gas systems can become extremely hazardous when pressure or temperature drop rapidly. Rapid drops in pressure can prevent gas delivery while temperature drops can lead to dew pointing and solids traveling with the gas. Previous simulation experiments employed an external control system to trip (switch off) a power plant when its pressure or temperature reached the set values. However, in the experiments, it was desired to keep switch-off control inside the process model to model a power plant engineer tripping the plant when the gas pressure or temperature reaches the set values. In the gas system model, a MATLAB function block was incorporated to set a power plant load to zero and switch it off for a number of seconds specified by a parameter at the beginning of the simulation. The shutoff duration of a power plant was set to 3,600 seconds (one hour). This time represents how long after a shutoff it takes power plant engineers to run through their safety procedures and ramp the plant back up to meet the current load. The goal of the experiments was to get power plants to trip their automatic shutoffs by dropping the gas pressure in the system.

The gas system model uses a dynamic load distribution algorithm that enables it to simulate a systemwide load that different power plants in the system have to cooperate to meet. Every load was specified individually in previous experiments. However, in this case, a single load could be specified to model a realistic scenario. The advantage of this approach is that when one power plant in the system trips, the load switches to other power plants in the system. This effectively models scenarios where the loss of a power plant can possibly cause a cascading failure because gas demands increase very rapidly in other parts of the system.

Each power plant in the system is specified with a gas load capacity (kg/s), which helps determine its current load. If the gas load capacity of a plant is p_c, total system gas load capacity is s_c and the current total gas load at time t is l_t, then the current gas load of the plant at time t is $p_c/s_c \cdot l_t$.

Also, a scenario must be considered where the total gas system load exceeds the capacity of the available power plants. In this case, each plant outputs at its maximum load, but the systemwide demand will not be met. This scenario corresponds to a situation where the gas system is not generating enough electrical power to meet demand.

The control system used in the experiments has considerable complexity. The compressors in the system are designed so that the power capacity of a power plant can be modified. When compressing gas, a compressor examines the value δ_p corresponding to the difference in pressure between the desired set point (800 psi in the model) and the current pressure reading. As δ_p increases, more power is required to compress gas to meet the pressure differential. In order to render the system realistic, there must be a limit on the amount of power that a compressor can use to achieve its goal. The limit has a base value of 5 MW. When the system requires more power than is available, δ_p is modified to the maximum compression available for the current maximum amount of power. This plays into the control system as the system operators desire to minimize the amount of power being used by compressors whenever possible.

The control algorithm for the gas model increases the power available to upstream compressors based on the current pressure readings at downstream power plants and compressors. The controller iteratively checks the state of the system and updates the power available to each immediate upstream compressor. Power is updated in 5 MW increments. If the pressure is less than 750 psi then power is increased by 5 MW whereas if the pressure is at 800 psi the available power is decreased by 5 MW to conserve energy. Upstream compressors are identified by consulting the directed graph that represents gas flow in the system. Each node in the graph is either a power plant or a compressor. Every power plant is always a leaf node because gas does not flow through a power plant to other nodes in the system.

Gas System Scenario. The gas model was set up in a scenario to conduct two experiments. The scenario covers a period of time when the gas system is placed under a high level of stress. This is important because cyber attacks are especially serious when systems are under high stress.

The scenario, which covered three days, was intended to demonstrate the potential impacts of data manipulation in a SCADA system. During the first day, the system operates under a moderate load. Such a situation occurs when a renewable energy source like wind provides a large portion of the electricity demand [1]. Although this may be slightly contrived, it is a good starting point for demonstrating the value of SCADA system simulation.

On the second day, there is a sudden loss of wind power coupled with an increase in electric power demand. As a result, the natural gas power plants ramp up to generate enough electricity to meet the demand. After a 12-hour period, things return to normal because wind power comes back up and electricity demand drops.

Figure 1 shows that the power generation matches the required power load over the three days of the scenario. This is because, during the high-stress period, when natural gas power plants ramp up to generate electricity, control systems in the gas system adjust the compressors to deliver gas to the power plants. When wind power comes back up and electricity demand drops, the control systems enable the gas system to ramp down to match the required power load.

When natural gas power plants ramp up to generate electricity, the demand for natural gas in the gas system increases dramatically, which reduces the pressure in the gas system. If the compressors in the gas system are not adjusted by the control systems to meet the demand, power plants begin to trip because gas is not delivered at a high enough pressure. Figure 2 shows the rapid loss in power generation when the control systems do not intervene.

The goal of measurement attacks in the scenario is to prevent control systems from adjusting gas pressure at the beginning of the high-stress

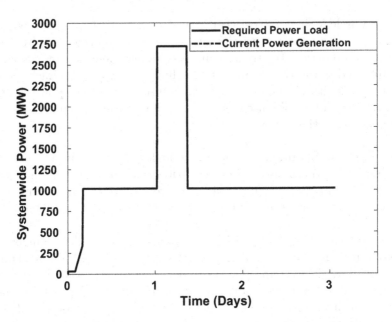

Figure 1. Electric power generation and power load over the three-day scenario.

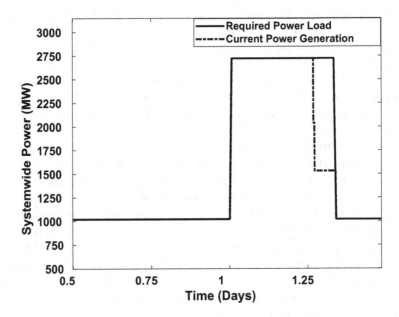

Figure 2. Rapid power generation loss without control system intervention.

period. An attack is successful if it causes a power plant to trip during the high-stress period.

Data Collection. Data was collected in several places in the simulated system to demonstrate consistency and the effects of control system compromises. The Simulink model logged all the data during the simulation and data coming from the programmable logic controllers to the simulated operator was tracked. This data was marked on the operator side. Thus, there is a copy of the authentic data as well as a copy of the compromised data. The two sets of data can be compared to show how the real state of the system is affected by the control actions made using the compromised data.

4. Single Point of Failure

The first experiment explored the impacts of a single point of failure on the gas system during the 12-hour high-stress window. When gas loads on the system increase, gas pressure drops at the natural gas power plants as they start evacuating their upstream gas lines. It is vital that the power plant controllers recognize the pressure drops and make more power available to the upstream compressors. Therefore, the attacks in the first experiment provide false pressure readings to the power plant controllers. The false pressure readings at the power plants would prevent upstream compressors from ramping up, dropping the gas pressure at the power plants to levels at which they cannot operate.

The compromise used in the experiment was very simple – no matter the system state, a compromised power plant would always report 800 psi. The experiment comprised five trials, each trial involving the application of the compromise to each power plant and running the simulation. An attack was deemed successful if a power plant failure occurred within the 12-hour window of high stress. The goal of the experiment was to determine if a single compromise could induce catastrophic effects on the gas system.

Interesting results were obtained in the experiment. In four of the five trials, although a measurement attack was taking place, the compressor immediately upstream of the attack was not affected. This is because multiple downstream entities showed low pressure values and a single false pressure value did not prevent the control system from updating the pressure value at the compressor. In the case of power plants that were isolated, the measurement attacks could have disabled their compressors, but as the compressors on the main lines in the simulation were still running, there would be enough gas being pushed through the system to prevent failures.

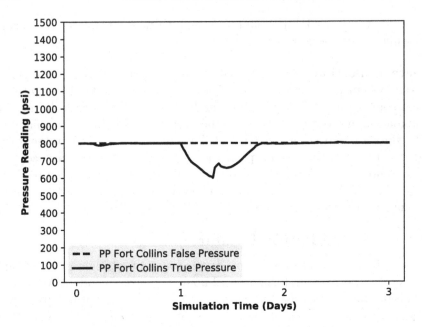

Figure 3.   True and false pressure readings at the Fort Collins plant.

The one trial that resulted in failure provided interesting insights. Compromising the pressure reading at the Fort Collins power plant led to its compressor being temporarily disabled, which caused the Fort Collins plant to go offline. Figure 3 shows the true and false pressure reading differentials at the Fort Collins plant over the simulation.

The increased gas demand imposed on the auxiliary line from Fort Morgan caused the Fort Morgan plant to trip. Figure 4 shows the failure of the Fort Collins plant followed by the failure of the Fort Morgan plant near the end of the 12-hour window.

The interesting takeaway is that the Fort Collins compressor is a critical point in the system because it feeds gas to a number of downstream power plants. When the Fort Collins compressor does not meet the demand of the downstream plants, increased loads are induced on the auxiliary lines, leading to the failure of the Fort Morgan plant.

5.   Sophisticated Measurement Attack

The second experiment explored compromises of multiple sensors in the system to induce a rapid failure. The objective was to prevent a compressor from ramping up when it should while encouraging other compressors to ramp up when they need not. The attack is similar to

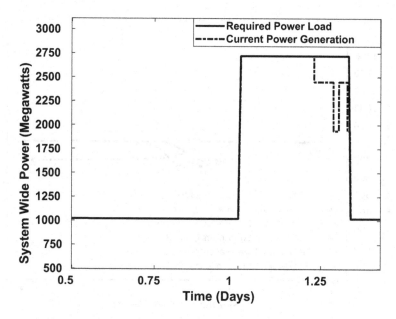

Figure 4. Failures of the Fort Collins and Fort Morgan plants.

the one in the first experiment because it falsifies data, but it is more sophisticated in that the false data manipulates the actions of multiple upstream compressors.

The first experiment revealed that the Fort Collins compressor is a critical asset in the gas system. Therefore, the second experiment sought to target the immediate downstream neighbors of the Fort Collins compressor – the Fort Collins power plant and the Longmont compressor. The attack caused the Fort Collins power plant and Longmont compressor to always read 800 psi regardless of the actual pressure. Additionally, the attack set the Denver power plant pressure reading low to ramp up the Denver compressor, pulling gas through the line from Fort Collins to Denver. The objective was to pull gas down the line while preventing the Fort Collins compressor from ramping up to meet the new demand. This would empty the gas lines and induce failures in the system. Figure 5 shows the discrepancies between the true and false pressure readings.

The second experiment yielded interesting results related to measurement attacks. The compromised high readings at the Fort Collins power plant and Longmont compressor prevented the Fort Collins compressor from ramping up during the period of high stress. Additionally, the control system increased the power to the Denver compressor to compensate for the false low pressure reading. This caused the pressure in the Fort

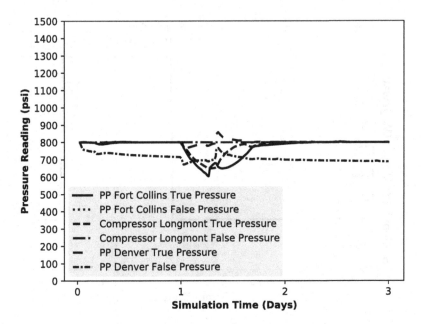

Figure 5.   Discrepancies between the true and false pressure readings.

Collins to Longmont line to drop (Figure 6) as well as increase the demand on the auxiliary line from Fort Morgan. As gas was evacuated from the two lines coming into Longmont, the pressure dropped rapidly in both lines. As a result, the Fort Collins and Fort Morgan plants tripped in rapid succession (Figure 7). This resulted in the gas and power generation systems not being able to meet their total demands. The total loss of capacity of gas load (in kg/s) translates roughly to a loss of about 800 MW in just five minutes (Figure 8).

6.   Discussion

The experimental results provide insights into the hazards posed by measurement attacks. The first experiment explored how a single point of failure can affect a complex system. The results show that, although there could be catastrophic effects at critical points in the system, isolated portions of the system tend to incur minimal impacts. Therefore, the isolated portions do not require comprehensive defenses. It may be adequate to secure the overall system from catastrophic failures by identifying and applying maximal defenses at the critical points.

The second experiment is interesting, albeit troubling, because it demonstrates that an attacker with intimate knowledge of system dy-

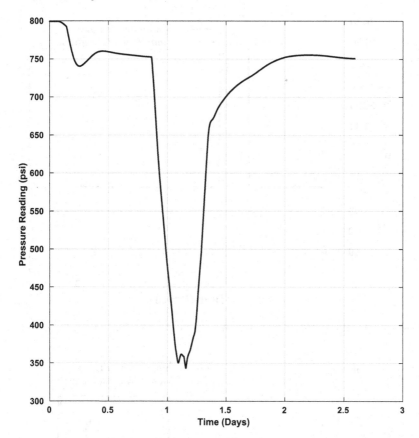

Figure 6. Pressure drop in the Longmont gas line during the high-stress period.

namics could use measurement attacks to manipulate the control response. Measurement attacks can put the system into a state that induces failures that would not occur with normal control behavior. As more sensors are compromised, measurement attacks become increasingly complex and likely more difficult to detect. However, they require the attacker to have knowledge of how the control system operates, the gas system topology and when the system is in a period of high stress.

The experiments also show that the responses of gas systems to cyber attacks are very different from the responses of electrical systems. Failures in electrical systems occur very rapidly. For example, in the case of the August 14, 2003 blackout in the United States and Canada, system operators noticed anomalies around 4:06 pm, just four minutes before a power surge took out a large power line that induced cascading failures leading to the blackout [16]. In the case of the San Diego

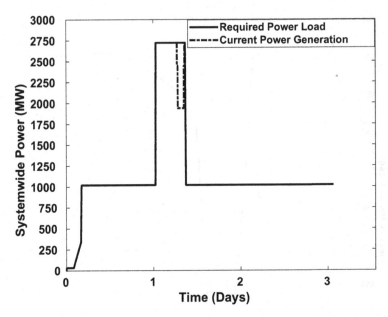

Figure 7.   Load profiles show that power plants trip and fail to meet the demand.

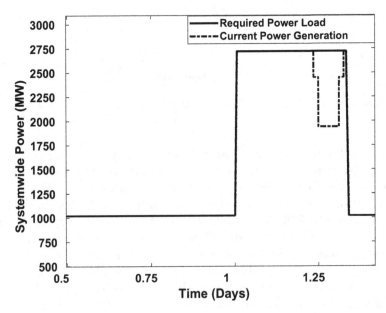

Figure 8.   Load profiles show that power plants trip and fail to meet the demand.

blackout of 2011, a system supported primarily by a 500 kV line went down in roughly 10 minutes following a maintenance problem at a remote substation [13].

Unlike in electrical systems, physical effects in gas systems have high latency. This is seen in the experimental results – even under a sustained measurement attack, several hours passed before a drop off in electricity production occurred. This is partly due to how the scenario was set up. But this could also be because it takes a long time (relative to electricity) to physically move gas through pipes. This could also explain why isolated attacks have less impact on the system.

Additionally, large pipes hold substantial amounts of gas. The stored gas can prevent failures during rapid increases in gas load because there is not an immediate reaction to the change in system state. This was seen in the scenario, where even with no control response, the system did not fail until the near the end of the 12-hour window. This suggests that there is ample time to react when the system is not operating normally. The positioning of gas storage tanks at strategic locations on gas lines is another way to avoid failures during periods of high stress. This does not bode well for attackers intending to damage a gas system, but it also does not mean that the system is safe from strategic and coordinated attacks.

The principal takeaway from the experiments is that cyber attacks have to be sustained for hours or even days to have impacts on gas systems. For example, in the single point of failure scenario, where the system was sustained by a primary source of gas (like the 500 kV line in the San Diego blackout example), a measurement attack had to be sustained for nearly 12 hours before any impact was observed. A variety of scenarios would have to be investigated to advance this hypothesis. The single point of failure scenario was designed to be challenging for a gas system in order to demonstrate the value of simulation and the impacts of measurement attacks. Regardless, the length of time a measurement attack would have to be sustained to produce a negative impact is encouraging because it would be very difficult to trick system operators for hours on end. Redundant sensors and frequent communication between operators could enable them to identify false data before failures occur. However, because cyber attacks on gas pipelines are rare, a gas system operator would likely attribute anomalous phenomena to faulty sensors or devices instead of attacks. Of course, the important point is that a sustained measurement attack on a gas system that goes undetected long enough could cause rapid cascading failures as seen in the second experiment.

7.   Future Work

An important area of future research is to detect measurement attacks using machine learning techniques. One approach is to employ statistical methods for outlier identification; these methods could enable control systems to identify sensor readings as outliers in time series data. Another approach is to apply deep learning and classification algorithms to identify anomalies in time series data.

SCADA system data could also be analyzed to identify constraints within and between sensor data streams. An example constraint within a data stream is that a pressure sensor reading should be in a certain range during normal operations. A constraint between data streams is the mathematical relationship between the temperature and pressure of a gas. Another such constraint is that pressure readings at power plants downstream of a large compressor vary together in response to changes in the compressor output. An intelligent SCADA system could be trained to identify and report constraint violations to system operators for analysis and mitigation.

A primary issue with identifying constraints in SCADA systems is that as the systems scale, the constraints become increasingly complex and interconnected. Identifying constraints between multiple components requires considerable expertise, and is time-consuming and error-prone. Researchers have developed an automated methodology for identifying and verifying constraints in large data sets using a feedback loop with subject matter experts [8]; this methodology is certainly applicable to automated constraint discovery in SCADA system time series data.

Another area of future research is the automated discovery of critical points to prioritize the application of security controls. This research has shown that compromises of certain controllers can be much more devastating than compromises of others. For example, in the first experiment, compromising the Fort Collins power plant controller prevented the Fort Collins compressor from feeding gas to several downstream power plants, resulting in a partial failure of the gas system. Automated discovery would require the simulation of a real-world gas system and iteratively applying measurement or command injection attacks to each controller. Analysis of compromises and the failures they induce would help determine the critical points and their relative importance.

8.   Conclusions

Realistic SCADA system simulations are vital to understanding the behavior of real-world systems and the impacts of cyber attacks. The principal contributions of this research are the development of a high-fidelity gas system simulation and the application of measurement attacks to understand their local and overall gas system impacts. The simulation experiments show that an intelligent attacker can cause considerable harm to a gas system via measurement attacks. The experiments also provide useful insights about critical points in gas systems and the propagation of the negative impacts of attacks. The simulation environment supports high-level reasoning about SCADA system security without having to work on a real system. Additionally, it enables the exploration of diverse scenarios that would simply not be possible on real gas system.

Acknowledgements

This research was supported by the National Science Foundation under Grant no. CNS 1822118 and by the National Institute of Standards and Technology, American Megatrends Inc., CyberRiskResearch, Statnett and the Colorado State Cyber Security Center and Energy Institute at Colorado State University. The authors wish to acknowledge the Colorado State University Powerhouse and METEC Gas Testing Site for their assistance in modeling high-fidelity gas systems. The authors also wish to thank Aeric Walls for his assistance with the experiments and presenting the results.

References

[1] V. Akhmatov, Analysis of Dynamic Behavior of Electric Power Systems with Large Amount of Wind Power, Ph.D. Thesis, Department of Electric Power Engineering, Technical University of Denmark, Lyngby, Denmark, 2003.

[2] A. Ashok, P. Wang, M. Brown and M. Govindarasu, Experimental evaluation of cyber attacks on automatic generation control using a CPS security testbed, *Proceedings of the IEEE Power and Energy Society General Meeting*, 2015.

[3] B. Cakir Erdener, K. Pambour, R. Bolado Lavin and B. Dengiz, An integrated simulation model for analyzing electricity and gas systems, *International Journal of Electrical Power and Energy Systems*, vol. 61, pp. 410–420, 2014.

[4] C. Correa-Posada, P. Sanchez-Martin and S. Lumbreras, Security-constrained model for an integrated power and natural gas system, *Journal of Modern Power Systems and Clean Energy*, vol. 5(3), pp. 326–336, 2017.

[5] D. Duggan, Penetration Testing of Industrial Control Systems, Sandia Report SAND2005-2846P, Sandia National Laboratories, Albuquerque, New Mexico, 2005.

[6] S. Duque Anton, M. Gundall, D. Fraunholz and H. Schotten, Implementing SCADA Scenarios and Introducing Attacks to Obtain Training Data for Intrusion Detection Methods, arXiv: 1905.12443 (arxiv.org/abs/1905.12443), 2019.

[7] K. Hemsley and R. Fisher, History of Industrial Control System Cyber Incidents, INL/CON-18-44411-Revision-2, Idaho National Laboratory, Idaho Falls, Idaho, 2018.

[8] H. Homayouni, S. Ghosh and I. Ray, ADQuaTe: An automated data quality test approach for constraint discovery and fault detection, *Proceedings of the Twentieth IEEE International Conference on Information Reuse and Integration for Data Science*, pp. 61–68, 2019.

[9] R. Langner, Stuxnet: Dissecting a cyberwarfare weapon, *IEEE Security and Privacy*, vol. 9(3), pp. 49–51, 2011.

[10] T. Li, M. Eremia and M. Shahidehpour, Interdependency of natural gas network and power system security, *IEEE Transactions on Power Systems*, vol. 23(4), pp. 1817–1824, 2008.

[11] B. Masset and O. Taburiaux, Simulating Industrial Control Systems Using Mininet, M.S. Dissertation, Department of Computer Science, Catholic University of Louvain, Louvain-la-Neuve, Belgium, 2018.

[12] K. Mathioudakis, N. Frangiadakis, A. Merentitis and V. Gazis, Towards generic SCADA simulators: A survey of existing multipurpose co-simulation platforms, best practices and use cases, *Proceedings of the Scientific Cooperations International Conference on Electrical and Electronics Engineering*, pp. 33–40, 2013.

[13] J. McDonald and M. Lee, Blackout sparks multiple investigations, *San Diego-Union Tribune*, September 9, 2011.

[14] T. Morris, A. Srivastava, B. Reaves, W. Gao, K. Pavurapu and R. Reddi, A control system testbed to validate critical infrastructure protection concepts, *International Journal of Critical Infrastructure Protection*, vol. 4(2), pp. 88–103, 2011.

[15] T. Morris, Z. Thornton and I. Turnipseed, Industrial control system simulation and data logging for intrusion detection system research, *Proceedings of the Seventh Annual Southeastern Cyber Security Summit*, 2015.

[16] North American Electric Reliability Council, Technical Analysis of the August 14, 2003 Blackout: What Happened, Why and What Did We Learn? Report to the NERC Board of Trustees by the NERC Steering Group, Princeton, New Jersey, 2004.

[17] Public Service Company of Colorado, Colorado Generating Stations, Denver, Colorado, 2017.

[18] Q. Qassim, N. Jamil, I. Abidin, M. Rusli, S. Yussof, R. Ismail, F. Abdullah, N. Ja'afar, H. Che Hasan and M. Daud, A survey of SCADA testbed implementation approaches, *Indian Journal of Science and Technology*, vol. 10(26), 2017.

[19] N. Schubert, KMI System Map, Kinder Morgan, Houston, Texas, 2014.

Chapter 8

A COMMUNICATIONS VALIDITY DETECTOR FOR SCADA NETWORKS

Prashant Anantharaman, Anmol Chachra, Shikhar Sinha, Michael Millian, Bogdan Copos, Sean Smith and Michael Locasto

Abstract   Supervisory control and data acquisition systems (SCADA) are attractive targets due to their widespread use in the critical infrastructure. A large percentage of attacks involve crafted inputs. Buffer overflows, a form of crafted input attack, are still common. These attacks can be used to take over SCADA systems or force them to crash. The compromised systems could be leveraged to issue commands to other devices in a SCADA network and cause harm.

This chapter presents a novel forensic tool that enables operators to detect crafted input attacks and monitor SCADA systems and networks for harmful actions. The tool incorporates several language-theoretic security-compliant parsers to ensure the syntactic validity of communications, enabling the detection of zero-day attacks that leverage crafted packets. The tool also detects attacks triggered using legacy protocols and includes graphical user interfaces, command-line interfaces and tools for comparing network traffic against configuration files to detect malicious activities. Experimental evaluations of the parsers using a large SCADA network traffic dataset demonstrate their efficacy. Fuzzing experiments demonstrate the resilience of the parsers as well as the tool itself.

Keywords: SCADA systems, language-theoretic security, forensics

1.   Introduction

Supervisory control and data acquisition (SCADA) protocols are used throughout modern power grids for automation and "smart" operation. Substations in power grids are increasingly unstaffed and are managed from control centers using SCADA protocols such as Distributed Network Protocol 3 (DNP3) and IEC 61850 Manufacturing Message Spec-

© IFIP International Federation for Information Processing 2022
Published by Springer Nature Switzerland AG 2022
J. Staggs and S. Shenoi (Eds.): Critical Infrastructure Protection XV, IFIP AICT 636, pp. 155–183, 2022.
https://doi.org/10.1007/978-3-030-93511-5_8

ification (MMS). These critical infrastructure assets have historically separated operational technology systems from information technology systems using non-routable interfaces and legacy hardware. However, the air gaps are disappearing as the assets are increasingly being operated remotely [8].

The interconnectivity of SCADA systems has also increased their attack surfaces. In December 2015 and 2016, attackers leveraged spear-phishing email to access computer systems of electric utility operators in Kiev, Ukraine [15], eventually taking several substations offline by opening electrical relays remotely. Iran's uranium hexafluoride centrifuges in Natanz were targeted by multiple zero-day attacks using a USB drive to breach the air gap [16].

Securing SCADA systems is challenging. Commands received by SCADA devices often have physical effects, and availability and timeliness are of paramount importance. Additionally, the devices are usually resource-constrained and security schemes often do not meet the strict real-time guarantees [41].

Meanwhile, anomaly and intrusion detection schemes for SCADA systems rely on the physics of the systems and/or communications patterns. Such schemes cannot detect crafted input attacks and zero-day attacks that are of increasing concern.

Forensic tools for SCADA systems must detect attacks that leverage invalid communications. In SCADA systems, invalid communications exploit weaknesses in programs due to insufficient syntax checking. Programs often fail to implement communications protocols correctly, leading to vulnerabilities. An attacker can exploit these vulnerabilities to crash programs or gain access to the devices that execute the programs.

Forensic tools must detect syntactically-valid but semantically-invalid communications. For each device in a SCADA network, an operator has a specifications document that lists all the IP addresses and endpoints. For SCADA protocols such as DNP3 and IEC 61850 MMS, a device only supports a specific set of requests known as setpoints. A SCADA operator also maintains documents showing the setpoints supported by SCADA devices. Communications that violate any of the network or setpoint configurations are semantically invalid.

SCADA forensic tools must also help detect communications triggered by malicious programs and devices. Differentiating between human actions and malicious program/device actions is a difficult problem. SCADA forensic tools must provide visual feedback or confirmation of human-triggered actions and malicious actions.

To address these challenges, this chapter presents a communications validity detection tool for SCADA networks. The tool detects malformed packets in a wide range of SCADA protocols. Packets that do not conform to the protocol specifications are flagged, providing the ability to detect potential zero-day attacks. The tool detects various web-based, Telnet-based and DNP3 commands leveraged in attacks. Also, it detects configuration and communications mismatches in SCADA networks. Indeed, this work heralds a new forensic paradigm that permanently positions devices across a large SCADA network to monitor traffic and provide early warnings of cyber attacks.

2.   Background and Related Work

This section presents background information and related research on SCADA systems, SCADA network attacks, language-theoretic security, SCADA system forensics, software-defined networks and anomaly detection.

2.1   SCADA Systems

SCADA systems are deeply embedded in critical infrastructure assets [13]. These systems are used to monitor and control assets such as railroads, aircraft, nuclear power plants, electric power grids, water treatment plants and petrochemical refineries.

SCADA systems in the electric grid are housed in two principal types of facilities, substations and control centers. Substations usually span large geographic areas. Multiple substations are typically managed by a single control center. A control center houses real-time automation controllers (RTACs), master terminal units (MTUs) and human-machine interfaces (HMIs). Substations house intelligent electronic devices (IEDs), relays, programmable logic controllers (PLCs) and remote terminal units (RTUs). These devices are responsible for physical tasks such as opening and closing circuits at substations, among others.

Devices in a substation such as programmable logic controllers and remote terminal units communicate with the real-time automation controllers and human-machine interfaces at the control center. The control center aggregates data such as phasor information and the states of all the relays in the substation. Operators use the human-machine interfaces to send commands to relays via the remote terminal units.

SCADA systems use various communications protocols. This research focuses on the DNP3, IEEE C37.118, IEC 61850 MMS, IEC 61850 GOOSE, SEL Fast Message and SES-92 protocols. Of these protocols, DNP3, IEC 61850 MMS and SES-92 can be used interchangeably to poll remote terminal units and send commands from human-machine interfaces.

The IEEE C37.118 and SEL Fast Message protocols are used to send phasor measurements from phasor measurement units to phasor data concentrators. Phasor measurements are useful for estimating the state of a power system, detecting wide-area power events and monitoring power flows. Some substations use dedicated phasor measurement units and phasor data concentrators, but these features are often incorporated in relays.

SCADA systems reside in operational technology networks that have distinct characteristics from conventional information technology networks [36]. First, operational technology networks operate under hard real-time constraints [40]. Network packets received after deadlines are often useless and may have adverse effects on the power system state. For example, the IEC 61850 GOOSE protocol has a packet reception deadline of 4 ms. Any packets received after this time are ignored.

Furthermore, devices in substations often operate continuously for long periods of time. Most of the devices run real-time operating systems, which handle memory differently from conventional operating systems. In particular, the operating system kernel and user memory are not separated. This feature of real-time operating systems renders them prime targets for buffer overflow attacks.

Some SCADA devices only support serial protocols. As a result, IP-based sniffers on routers and switches are mostly ineffective for these devices. Also, most attacks that target information technology systems exploit various features of IP-based protocol stacks. SCADA devices may be immune to such attacks, but they are still prone to buffer overflow and crafted packet attacks.

Finally, most SCADA protocols do not support encryption. Even when the implementations support protocol encryption, communications are unencrypted because encryption adds latency. Most SCADA protocols also do not support authentication mechanisms, which enables SCADA devices to be spoofed easily.

2.2   SCADA Network Attacks

Historically, SCADA networks have used proprietary protocols and devices that were separated from other components. The air gaps are disappearing as corporate and cloud networks increasingly connect to SCADA networks [6]. The absence of air gaps enables attackers who enter corporate or cloud networks to make their way into SCADA networks.

In December 2015 and 2016, attackers leveraged spear-phishing email with malicious Word documents to access computer systems of electric utility operators in Kiev, Ukraine [15]. The attackers observed operator actions and collected virtual private network (VPN) credentials to access the SCADA networks. The attackers then took several substations offline by opening electrical relays remotely.

One of the earliest recorded SCADA system attacks was in 1982 [9]. A trans-Siberian gas pipeline ran software that incorporated a Trojan horse. The malware executed when pipeline operators were conducting a routine pressure test, increasing the pipeline pressure and causing an explosion.

In 2017, a Saudi Arabian petrochemical plant was targeted by the Triton malware [29]. As in the Ukraine attacks, the attackers pivoted from the information technology network to the operational technology network to infect engineering workstations. The Triton malware reprogrammed the Triconex industrial safety system to induce an automatic shutdown.

In contrast, the Stuxnet malware entered a highly-secure air-gapped operational technology network in Natanz, Iran via an infected USB drive [16]. The malware injected a rootkit into a Siemens programmable logic controller that sent malicious commands to uranium hexafluoride centrifuges while reporting normal readings to plant operators. In 2010, it was reported that Stuxnet destroyed almost 20% of Iran's centrifuges.

Meanwhile, researchers have discovered several vulnerabilities that could have been exploited by attackers. For example, Lee et al. [21] have demonstrated several simulated attacks on DNP3 systems. Crain and Sistrunk [11] have discovered several vulnerabilities in DNP3 vendor implementations.

SCADA systems often have buffer overflow weaknesses [40]. In addition to the buffer overflows discovered by Crain and Sistrunk [11], researchers have found heap-based buffer overflows in WellinTech King-View servers that are widely used in China. Triangle Microworks [26] reported buffer overflows in their DNP3 library that could be exploited using crafted packets.

2.3 Language-Theoretic Security

Language-theoretic security is a programming paradigm that mandates that all inputs received by a program must be treated as sentences in a formal language, such as one generated by a regular or context-free grammar. Moreover, all inputs must be validated by a recognizer for the formal language before they are processed.

Most protocol specifications constitute pages of verbose text without machine-recognizable grammars. Developers have to read through the entire specifications and implement code that conforms to the un-documented grammars. As a result, they often leave certain features unimplemented and/or do not implement features correctly. For example, a stack overflow bug was found in the Triangle Microworks DNP3 library [26]. The CVE description of the bug acknowledges that it was due to "poor validation of user-supplied data."

In a language-theoretic security methodology, a protocol specification is expressed in terms of a formal grammar. A parser-combinator toolkit such as Hammer [28] is used to implement a parser based on the grammar. Parser combinators make it easy to implement grammars using programming languages.

Several attempts have been made to implement parsers for SCADA protocols. Bratus et al. [7] were the first to implement a parser for the popular DNP3 protocol. However, they discovered that the Hammer toolkit constructs were inadequate to implement the protocol and had to incorporate additional constructs. The resulting DNP3 parser is incorporated in the communications validity detection tool described in this work.

Anantharaman et al. [4] have developed a tool that filters invalid and malformed IEEE C37.118 packets using a language-theoretic security parser. This parser is also incorporated in the communications validity detection tool with the caveat that the parser is only used to detect anomalous traffic and not perform filtering. When malformed packets are detected, only alerts are sent because availability in SCADA systems is of paramount importance. Specifically, a packet that is filtered as a false negative could prevent a SCADA device from performing a time-critical task with adverse consequences.

Millian et al. [23] have demonstrated how a power grid utility network could be converted to use language-theoretic security-compliant protocol implementations. They explored the steps it would take to include language-theoretic security filters, i.e., software that would not allow any malformed traffic to pass. In contrast, given the risk posed by false negatives, this work allows all traffic to pass while operators are alerted to malformed inputs.

2.4   SCADA System Forensics

After a cyber attack occurs, digital forensic practitioners apply various techniques and tools to gather evidence to retrace the attack steps and prevent similar attacks in the future. Wright et al. [38] have proposed a model for investigating cyber attacks on SCADA systems. The model has four sequential steps: examination of evidence sources, identification of an attack, collection of evidence and documentation of evidence. The communications validity detection tool described in this research follows these forensic analysis steps. The tool gathers evidence from network packets and identifies packets that violate specifications as potential crafted packets. This evidence is logged in a local database.

Valli et al. [35] have proposed a framework for creating Snort signatures for various vulnerabilities. They examined multiple vulnerabilities in SCADA protocols such as DNP3 and Modbus to create signatures. They performed attacks in a test environment and constructed a system to generate Snort rules from packet captures. The communications validity detection tool differs from this framework in a fundamental manner. Rules are not created for known attacks; instead, parsers that validate all inputs are developed for SCADA protocols.

Ahmed et al. [2] have discussed the challenges encountered when investigating attacks on SCADA systems. They point out that operators would rather keep SCADA systems online than turn them off for evidence gathering. Therefore, SCADA systems need live forensic tools [1, 24]. Additionally, intrusion detection tools based on prior data or rule sets may be too strict for forensic tools, causing the tools to raise too many false alarms. Also, substation devices are often very resource-constrained and storing forensic data on the devices may not be an option.

The communications validity detection tool described in this research addresses these challenges in various ways. First, the tool connects to a live network tap interface. A router or switch duplicates all network traffic and sends the duplicated traffic to the tap interface, enabling the tool to validate the packets. Second, since the tool runs its own analysis, it ignores the packets it creates, which reduces false alarms. Finally, the tool employs a PostgreSQL database to store forensic data.

2.5   Software-Defined Networks

Software-defined networks (SDNs) allow for packet processing, forwarding and filtering at virtual switches [14]. These networks disassociate network forwarding rules in a data plane and routing rules in a control plane. In the case of an operational technology network, a software-defined network would manage network access control and Ethernet forwarding for SCADA devices. Kalra et al. [20] describe a software-defined operational technology network that meets the network performance and cyber security requirements. However, their cyber security requirements only overlap with a portion of the semantic errors considered in this research, namely, issues with missing and newly-added devices.

Urias et al. [34] explore how software-defined operational technology networks can be used to deceive attackers and learn about their techniques. However, the work described in this chapter is closest to the approaches of Chang et al. [10] and Kalra et al. [20]. Chang and colleagues use software-defined operational technology networks to collect network situational awareness information. They gather system logs and event logs from operational technology networks in near real time using software-defined networks. However, this technique can only detect network configuration issues and malicious devices in the networks. The work described in this chapter goes beyond the systems proposed by Chang et al. and Kalra et al. by providing situational awareness about SCADA-system-specific semantic issues and the syntactic validity of SCADA protocols.

Since software-defined networks traditionally support only network-header-based filtering, they are conducive to providing situational awareness via event logging. More research is needed to understand how to build on existing software-defined networking technologies to validate the syntactic correctness of SCADA protocol packets.

2.6   Anomaly Detection

Anomaly detection techniques are classified as specification-based [5], signature-based [37] or learning-based [22, 25]. Specification-based techniques employ manually-specified behavior to detect anomalies. Signature-based techniques look for packets that appear to be replicating known attacks. Learning-based techniques use statistical or machine learning techniques to identify normal and abnormal operations.

These anomaly detection techniques can be used in conjunction with the communications validity detection tool to gather forensic data. Although the anomaly detection techniques can identify fuzzing attacks, they are ineffective against zero-days because they cannot protect against attacks they have not encountered before. In contrast, the communications validity detection tool can identify attacks that have not been seen previously while also detecting malicious SCADA commands.

The communications validity detection tool can be used in conjunction with device fingerprinting techniques [18] to prevent forgery attacks. Physics-based defenses [33] can also be used with the tool. In fact, the communications validity detection tool neither fingerprints SCADA devices nor considers the underlying physics of the devices; instead, it focuses on SCADA network protocols.

Berthier et al. [5] use specification-based intrusion detection, which analyzes the security properties at the transport, network and application layers; the technique is demonstrated using metering infrastructure protocols. Hong et al. [19] combine host-based and network-based intrusion detection to obtain better detection coverage. However, neither technique can identify zero-day attacks that employ novel crafted packets.

Ren et al. [30] categorize smart grid network traffic into transport, operations and content traffic, and proceed to construct multilevel anomaly detection frameworks. The communications validity detection tool uses some similar techniques while differing in the core approach. Ren and colleagues rely on the Zeek (formerly Bro) intrusion detection system to provide attack alerts whereas the communications validity detection tool employs language-theoretic security-compliant parsers to detect attacks. The attacks detected by the parsers are significantly different from those detected by Zeek.

Of course, the Zeek intrusion detection system could be used in conjunction with the communications validity detection tool. Zeek would detect brute-force attacks and SQL injection attacks whereas the communications validity detection tool would detect misconfigurations and crafted input attacks that target electric power sector protocols.

3.   Tool Design

The following technical goals were set for the communications validity detection tool to support forensic data collection in SCADA networks:

- **Live Forensics:** The tool must be connected to SCADA network traffic to continuously monitor and collect forensic data. When suspicious network activities are encountered, operators can review the collected data.

- **Syntactically-Invalid Message Detection:** The tool must detect messages that violate protocol specifications.

- **Semantically-Incorrect Packet Detection:** The tool must detect communications flow violations based on SCADA network configuration files.

- **Non-Human-Triggered Action Detection:** Most SCADA system commands with physical effects such as opening and closing breakers and relays are triggered by human operators. Since a compromised device can send these SCADA commands over a network, the tool must detect and visualize all commands with physical effects.

The following design goals were set to ensure that the communications validity detection tool would be extensible and usable:

- **Adaptive:** The tool must not depend on attack scenarios and heuristics, but should detect crafted packet attacks. Since zero-day attacks exploit patterns and vulnerabilities that have not been seen before, the language-theoretic security paradigm is leveraged to detect new attacks.

- **Scalable:** The tool must support a range of smart grid protocols and application program interfaces to support future protocols. The tool must detect syntactically-malformed packets for all the supported protocols. The tool must have a flexible architecture so that unsupported SCADA protocols can be handled by adding parsers with minimal effort.

- **Distributed:** Since copious amounts of data are generated at each substation, as much data analysis as possible should be performed locally at the substations. The control center would primarily perform aggregated operations. This is vital to reduce SCADA network overhead during tool operation.

- **Usable:** The tool must provide alerts in a useful and visually-appealing manner while not overwhelming operators with information.

3.1   Design Techniques

Several techniques are leveraged to realize the design goals of the communications validity detection tool. First, the tool uses a comprehensive set of language-theoretic security-compliant parsers for the protocols commonly used in smart grid substations. The supported protocols include DNP3, IEEE C37.118 and IEC 61850. The parsers are adaptive in that they do not rely on previous attack samples to detect crafted input attacks.

Second, the tool employs a producer-consumer model in each implementation. This design, which uses an Apache Kafka broker, renders the tool highly scalable. Future protocol support merely involves adding consumers. The producers extract the payload portions of the packets and broadcast them to all the consumers simultaneously.

Third, the tool uses a distributed master-minion system, where minions are placed at substations and the master is positioned at the control center. Figure 1 shows the distributed master-minion system. Minions, which are connected to substation routers, collect traffic from two interfaces. The shaded boxes show the communications validity detection

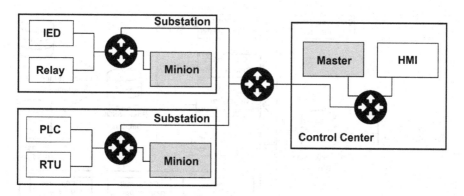

Figure 1. Distributed master-minion system.

devices. Note that the master performs data aggregation and correlation whereas the minions perform data collection and parser checks.

Finally, the tool incorporates strong visual components such as web user interfaces and command-line interfaces. The web user interfaces present smart grid operators with alerts and visual representations of specific traffic, giving operators the ability to monitor network traffic that may be well-formed but not sent by operators. For example, an attacker could use a relay device compromised via a side-channel attack to send DNP3 commands to other circuit breakers. Operators can easily detect such attacks using the visual component that displays DNP3 protocol commands.

3.2 Continuous Data Collection and Monitoring

The communications validity detection tool engages a novel paradigm of continuous data collection and monitoring. Most forensic investigation tools are deployed after attacker actions are complete. Instead, the communications validity detection tool is deployed in SCADA networks to continuously monitor network traffic. If a cyber attack is suspected, an operator can retrace the attacker's actions using the tool database.

A live network tap interface must be created by duplicating all the traffic going through a router. The duplication ensures that the communications validity detection tool does not add significant overhead to the network. The tool asynchronously processes all the packets forwarded by the router, alerting to suspicious packets. The alerts are continuously pushed to the database along with observed network traffic metadata. Leaving the tool connected to a SCADA network tap before a cyber attack to support forensic investigations enables operators to reproduce attacker steps rapidly.

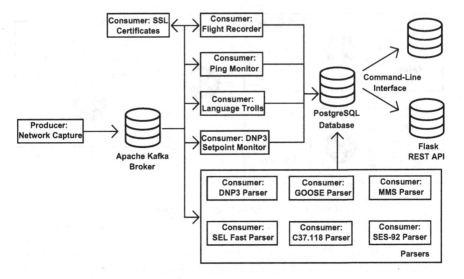

Figure 2.   Publish-subscribe minion model.

3.3   Distributed Data Collection

Data is collected by minions at the substations. The minions collect
and store data at the substations as well as across them. The data
mostly includes SCADA commands, but could also include ARP, NTP
and DNS routing data.

Since the minions and master are part of substation networks, network
traffic originates from these devices as well. However, the data does not
contribute to the forensic data gathered by the parsers because all traffic
originating from the tool is whitelisted.

3.4   Publish-Subscribe Minion Model

A key goal is to run a given packet received from the network through
the parsers in parallel to check if the packet conforms to any of the
supported protocols. This is accomplished using a publish-subscribe
model for minions.

Figure 2 shows the publish-subscribe minion model. The producers
process network packets and forward them to the Apache Kafka broker,
which broadcasts them to all the consumers. The consumers perform
their analyses and store the results in a PostgreSQL database. Operators can consume information from the PostgreSQL database using
web user interfaces or command-line interfaces. This publish-subscribe

Table 1. Parsers included in the current tool version.

Protocol	Language	Availability
DNP3	C/C++	Yes [7]
IEEE C37.118	C/C++	Yes [4]
IEC 61850 MMS	Python	Not yet
IEC 61850 GOOSE	Python	Not yet
SEL Fast Message	Python	Not yet
SES-92	C/C++	Not yet

model provides the flexibility to add future protocols and other analyzers without much effort.

Producers. The Apache Kafka producers accept inputs in two formats. They accept packet capture files or attach directly to live network interfaces. In either case, the producers read each packet, convert it to a string and send it to all the consumers. The producers do not do pre-processing because each consumer analyzes the packet at a different layer of the protocol stack.

Consumers. The Apache Kafka consumers receive all the packets from the producers and process them in various ways as described below. As shown in Figure 2, the consumers store the results of their analyses in a PostgreSQL database.

3.5 Detecting Syntactically-Invalid Packets

Table 1 shows the language-theoretic security-compliant parsers currently deployed in the tool; the remaining parsers will be available in the near future. Parser construction required the specifications of all the SCADA protocols of interest to be procured or purchased.

After carefully analyzing the specifications, protocol state machines and message formats corresponding to the protocols were created. The protocol state machines specify the correct sequences of packets as well as prohibited sequences. The message formats specify the structures of packets conforming to the protocols. The message formats were subsequently converted to formal grammars.

Parser-combinators, such as Hammer, were used to convert the formal grammars to code that visually resembles the formal grammars. Figure 3 shows a code snippet in the IEC 61850 GOOSE protocol parser. Note that **h.sequence()** is a function provided by the Hammer parser-combinator toolkit.

```
IECGoosePdu = h.sequence(gocbRef, timeAllowedToLive, datSet, goID, T,
                         stNum, sqNum, simulation, confRev, ndsCom,
                         numDatSetEntries, allData)
```

Figure 3. Code snippet in the IEC 61850 GOOSE protocol parser.

The language-theoretic security-compliant parsers detect packets that violate the formal protocol specifications. Although it is difficult to identify specific semantic bugs where well-formed packets crash applications, state-of-the-art fuzzers should be able to find such bugs. The parsers or syntax validators cannot detect other types of attacks. However, previous research has determined that most zero-day attacks are crafted input attacks such as buffer overflows that are handled by the parsers [3].

The parsers are Apache Kafka consumers that accept raw byte strings. The parsers process the byte strings and decide whether or not the corresponding packets are safe. Often, the packets may conform to protocols that are not yet supported. However, packets can be shortlisted by checking the packet metadata (first two bytes of payloads and Ethernet frames) to see if they conform to a supported protocol.

The consumers run in Docker containers to ensure functional separation. A parser returns the parsed object if the parse is successful and `null` if the parse has failed. The parsed object is essentially an abstract syntax tree. The parser interacts with the abstract syntax tree to store information. Based on the data extracted by the parsers, all instances of failed parses due to malformed packets are saved in a local database. After ascertaining if a particular packet is making a setpoint change, the new setpoint value is also stored in the database.

3.6   Setpoint Monitors

Operators use human-machine interfaces to interact with SCADA devices. The human-machine interfaces communicate with SCADA devices using various protocols.

Monitoring and changing setpoints are important actions performed by operators. The setpoint monitoring consumer of the communications validity detection tool records the setpoints transmitted over HTTP and DNP3 to SCADA devices. Along with the setpoints and their values, the setpoint monitoring consumer also stores the source and destination MAC addresses, IP addresses and ports. The consumer adds these records to the database and the setpoints can be visualized on a timeline.

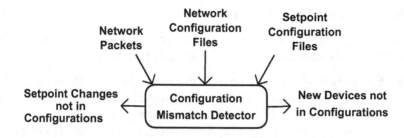

Figure 4. Configuration mismatch detection.

3.7 Detecting Semantically-Incorrect Packets

SCADA operators maintain several configuration files. The files specify setpoint mappings from point numbers in a human-readable format. Configuration files also specify IP and MAC addresses of all the SCADA network devices. To ensure availability, SCADA operators do not strictly enforce the configurations on routers and switches that filter traffic.

The configuration files are accessed during communications validity detection tool setup. Operators upload the files using a web user interface. The tool stores the configurations in the database, enabling the consumers to use them to make semantic decisions. When the configurations change, the tool enables operators to make modifications manually via the web user interface or by uploading new files.

The communications validity detection tool detects two types of semantic violations. The first type of semantic violations are due to devices that generate network traffic, but are not present in the network configurations. These could be rogue devices introduced by attackers. Adversarial code on devices can also change their network interfaces, so the tool detects them as new devices. The tool checks the IP and MAC addresses of every device in the SCADA network.

The second type of semantic violations involve setpoint mappings. Each SCADA device has a list of configured points and the types of communications (digital or analog). The parsers extract the setpoint information. The configuration files are checked to ensure that each setpoint is valid. Semantic violations are logged and alerts are sent to operators. The misconfigurations can be due to malicious code executing on SCADA devices or human error. The communications validity detection tool assists operators in detecting such semantic error conditions.

Figure 4 shows the configuration mismatch detection module. The module consumes network packets, configuration files and setpoint configuration files, and finds mismatches in the files.

3.8   User Interfaces

The communications validity detection tool provides two types of user interfaces, web interfaces and command-line interfaces:

- **Flask-Based Web User Interfaces:** Important features of a SCADA system forensic tool are supporting the visualization of actions and logging them. The communications validity detection tool incorporates a robust visual component to aid operators in detecting problems in a SCADA network. This is provided by Python Flask-based web user interfaces.

  The web user interfaces assist operators in setting up the communications validity detection tool in a SCADA network. Operators may use the interfaces to upload various network and setpoint configuration files to the tool. After operators start capturing traffic using the tool, the configuration files provide insights into misconfigurations and missing devices.

  Timeline interfaces are also provided to enable operators to check DNP3 protocol actions. Although most DNP3 actions are automated, some critical functions such as OPERATE, DIRECT-OPERATE and WRITE are triggered by humans. Operators can continuously monitor the user interfaces to ensure that all the critical functions were initiated by them and not by malicious programs. Operators can also monitor network interface visuals to check if devices have not communicated in some time and to pinpoint unidentified devices.

  The overall states of crank paths are presented as one-line diagrams. Multiple substations are connected using crank paths. During a power failure, crank paths enable troubleshooters to restore power to one substation at a time. Using various codes, the user interfaces identify whether substations are clean and have the communications validity detection tool running on them. A web user interface running on a master provides a single location for monitoring tool instances running on SCADA devices. The same interface helps pinpoint network and communications validity detection tool problems.

- **Command-Line Interfaces:** The command-line interfaces enable operators to initialize the communications validity detection tool and specify live network capture interfaces for running the tool. Packets from the interfaces are provided to all the producers and consumers. The command-line interfaces also enable individual producers and consumers to be restarted. Several commands

Table 2. Sampling of commands supported by command-line interfaces.

Command	Description
map	Start the communications validity detection tool against a packet capture file or network interface.
dnppoints	Print the observed DNP3 setpoints. The command provides several options for querying the database based on various timeframes and for DNP3 commands such as OPERATE and DIRECT-OPERATE.
cmds	Print the Telnet commands observed using the communications validity detection tool. Cyber attacks often leverage Telnet interfaces on SCADA devices to gain entry.
malformed	Print the observed malformed packets for all protocols. The command provides an overall summary or protocol-specific summary with the bytes observed in the protocols.
flows	Print the TCP and UDP connections entering and leaving a substation.
layer2	Print the MAC addresses of the observed devices.
certs	Print the observed SSL certificates.
roles	Print the SCADA device roles inferred by the communications validity detection tool. The device roles are inferred based on communications patterns and MAC addresses.
stop	Stop the communications validity detection tool and all the producers and consumers launched by the tool.

are available for querying multiple portions of the database, such as setpoints, Telnet commands and malformed packets for any protocol. Table 2 shows a sampling of commands supported by the command-line interfaces.

4. Tool Evaluation

Experiments were conducted to evaluate the communications validity detection tool. The experiments were conducted on a workstation with an Intel Xeon E31245 3.30 GHz processor with four cores and 16 GB RAM. Apache Kafka version 0.10 and Hammer toolkit version 1.0-rc3 were employed in the experiments.

The following metrics were employed to evaluate the communications validity detection tool:

- Correctness of the implemented language-theoretic security parsers.

- Resilience of the implemented language-theoretic security parsers to fuzzing.

- Resilience of the network interfaces of the tool to fuzzing.

- Detection of crafted packet attacks for the supported protocols.

- Ability to handle high SCADA network traffic rates.

- Visualization of operator actions.

4.1   Parser Correctness

To verify that the parsers cover a wide range of features in SCADA protocols, data collected from a SCADA tested was input to the parsers. In addition to running live network captures, the communications validity detection tool can replay and process packet capture (PCAP) files.

A dataset provided by Yardley [39] was used. The dataset contained data from 20 substations and three control centers. The substations and control centers did not belong to an actual utility, but they were otherwise realistic, simplified physical substations with SCADA communications and power equipment in a field-deployed testbed.

The experimental substations were spread over two square miles representing three independent crank paths. The substations were fed by three generators connected by real overhead and underground cables. Also included were high-voltage substations handling electricity at 13 kV. Each substation had at least four relays and a remote terminal unit. The three control centers had real-time automation controllers and human-machine interfaces from at least four manufacturers.

The dataset comprised five hours of traffic. Although most of the substations and control centers ran the DNP3 protocol. At least one substation ran each of the other SCADA protocols: IEEE C37.118, IEC 61850 MMS, IEC 61850 GOOSE, SEL Fast Message and SES-92.

Table 3 shows the parser correctness results. The parsers ran with a minimum accuracy of 94.5% and most of them had accuracies of 98% or higher. The experiments demonstrate that the parsers successfully cover an extensive feature set of the six SCADA protocols. However, several practical DNP3 implementations provide experimental and error-prone features that are not supported at this time.

4.2   Resilience to Fuzzing

Fuzzing SCADA devices can lead to crashes and denial-of-service attacks if the parsers are vulnerable [32]. The communications validity detection tool includes a set of parsers to ensure the syntactic validity

Table 3. Parser correctness results.

Protocol	Number of Substations	Packets Parsed Successfully	Total Number of Packets	Packets Parsed Correctly
DNP3	25	1,888,861	2,007,277	94.5%
IEEE C37.118	2	1,619,479	1,619,582	99.9%
IEC 61850 MMS	1	35,635	36,262	98.2%
IEC 61850 GOOSE	1	4,501	4,511	99.7%
SEL Fast Message	1	45,802	46,737	98.1%
SES-92	2	488,147	503,244	97.0%

of SCADA network packets. Since the tool is designed to detect crafted packet attacks on SCADA protocols, it was necessary to ensure that fuzzing does not crash the tool itself.

Fuzzing the communications validity detection tool was intended to serve two purposes. The first is parser resilience in that the parsers do not crash on any input (well-formed, malformed or random). The second is network resilience in that the network interfaces of the consumers can handle large volumes of SCADA network traffic.

Parser Resilience. In this set of experiments, separate fuzzers had to be used for the C/C++ and Python parsers. The C/C++ parsers were fuzzed using AFL++ [17] and the Python parsers were fuzzed using pythonfuzz [27], both coverage-guided fuzzers. To create a fuzzing target for AFL++, additional C files were created that invoked the parsers. AFL++ required the programs with instrumentation to be compiled using an afl-cc compiler. Next, afl-fuzz was executed on the binaries generated with a seed folder. A corpus of valid packets was created for the seed.

Each fuzzer was executed for 48 hours. Table 4 shows the parser fuzzing results. None of the fuzzing executions led to any crashes or unresponsive parsers. Each pythonfuzz target ran at least one million permutations through the parsers. In comparison, the AFL++ targets ran a minimum of three million executions through the parsers.

Network Resilience. In the experiments, the parsers were implemented as Apache Kafka consumers. The consumers received raw bytes from the producers that they parsed to decide if they were safe or not. Since the parsers included network interfaces, they were fuzzed using fuzzotron [12]. The fuzzing experiments sought to determine if the net-

Table 4. Parser resilience results.

Protocol	Parser Resilience			
	Number of Packets	Unique Paths	Crashes	Hangs
DNP3	3.62 million	623	0	0
IEEE C37.118	112 million	5	0	0
IEC 61850 MMS	2.2 million	13	0	0
IEC 61850 GOOSE	1.2 million	254	0	0
SEL Fast Message	1 million	6	0	0
SES-92	637 million	6	0	0

work interfaces were resilient and could withstand several connections and drops in connections every second.

The `fuzzotron` tool targeted the ports used by each consumer. Specifically, it created and dropped connections to the ports, often violating the TCP state machines. Once connections were established, `fuzzotron` sent random bytes on the open TCP ports.

Table 5. Network resilience results.

Protocol	Network Resilience	
	Number of Connections	Crashes
DNP3	900,000	120
IEEE C37.118	900,000	0
IEC 61850 MMS	900,000	0
IEC 61850 GOOSE	900,000	0
SEL Fast Message	900,000	5
SES-92	900,000	6

The network interfaces were fuzzed using `fuzzotron` while setting a maximum limit on the number of attempts. Table 5 shows the total numbers of connections that `fuzzotron` attempted to establish with the consumers. The numbers of network timeouts or crashes were recorded. Three consumers encountered no timeouts or crashes. The other three consumers had at most 0.1% of the packets cause crashes. Most of the crashes were due to heavy network loads. None of the crashes could be reproduced.

4.3   Crafted Packet Detection

Malformed DNP3 packets from the Aegis fuzzer [31] were employed to evaluate the communications validity detection tool against crafted packets. The dataset comprised 198 malformed DNP3 packets that were generated by mutating well-formed DNP3 packets. The malformed packets leveraged some of the DNP3 vulnerabilities identified by Crain and Sistrunk [11]. Most of the vulnerabilities were structural or syntactic.

Since the Aegis fuzzer only supports the Modbus and DNP3 protocols, mutations of well-formed packets corresponding to the IEEE C37.118, IEC 61850 MMS, IEC 61850 GOOSE, SEL Fast Message and SES-92 protocols were created. The mutated packets mostly conformed to the protocols, but violated the specifications in certain locations. A dataset comprising 198 packets was generated for each protocol.

The mutated packets were fed to the producers, which passed the packets on to their consumers. The communications validity detection tool was able to detect all the mutated packets as malformed. Also, none of the malformed packets caused any of the parsers to crash.

4.4   Parser Performance

Parser performance was assessed by measuring the time taken to decide whether packets are well-formed or malformed. The same dataset used to evaluate parser correctness was employed.

Figure 5 shows the parser performance results. The times required by most of the parsers was constant with minor variations. The times are in the order of microseconds for the IEEE C37.118, IEC 61850 MMS and IEC 61850 GOOSE parsers whereas they are in the order of milliseconds for the DNP3 and SES-92 parsers. The time taken does not directly depend on packet size. Also, latency is introduced by the publish-subscribe model.

The Python-based parsers performed much better than the parsers implemented in C. The tool incorporated Python code even for the C implementations to ensure seamless interoperability across the containers. However, this feature was found to add latency.

4.5   Visualization Capabilities

One of the core features of the communications validity detection tool is the visual component for operators to confirm actions. Several scenarios were developed to validate the operator interfaces. Network configurations were created for the test network using three relays, two remote terminal units and one real-time automation controller from three man-

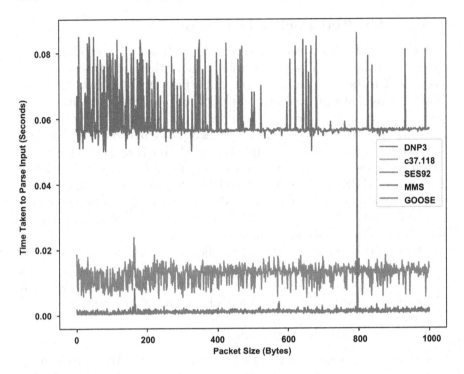

Figure 5. Parser performance results.

ufacturers. This was exclusively a SCADA system network because the relays did not control any live power settings.

Figure 6 shows the network user interface. Unidentified devices are shaded and the numbers at the edges indicate the numbers of packets observed. Various devices were removed from the network configuration and the communications validity detection tool was applied to the network. The tool was successfully able to detect all the network devices not present in the configurations. Additionally, the network configuration mismatch analyzer triggered the appropriate alerts.

The DNP3 timeline user interface was evaluated by crafting a scenario where a malicious program injects DNP3 WRITE commands in the network. In this scenario, operators must monitor the DNP3 timeline to ensure that no malicious WRITE or OPERATE commands enter the network (only human users should trigger these commands).

When the DNP3 WRITE commands were injected, the communications validity detection tool raised alerts and generated the timeline shown in Figure 7. An operator viewing the timeline on a web user inter-

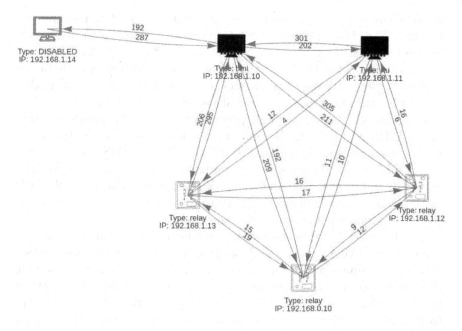

Figure 6. Network user interface.

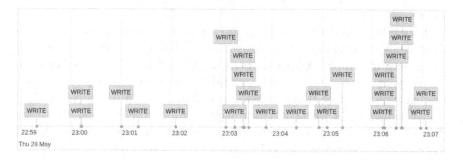

Figure 7. Web user interface with DNP3 WRITE commands in a 10-minute window.

face would see immediately that a network device is sending malicious commands.

5. Discussion

The communications validity detection tool filters packets to decide if they match the headers of a specific protocol and then run the associated parser on the packets. If the parser fails, the result is logged. This approach is effective for most protocols, but it proved challenging for the SEL Fast Message and SES-92 protocols. These protocols do not have a fixed set of bytes designated as the header. Instead, the parsers have to be executed to determine if the packets conform to one of the two protocols. Although the parsers may detect several crafted packet attacks for the two protocols, several packets could be missed.

For example, suppose a single packet is processed by the DNP3, IEC 61850 MMS and SES-92 parsers. Then, the question is, if the packet header does not match the DNP3 and IEC 61850 MMS protocols and the SES-92 parser does not parse the packet successfully, whether the packet should be as logged an invalid SES-92 packet. This is problematic because the packet could correspond to any protocol, such as DNS or NTP, for which a parser has not been developed.

The Hammer parser-combinator toolkit was employed to construct parsers for SCADA protocols. Hammer uses two data structures, parser objects to define a parser and a parsed abstract syntax tree to provide the parsed output for a specific input. Hammer provides functions to free the parsed abstract syntax tree but does not provide a mechanism to free parser objects. This issue was discovered during the fuzzing efforts because some of the fuzzers reached their memory limits much earlier than anticipated. Discussions are underway with the Hammer development team about facilitating fuzzing by adding functions to free parser objects.

Formally verifying the language-theoretic parsers is another challenge. No formal parsing algorithms are available to handle the context-sensitive languages used in SCADA communications. Efforts have been made to construct parsers that extend beyond regular grammars and context-free grammars. The Hammer parser-combinator tool provides bindings to parse languages with context-sensitive properties. However, Hammer has not been verified. Therefore, the parser implementations were fuzzed extensively to ensure that no bugs had been introduced.

Although the communications validity detection tool was designed as a forensic analysis toolkit to gather data from SCADA networks, it can also be deployed for network intrusion detection and prevention. The primary reason for not pursuing this direction is that latency of a few milliseconds was introduced due to tool limitations. Protocols such as IEC 61850 GOOSE specify that the latency must not exceed 4 ms. This latency requirement would be violated if the communications validity detection tool in its current state were to be used as an intrusion prevention system. However, the tool could be repurposed for such applications with engineering improvements and parsers running on field programmable gate array (FPGA) hardware.

TCP reassembly poses another challenge to parsing. Although most SCADA packets are small enough not to be fragmented, the DNP3 and IEC 61850 MMS protocols have large packets in rare conditions. In its current state, the communications validity detection tool cannot handle fragmented packets. However, introducing a TCP reassembly engine in the parsers would introduce significant overhead. It would require maintaining the TCP state as well as buffering packets before decisions can be made. Nevertheless, future plans involve creating a TCP reassembly engine to go with the proposed FPGA-based parser implementations.

6.   Conclusions

The communications validity detection tool presented in this chapter is designed to monitor SCADA networks for crafted input and malformed packet attacks. It incorporates language-theoretic security-compliant parsers and continuous monitoring and data collection to gather forensic data from SCADA networks.

The parsers incorporated in the communications validity detection tool cover a range of SCADA protocols and experimental evaluations using a large dataset of SCADA network traffic demonstrate their efficacy. Fuzzing experiments with the tool demonstrate the resilience of the parsers and the use of the tool in SCADA networks. Graphical user interfaces are also provided to facilitate security decision making by SCADA system operators.

Future research will formally verify the parsers and build a new toolkit to generate verified parsers. Other research will focus on new parsing algorithms for context-sensitive grammars and well as implementing highly-parallelized parsing algorithms on FPGAs to reduce latency. Additionally, attempts will be made to understand SCADA operator needs with regard to the tools needed to detect attacks on SCADA networks.

Any opinions, findings and conclusions or recommendations expressed in this chapter are those of the authors and do not necessarily reflect the views of the U.S. Air Force or DARPA.

Acknowledgement

This research was supported by the U.S. Air Force and by DARPA under Contract no. FA8750-16-C-0179.

References

[1] F. Adelstein, Live forensics: Diagnosing your system without killing it first, *Communications of the ACM*, vol. 49(2), pp. 63–66, 2006.

[2] I. Ahmed, S. Obermeier, M. Naedele and G. Richard, SCADA systems: Challenges for forensics investigators, *IEEE Computer*, vol. 45(12), pp. 44–51, 2012.

[3] P. Anantharaman, V. Kothari, J. Brady, I. Jenkins, S. Ali, M. Millian, R. Koppel, J. Blythe, S. Bratus and S. Smith, Mismorphism: The heart of the weird machine, in *Security Protocols XXVII*, J. Anderson, F. Stajano, B. Christianson and V. Matyas (Eds.), Springer, Cham, Switzerland, pp. 113–124, 2020.

[4] P. Anantharaman, K. Palani, R. Brantley, G. Brown, S. Bratus and S. Smith, PhasorSec: Protocol security filters for wide-area measurement systems, *Proceedings of the IEEE International Conference on Communications, Control and Computing Technologies for Smart Grids*, 2018.

[5] R. Berthier and W. Sanders, Specification-based intrusion detection for advanced metering infrastructures, *Proceedings of the Seventeenth IEEE Pacific Rim International Symposium on Dependable Computing*, pp. 184–193, 2011.

[6] D. Bradbury, The "air gap" between IT and OT is disappearing, and we're not ready to manage the risk, *Infosecurity Magazine*, February 26, 2019.

[7] S. Bratus, A. Crain, S. Hallberg, D. Hirsch, M. Patterson, M. Koo and S. Smith, Implementing a vertically-hardened DNP3 control stack for power applications, *Proceedings of the Second Annual Industrial Control System Security Workshop*, pp. 45–53, 2016.

[8] J. Brenner, Eyes wide shut: The growing threat of cyber attacks on industrial control systems, *Bulletin of the Atomic Scientists*, vol. 69(5), pp. 15–20, 2013.

[9] E. Byers, Cyber security and the pipeline control system, *Pipeline and Gas Journal*, pp. 58–59, February 2009.

[10] L. Chang, T. Bryan, A. McKinnon and M. Hadley, Enabling situational awareness in operational technology environments through software-defined networking, *Journal of Information Warfare*, vol. 18(4), pp. 156–166, 2019.

[11] A. Crain and C. Sistrunk, S4x14 Video: Crain/Sistrunk – Project Robus, Master Serial Killer, Digital Bond, Sunrise, Florida (dale-peterson.com/2014/01/23/s4x14-video-crain-sistrunk-project-robus-master-serial-killer), 2014.

[12] denandz, fuzzotron: A TCP/UDP Based Network Daemon Fuzzer, GitHub (github.com/denandz/fuzzotron), 2018.

Ananthayraman

[13] P. Eden, A. Blyth, P. Burnap, Y. Cherdantseva, K. Jones and H. Soulsby, A forensic taxonomy of SCADA systems and approach to incident response, *Proceedings of the Third International Symposium on ICS and SCADA Cyber Security Research*, pp. 42–51, 2015.

[14] M. Ehrlich, D. Krummacker, C. Fischer, R. Guillaume, S. Perez Olaya, A. Frimpong, H. de Meer, M. Wollschlaeger, H. Schotten and J. Jasperneite, Software-defined networking as an enabler for future industrial network management, *Proceedings of the Twenty-Third IEEE International Conference on Emerging Technologies and Factory Automation*, pp. 1109–1112, 2018.

[15] Electricity Information Sharing and Analysis Center, Analysis of the Cyber Attack on the Ukrainian Power Grid, Washington, DC, 2016.

[16] N. Falliere, L. O'Murchu and E. Chien, W32.Stuxnet Dossier, Version 1.4, Symantec, Mountain View, California, 2011.

[17] A. Fioraldi, D. Maier, H. Eissfeldt and M. Heuse, AFL++: Combining incremental steps of fuzzing research, *Proceedings of the Fourteenth USENIX Workshop on Offensive Technologies*, 2020.

[18] D. Formby, P. Srinivasan, A. Leonard, J. Rogers and R. Beyah, Who's in control of your control system? Device fingerprinting for cyber-physical systems, *Proceedings of the Twenty-Third Annual Network Distributed System Security Symposium*, 2016.

[19] J. Hong, C. Liu and M. Govindarasu, Integrated anomaly detection for cyber security of substations, *IEEE Transactions on Smart Grid*, vol. 5(4), pp. 1643–1653, 2014.

[20] A. Kalra, D. Dolezilek, J. Mathew, R. Raju, R. Meine and D. Pawar, Using software-defined networking to build modern, secure IEC 61850 based substation automation systems, *Proceedings of the Fifteenth International Conference on Developments in Power System Protection*, 2020.

[21] D. Lee, H. Kim, K. Kim and P. Yoo, Simulated attack on the DNP3 protocol in SCADA systems, *Proceedings of the Thirty-First Symposium on Cryptography and Information Security*, 2014.

[22] L. Maglaras and J. Jiang, Intrusion detection in SCADA systems using machine learning techniques, *Proceedings of the Science and Information Conference*, pp. 626–631, 2014.

[23] M. Millian, P. Anantharaman, S. Bratus, S. Smith and M. Locasto, Converting an electric power utility network to defend against crafted inputs, in *Critical Infrastructure Protection XIII*, J. Staggs and S. Shenoi (Eds.), Springer, Cham, Switzerland, pp. 73–85, 2019.

[24] M. Naedele, Addressing IT security for critical control systems, *Proceedings of the Fortieth Annual Hawaii International Conference on System Sciences*, 2007.

[25] V. Narayanan and R. Bobba, Learning-based anomaly detection for industrial arm applications, *Proceedings of the Workshop on Cyber-Physical Systems Security and Privacy*, pp. 13–23, 2018.

[26] National Institute of Standards and Technology, CVE-2020-10613 Detail, National Vulnerability Database, Gathersburg, Maryland (nvd.nist.gov/vuln/detail/CVE-2020-10613), April 22, 2020.

[27] Y. Pats, pythonfuzz: Coverage-Guided Fuzz Testing for Python, GitLab (gitlab.com/gitlab-org/security-products/analyzers/fuzzers/pythonfuzz), 2020.

[28] M. Patterson, Hammer, GitLab (gitlab.special-circumstanc.es/hammer/hammer), 2020.

[29] N. Perlroth and C. Krauss, A cyberattack in Saudi Arabia had a deadly goal. Experts fear another try, *New York Times*, March 15, 2018.

[30] W. Ren, T. Yardley and K. Nahrstedt, EDMAND: Edge-based multilevel anomaly detection for SCADA networks, *Proceedings of the IEEE International Conference on Communications, Control and Computing Technologies for Smart Grids*, 2018.

[31] Step Function I/O, Aegis Fuzzer, Bend, Oregon (stepfunc.io/products/aegis-fuzzer), 2021.

[32] F. Tacliad, T. Nguyen and M. Gondree, DoS exploitation of Allen-Bradley's legacy protocol through fuzz testing, *Proceedings of the Third Annual Industrial Control System Security Workshop*, pp. 24–31, 2017.

[33] D. Urbina, J. Giraldo, A. Cardenas, N. Tippenhauer, J. Valente, M. Faisal, J. Ruths, R. Candell and H. Sandberg, Limiting the impact of stealthy attacks on industrial control systems, *Proceedings of the ACM SIGSAC Conference on Computer and Communications Security*, pp. 1092–1105, 2016.

[34] V. Urias, W. Stout and B. Van Leeuwen, On the feasibility of generating deception environments for industrial control systems, presented at the *IEEE International Symposium on Technologies for Homeland Security*, 2018.

[35] C. Valli, SCADA forensics with Snort IDS, *Proceedings of the International Conference on Security and Management*, pp. 618–621, 2009.

[36] R. van der Knijff, Control systems/SCADA forensics, what's the difference? *Digital Investigation*, vol. 11(3), pp. 160–174, 2014.

[37] J. Verba and M. Milvich, Idaho National Laboratory Supervisory Control and Data Acquisition Intrusion Detection System (SCADA IDS), *Proceedings of the IEEE Conference on Technologies for Homeland Security*, pp. 469–473, 2008.

[38] C. Wright, Forensics management, in *Handbook of SCADA/Control Systems Security*, R. Radvanovsky and J. Brodsky (Eds.), CRC Press, Boca Raton, Florida, pp. 169–200, 2016.

[39] T. Yardley, Building a physical testbed for black start restoration, presented at the *ICS Village at DEF CON Safe Mode*, 2020.

[40] B. Zhu, A. Joseph and S. Sastry, A taxonomy of cyber attacks on SCADA systems, *Proceedings of the International Conference on Internet of Things and Fourth International Conference on Cyber, Physical and Social Computing*, pp. 380–388, 2011.

[41] B. Zhu and S. Sastry, SCADA-specific intrusion detection/prevention systems: A survey and taxonomy, *Proceedings of the First Workshop on Secure Control Systems*, 2010.

III

TELECOMMUNICATIONS SYSTEMS SECURITY

Chapter 9

INFINIBAND NETWORK MONITORING: CHALLENGES AND POSSIBILITIES

Kyle Hintze, Scott Graham, Stephen Dunlap and Patrick Sweeney

Abstract   The InfiniBand architecture is among the leading interconnects that support high performance computing. The high bandwidth and low latency provided by InfiniBand are increasing its applications outside the high performance computing domain. One of the important application domains is the critical infrastructure.

However, InfiniBand is not immune to security risks. Previous research has shown that common traffic analysis tools cannot effectively monitor InfiniBand traffic transmitted between hosts. This is due to the kernel bypass nature of the InfiniBand architecture and remote direct memory access operations. However, if the Remote Direct Memory Access over Converged Ethernet (RoCE) protocol is employed, it is possible to restore traffic visibility in novel ways. This research demonstrates that the approach, coupled with an InfiniBand-capable adapter, enables common traffic analysis tools to be used to monitor InfiniBand network traffic without sacrificing bandwidth and performance.

Keywords: InfiniBand architecture, network security, network monitoring

1.   Introduction

While the capabilities of modern computer processors continue to improve by optimizing current architectures or introducing new architectures, other computing technologies have been unable to keep pace. In particular, the majority of industry-standard input/output bus systems cannot keep up with the raw power of modern computer processors [3].

A promising solution is the InfiniBand architecture interconnect technology [4]. InfiniBand offers higher bandwidth and lower memory latency than Ethernet, and is a powerful technology with promising capabilities. According to the most recent Top 500 ranking [18], which tracks the 500 most powerful supercomputers in the world, seven of the top ten

This is a U.S. government work and not under copyright protection in the U.S.;
foreign copyright protection may apply 2022
Published by Springer Nature Switzerland AG 2022
J. Staggs and S. Shenoi (Eds.): Critical Infrastructure Protection XV, IFIP AICT 636, pp. 187–208, 2022.
https://doi.org/10.1007/978-3-030-93511-5_9

supercomputers utilize the InfiniBand architecture. Network communications are key to the operation of critical infrastructure assets. As InfiniBand is adopted in the critical infrastructure, serious evaluations of its security issues are vital [6, 7, 15, 17, 19].

This research focuses on expanding the monitoring capability of the InfiniBand architecture. In particular, it evaluates the efficacy of common traffic analyzers at capturing and monitoring Remote Direct Memory Access (RDMA) over Converged Ethernet (RoCE) protocol traffic in InfiniBand networks. Several case studies are considered and the results are intended to guide future research focused on securing InfiniBand networks.

2.   InfiniBand Architecture

InfiniBand is a network protocol similar to Ethernet that is quickly becoming the standard for high performance computing clusters and data centers. While it is similar to the Ethernet protocol in several ways, InfiniBand was designed to handle higher network bandwidths with significantly reduced memory latency. This came as a direct response to the inability of traditional input/output systems to provide the speeds required to keep up with advancements in modern computing technology. At a high level, by treating input/output as communications, using point-to-point connections and transferring information between hosts and devices via messages instead of memory operations, the InfiniBand architecture is able to achieve the performance desired by the modern computing industry [5]. Figure 1 shows a high-level view of a generic InfiniBand network.

2.1   InfiniBand Hardware

An InfiniBand network has many of the components and connections found in Ethernet networks. Network interface cards (NICs) connect to workstations and processors handle certain workloads related to network traffic. Fundamentally, InfiniBand is an interconnect that enables multiple processors, switches and other devices to communicate with each another. In the InfiniBand architecture, channel adapters, switches and subnet managers play crucial roles that differentiate InfiniBand networks from their Ethernet counterparts.

- **Channel Adapter:** A channel adapter (CA) connects InfiniBand to other devices. A channel adapter can be a host channel adapter (HCA) or a target channel adapter (TCA). Both types of channel adapters generate and consume packets. A host channel adapter supports the functions specified by InfiniBand verbs (described

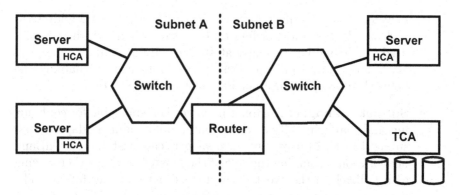

Figure 1. Generic InfiniBand network.

later) whereas a target channel adapter uses an implementation-dependent interface to the transport layer.

What sets a channel adapter apart from a normal interconnect interface (e.g., in Ethernet) is its ability to serve as a programmable direct memory access engine. This enables direct memory access operations to be made locally on hardware and independent of the central processing unit (CPU). Additionally, to identify devices in a network, a channel adapter is assigned a local identifier (LID) by the subnet manager and a globally unique identifier (GUID) by the manufacturer, analogous to the interface identifiers and media access control (MAC) addresses used in Ethernet networks [4].

Channel adapters communicate via work queues that comprise multiple sub-queues [4]. A work queue is initiated by the client (sending network interface card) and the traffic to be sent is placed in a sub-queue. After this is done, the channel adapter processes the received information from the sub-queue and sends it to the requesting device (receiving network interface card). After the information is received, the receiving network interface card returns a status response to the sending network interface card via a completion queue. Multiple queues can exist at a time, enabling a client to conduct other activities while transactions are being processed by channel adapters [11].

- **Switch:** As in the case of Ethernet, an InfiniBand network switch is responsible for forwarding decisions, acting as the fundamental routing component for intra-subnet routing [4]. Data is forwarded from one channel adapter to another based on the data link layer addresses. Forwarding decisions are made based on channel adapter local identifiers (analogous to Ethernet MAC addresses) and based on the forwarding table of the switch, which is configured by the subnet manager at startup. InfiniBand switches also allow for unicast and multicast packet forwarding, enabling the network to support Internet Protocol (IP) applications.

- **Subnet Manager:** A subnet manager is responsible for configuring and managing all switches, routers and channel adapters in a subnet [4, 10]. Multiple subnet managers can exist in an InfiniBand network, one assuming the role of the master and the other serving as a fallback in the event of master subnet manager failure. The master subnet manager communicates with every switch, channel adapter and slave subnet manager to ensure that all routing and forwarding tables are correct.

  The master subnet manager has four responsibilities: (i) discovering the subnet topology, (ii) configuring each channel adapter port with local identifiers, globally unique identifiers, subnet prefixes and partition keys, (iii) configuring each switch with a local identifier, subnet prefix and forwarding database and (iv) maintaining the end node and service databases for the subnet and providing a globally unique identifier to local identifier resolution service.

2.2   InfiniBand Software Architecture

The InfiniBand architecture is compatible with all the major operating systems. The architecture is abstracted away from user space to enable consumers to interact with InfiniBand without any knowledge about the processes executing in kernel space.

The InfiniBand software stack can be divided into the hardware, kernel and application levels [11]. The hardware level comprises the physical network components (i.e., input/output), which transmit electromagnetic signals along copper or fiber waveguides. Connections are made at the hardware level between multiple host devices in a variety of configurations to provide network communications. As with Ethernet communications, InfiniBand network traffic enters and exits through these access points before moving into the host machine.

In kernel space, physical components (host channel adapters) are controlled by input/output drivers to enable user space applications to directly control the hardware. An application is executed in user space through which the device driver maps to an operation [1]. In doing so, a user can leverage an array of InfiniBand capabilities.

In the next level of kernel space, core kernel modules provide the main InfiniBand services. Important services such as the verbs application programming interface and subnet administrator client reside in this level [11]. Indeed, these services distinguish InfiniBand from Ethernet.

Finally, upper layer protocols reside in the top level of kernel space. These protocols enable user applications to leverage the InfiniBand architecture.

2.3 InfiniBand Transport Services

While InfiniBand offers many transport services, this research focuses primarily on its use of the RoCE and IP over InfiniBand (IPoIB) protocols. In an Ethernet network, packets traverse the protocol stack, which involves the host operating system kernel. The kernel processes packets and determines where to send them, consuming many CPU clock cycles in the worst case, leading to lower throughput.

The InfiniBand architecture avoids this limitation by using remote direct memory access, the access of memory from one machine to another without direct CPU involvement. This means that the operating system kernel is bypassed, enabling data transfers to be done by applications directly from user space. User applications can move data directly between virtual memory on different network nodes without operating system intervention [9]. In the case of remote direct memory access, the CPU initiates the communications channel, after which the user application and hardware that perform message passing take control. Throughout the process, verbs are used to convey requests to the hardware.

This study focuses on the RoCE v1 protocol, which replaces the physical and data link layers of the InfiniBand protocol stack with Ethernet [9]. RoCE, which provides the same speed and low latency as remote direct memory access, comes in two versions: (i) RoCE v1 that supports communications between two hosts in the same Ethernet broadcast (link layer protocol) and (ii) RoCE v2 that enables packets to be routed outside a local area network (network layer protocol).

Since RoCE employs Ethernet as its link layer protocol, it supports the use of the IP over InfiniBand protocol [12]. This upper layer protocol implements a network interface using the InfiniBand architecture. It encapsulates IP datagrams over an InfiniBand transport service [15]. After the appropriate kernel modules are loaded, the service can be enabled using standard Linux tools such as `ifconfig` and `ip`. The tools provide standard IP addresses to the chosen interfaces. All applications configured to use the IP over InfiniBand protocol traverse the Transport Control Protocol/Internet Protocol (TCP/IP) stack in the kernel [15].

3.   Related Work

Due to the use of InfiniBand in high performance computing environments, early research was mainly directed at increasing bandwidth and reducing latency. Until recently, limited research focused on InfiniBand security.

Dandapanthula et al. [2] investigated the scalable monitoring and analysis of InfiniBand networks. They developed the INAM tool for monitoring an InfiniBand cluster in real time and querying subnet management entities. A web interface was provided for visualizing network performance and the communications patterns of target applications. The INAM tool provided a foundation for developing monitoring capabilities for InfiniBand networks.

Mireles et al. [15] demonstrated that network packets crafted using InfiniBand verbs could not be handled by standard networking monitoring tools. Unlike Ethernet, InfiniBand traffic uses verb semantics to describe operations between a host channel adapter and a consumer (receiver of network traffic) [4, 9]. Traffic crafted with verbs bypasses the operating system kernel to achieve high bandwidth and low latency via remote direct memory access operations. However, this prevents modern traffic analyzers from capturing and analyzing InfiniBand traffic because it bypasses the TCP/IP stack in the kernel. Mireles and colleagues concluded that hardware offloads are key to securing InfiniBand networks.

Lee et al. [7] focused on security enhancements to the InfiniBand architecture. Their research highlighted the promising features provided by InfiniBand for clusters and system area networks, but the lack of security features meant that InfiniBand networks could be exploited. The most serious vulnerability involved network traffic authentication based on the presence of plaintext keys in packets. Lee and colleagues proposed a new authentication mechanism that treated the Invariant Circular Redundancy Check (ICRC) field as an authentication tag, a solution that is compatible with the current InfiniBand specification. Experiments revealed that the new tag enhanced InfiniBand authentication capabilities with marginal performance overhead.

4.   Experimental Setup and Case Studies

This research sought to evaluate the ability of common network traffic analyzers to monitor the RoCE protocol in InfiniBand networks. Three experimental case studies were conducted to observe the capabilities of monitoring tools in various configurations and identify an approach for capturing the maximum amount of network traffic. This section de-

Figure 2. Network configuration of RoCE 100 Gbps with ConnectX-5 adapters.

scribes the experimental setup and network monitoring tools employed, the data collection metrics and the three case studies.

4.1 Experimental Setup

The experimental setup incorporated host workstations, network interface cards and virtual multilayer switches:

- **Host Workstations:** Two host workstations were employed in the experiments. Each workstation was powered by an Intel Xeon Silver 4114 processor (2.2 GHz, 10 cores and 20 logical processors) with 126 GB RAM. The workstations ran Ubuntu 18.04 LTS 64-bit, kernel version 5.0.4-56-generic.

- **Network Interface Cards:** Each workstation was installed with an Nvidia Mellanox Bluefield DPU Programmable SmartNIC [14]. The SmartNICs incorporated 16 ARMv8 A72 cores and 16 GB RAM. Each SmartNIC used a ConnectX-5 adapter as the host channel adapter to provide the physical network interface. Additionally, each SmartNIC ran Ubuntu 18.04 LTS 64-bit.

  Figure 2 shows the network configuration used in the experiments. The two ConnectX-5 adapters were connected in a "back-to-back" manner using a 100 Gbps active optical cable. A switch was not required for this configuration. Interconnect traffic adhered to the RoCE protocol.

  A SmartNIC has two modes of operation. In the default separated host mode, the host workstation and SmartNIC operating systems act as separated entities, communicating with each other or with the network via the ConnectX-5 module of the SmartNIC. This research employed the SmartNIC mode in which a host workstation communicates with the network only through the SmartNIC ARM cores [13].

- **Open vSwitches:** Each SmartNIC has an Open vSwitch application installed as part of its operating system. This multi-layer software switch provides security, monitoring functionality, quality of service and automated control. However, its principal purpose is to provide a switching stack for hardware virtualization environments [8]. In the experiments, Open vSwitch enabled network traffic from the host workstation to be directed through the ARM cores of the SmartNIC and then out to the wire. This provided an opportunity to directly monitor and manipulate traffic in an out-of-band manner, along with other capabilities supported by a software stack.

In addition to acting as a virtual switch, Open vSwitch provided the high bandwidth attributed to the InfiniBand architecture via a hardware offload. In a traditional network stack, all the incoming packets are processed by the operating system kernel. This is very CPU intensive and has low bandwidth because the CPU has to inspect each packet before forwarding it to its destination. By leveraging the Open vSwitch hardware offload, the ConnectX-5 adapter freed up the host workstation CPU and achieved higher bandwidth.

In the configuration, a packet reached the Open vSwitch daemon and kernel module within user and kernel space, respectively. Open vSwitch then made the decision to offload all subsequent packets to the InfiniBand hardware.

4.2   Network Monitoring Tools

InfiniBand network traffic was monitored using Wireshark/`tshark`, `tcpdump` and `ntopng`. These open-source tools are commonly employed for network traffic monitoring.

A network monitoring tool uses a packet capture library (such as `libpcap`) to capture packets from live network devices or files. In general, a packet capture library polls for suitable devices, gains control of the devices and proceeds to filter and capture the incoming network packets. In addition to `libpcap`, the `ntopng` tool also uses the PF_RING library, a newer network socket that dramatically improves packet capture speed. New versions of PF_RING provide packet capture speeds exceeding 10 Gbps (up to 100 Gbps is possible) on multiple network adapters with low packet loss.

PF_RING polls packets from the SmartNIC using the Linux NAPI, which copies the packets from the hardware to a circular buffer. The incoming packets are then distributed to multiple rings simultaneously, drastically improving the packet capture speed and reducing packet loss [16].

The iPerf tool was employed for traffic generation and bandwidth testing. The tool reports multiple metrics related to network health, including bandwidth, latency, jitter and datagram loss. In the simplest setup, a server is created that opens up a socket to receive traffic and a client is configured to send traffic at a specified interval and bandwidth.

4.3   Data Collection Metrics

The following data collection metrics were employed in the experiments to analyze the effectiveness of the monitoring tools:

- **Bandwidth:** The average bandwidth in each experimental trial determines how much TCP/IP traffic was sent from a client to a server, and the (potential) negative impact of a monitoring tool on the network.

- **Packets Received:** This metric measures the number of packets received by a monitoring tool.

- **Packets Dropped:** This metric measures the number of packets dropped by a monitoring tool.

- **Data Consistency:** Data consistency is measured using the mean, standard deviation and coefficient of variation (CV) of the experimental trials.

Additionally, a baseline was set using the Linux utility `ip` on the server host machine. The `ip` utility reports many statistics, but the experiments only used the packets received and packets dropped statistics. While the utility does drop some packets, it captures 99% of all TCP/IP traffic that enters and leaves a client host machine. This enabled the collection of statistics pertaining to the numbers of packets dropped by the monitoring tools due to their inability to handle high traffic flows.

4.4   Case Study 1

The first case study, involving host-based monitoring with hardware offload enabled, was designed to evaluate the efficacy of applying network monitoring tools in InfiniBand networks. The experiments used the Wireshark and `tcpdump` tools.

Under typical conditions, an InfiniBand application using remote direct memory access bypass the operating system kernel and would, therefore, be hidden from network monitors. Nvidia Mellanox adapters support the use of custom vendor tools such as the Offloaded Traffic Sniffer to capture TCP/IP packets on desired interfaces [15]. However, because

Ethernet was used as the link layer protocol in this research (along with the RoCE protocol for direct memory access), network packets could be captured without using custom tools on Nvidia Mellanox and other vendor-specific hardware. In general, capturing network traffic using remote direct memory access or RoCE is the same. Both use direct memory access operations; the main difference is that either Ethernet or InfiniBand is used as the link layer protocol for network communications. The main benefit of RoCE is that a custom tool is not needed to monitor incoming traffic. Any common network monitoring tool can see TCP/IP traffic on the network interface card interface with RoCE, a benefit that stems from using Ethernet as the underlying link layer protocol.

Case Study 1 employed InfiniBand/Ethernet 100 GbE with the Smart-NIC ConnectX-5 adapter network configuration. iPerf was used to send TCP/IP packets and report the average bandwidth. A total of 50 trials were performed, five trials for each of five bandwidth levels (1, 3, 5, 10 and 25 Gbps) for each of the two monitoring tools. The trial durations were 120 seconds and the average bandwidth was reported at one second intervals throughout the trials. Hardware offload was enabled in the case study. The goal was to determine whether the monitoring tools could capture TCP/IP traffic at bandwidths of 1 Gbps or higher because large volumes of packets are dropped at these bandwidths.

The experiments in Case Study 1 involved the following steps with each monitoring tool:

- **Step 1:** Configure the server and client host machines to enable IPoIB so that network traffic can be sent on Layer 3.

- **Step 2:** Run iPerf receiver on the server host at the desired bandwidth level.

- **Step 3:** Initiate the network monitoring tool on the server host and specify the interface for packet capture.

- **Step 4:** Run iPerf sender on the client host to send TCP/IP packets to the receiver.

- **Step 5:** Terminate the network monitoring tool after 120 seconds of capture.

- **Step 6:** Record the 120 samples captured during the trial.

- **Step 7:** Repeat Steps 2 through 6 for the remaining bandwidth levels.

After all the trials were completed, the baseline numbers of received and dropped packets were compared against the numbers of received and dropped packets in Case Study 1. The number of dropped packets reported by the ip tool was subtracted from the number of dropped packets reported by each monitoring tool.

Next, the variation of the data collected during each bandwidth level trial was computed. A statistical test of the mean, standard deviation and coefficient of variation (CV) of the dropped packets was conducted to evaluate data consistency. In this case study as well as the other two case studies, a coefficient of variation less than 10% was assumed to indicate that the collected data was consistent across all the bandwidth level trials.

4.5   Case Study 2

The second case study, involving SmartNIC monitoring with hardware offload disabled, was designed to evaluate the throughputs of the network monitoring tools for InfiniBand applications at the SmartNIC itself. In the case study, a degree of anonymity was gained because network traffic was captured from the network interface card hardware instead of the host workstation. The monitoring tools were configured as in Case Study 1. However, because the SmartNIC only had a command line interface, the experiments were performed using tshark, the command line equivalent of Wireshark.

The ntopng tool was selected to evaluate the efficacy of a flow-based traffic analyzer, a capability that arose from the SmartNIC having the Open vSwitch application in its Linux installation. In the experiments, ntopng collected NetFlow records that were configured on and transmitted by Open vSwitch running on the Smart NIC. NetFlow is a network protocol for collecting IP traffic information and monitoring network flows. The Open vSwitch application on the SmartNIC was configured to send NetFlow records to a collector (ntopng) running on the server host machine. The ntopng tool analyzed the flow and updated network statistics for observation and analysis on a web browser on the client host machine.

Case Study 2 employed InfiniBand/Ethernet 100 GbE with the Smart-NIC ConnectX-5 adapter network configuration. iPerf was used to to send TCP/IP packets and report the average bandwidth. A total of 45 trials were performed, five trials at each of three bandwidth levels (1, 3 and 5 Gbps) for each of the three monitoring tools; the maximum bandwidth was 5 Gbps instead of 25 Gbps because TCP/IP traffic could not be captured by the SmartNIC with hardware offload enabled. The trial durations were 120 seconds and the average bandwidth was reported at one second intervals throughout the trial.

All the packets captured on the SmartNIC were related to RoCE operations. This is because only the first packet reached the Open vSwitch daemon, all subsequent packets were instructed to be offloaded to the ConnectX-5 network interface card. The destinations of all the packets (server host workstation) were observed. TCP/IP traffic was observed in a parallel packet capture on the server host. This is why hardware offloading had to be disabled to see traffic on the SmartNIC in the Case Study 2.

The experiments in Case Study 2 involved the following steps with each of the two monitoring tools:

- **Step 1:** Configure the server and client host machines to enable IPoIB so that network traffic can be sent on Layer 3.

- **Step 2:** Run iPerf receiver on the server host at the desired bandwidth level.

- **Step 3:** Initiate the network monitoring tool on the SmartNIC and specify the interface for packet capture.

- **Step 4:** Run iPerf sender on the client host to send TCP/IP packets to the receiver.

- **Step 5:** Terminate the network monitoring tool after 120 seconds of capture.

- **Step 6:** Record the 120 samples captured during the trial.

- **Step 7:** Repeat Steps 2 through 6 for the remaining bandwidth levels.

As in Case Study 1, the numbers of dropped packets reported by the ip utility were subtracted from the numbers of dropped packets reported by the network monitoring tools. This was done to correct for the packets that were not dropped by the monitoring tools themselves. Statistical tests of the mean, standard deviation and coefficient of variation (CV) of the dropped packets were conducted to evaluate data consistency. A coefficient of variation less than 10% was assumed to indicate that the collected data was consistent across all the bandwidth level trials.

4.6   Case Study 3

The third case study, involving SmartNIC monitoring with hardware offload enabled, was designed to evaluate the throughputs of the network monitoring tools at the SmartNIC with the maximum bandwidth. The monitoring tools and their configurations were similar to those in Case Study 2, except that Open vSwitch was configured to allow for hardware offload. Hardware offload enables network traffic to be handled by the host channel adapter instead of having to traverse the host operating system kernel, reducing CPU intensive operations and improving bandwidth.

With hardware offload enabled, the full bandwidth of the ConnectX-5 adapter and InfiniBand applications can be achieved, and the efficacy of the network monitoring tools for InfiniBand applications can be evaluated. Case Study 3 employed InfiniBand/Ethernet 100 GbE with the SmartNIC ConnectX-5 adapter network configuration. Once again, iPerf was used to send TCP/IP traffic and report the average bandwidth. However, since Case Study 3 only used the ntopng tool, a total of 25 trials were performed, five trials at each of the five bandwidth levels (1, 3, 5, 10 and 25 Gbps). Only ntopng was used because the two previous case studies revealed that Wireshark and tcpdump were incapable of handling high bandwidths.

The experiments in Case Study 3 involved the following steps with the ntopng monitoring tool:

- **Step 1:** Configure the server and client host machines to enable IPoIB that allows network traffic to be sent on Layer 3.

- **Step 2:** Run iPerf receiver on the server host at the desired bandwidth level.

- **Step 3:** Initiate the ntopng network monitoring tool on the SmartNIC and specify the interface for packet capture.

- **Step 4:** Run iPerf sender on the client host to send TCP/IP packets to the receiver.

- **Step 5:** Terminate the ntopng network monitoring tool after 120 seconds of capture.

- **Step 6:** Record the 120 samples captured during the trial.

- **Step 7:** Repeat Steps 2 through 6 for the remaining bandwidth levels.

5. Results

This section presents the results of the three case studies and their implications with regard to traffic monitoring in InfiniBand networks.

Table 1.   Baseline packet losses reported by the ip tool.

Case Study	Bandwidth	Packets Received	Packets Dropped	Percent Dropped
Case Study 1	1 Gbps	10,414,492	0	0.0%
	3 Gbps	31,242,709	153	0.1%
	5 Gbps	52,070,648	193	0.0%
	10 Gbps	104,137,417	5,212	0.5%
	25 Gbps	225,989,529	10,987	0.5%
Case Study 2	1 Gbps	10,414,521	0	0.0%
	3 Gbps	31,242,631	148	0.1%
	5 Gbps	52,070,535	199	0.0%
Case Study 3	1 Gbps	10,414,537	0	0.0%
	3 Gbps	31,242,595	177	0.1%
	5 Gbps	52,070,499	201	0.0%
	10 Gbps	104,136,650	5,170	0.5%
	25 Gbps	260,115,117	11,086	0.4%

Before starting the experiments, a baseline of packets dropped by the operating system kernel was determined using the Linux tool ip running on the server host machine. Regardless of the network monitoring tool used, some packets will be dropped by the operating systems of the server hosts or by the hardware interfaces that receive packets. While many factors contribute to packets being dropped, these commonly occur due to hardware issues (e.g., faulty cables or hardware incapable of routing effectively), software problems or insufficient bandwidth, among others. Therefore, at the beginning of each case study, a test was conducted using iPerf at each bandwidth level used in the case study. To normalize the comparisons of monitoring tools, the number of packets dropped in the bandwidth test was subtracted from the total number of dropped packets reported by each monitoring tool.

Table 2 shows the baseline packet losses reported by the ip tool. The results show that for every bandwidth level, less than 1% of the packets during the test were dropped, which is well within the acceptable standards. Applying this data to the network monitoring tool results in the case studies makes it possible to make better claims about the effects of using the monitoring tools, especially if they impose negative effects on the network. While monitoring tools are expected to drop some packets for any number of reasons, it would be highly undesirable if the tools were to degrade the network.

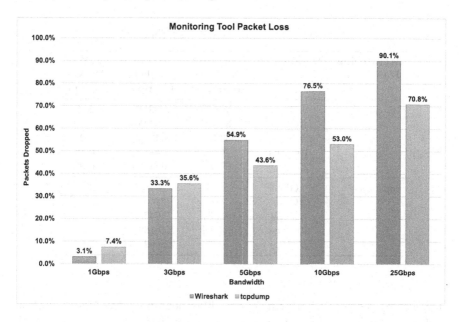

Figure 3. Dropped packets on the host workstation at various bandwidths.

5.1 Case Study 1 Results

The first case study was designed to explore the capabilities of common network monitoring tools in an InfiniBand network. The Wireshark and tcpdump tools were used to capture packets at the server host machine (192.168.1.30). In all the experiments, the two tools were able to capture TCP/IP traffic at the host workstations.

However, further analysis revealed that increasing the bandwidth reduced the ability to capture all the traffic. What started out as trivial at 1 Gbps became overwhelming at the maximum bandwidth. Figure 3 shows that both monitoring tools begin to lose their effectiveness rapidly beyond a bandwidth of 3 Gbps. Notably, Wireshark begins to drop off dramatically at 5 Gbps and is incapable of keeping up with traffic at higher bandwidths. The tcpdump performs better than Wireshark above 3 Gbps, but it still drops a large percentage of packets. A monitoring tool drops packets when its packet capture library is slow, when packets are copied between user and kernel space and/or when the buffer space allocated by the operating system kernel fills up quickly.

Next, the statistics of the dropped packets at the various bandwidth levels were used to provide estimates of collection accuracy. A total of 50 trials were performed, with five trials at each of the five bandwidth levels

Table 2. Case Study 1: Packet loss – data variance.

Monitoring Tool	Bandwidth	Mean of Packets Dropped	SD of Packets Dropped	CV of Packets Dropped
Wireshark	1 Gbps	3.1%	493.25	2.4%
	3 Gbps	33.3%	1,079.03	0.2%
	5 Gbps	54.9%	5,450.47	0.2%
	10 Gbps	76.5%	2,488.52	0.1%
	25 Gbps	90.0%	46,663.91	0.0%
tcpdump	1 Gbps	7.4%	372.61	0.8%
	3 Gbps	35.5%	5,240.27	0.7%
	5 Gbps	43.6%	9,643.42	0.7%
	10 Gbps	53.0%	169,169.98	4.7%
	25 Gbps	70.8%	229,920.93	2.9%

for each of the two monitoring tools. The mean and standard deviation (SD) of the dropped packets at each bandwidth level were computed. The coefficient of variation (CV) was then computed by dividing the standard deviation by the mean.

Table 2 shows that the coefficients of variation were all under 5%. The coefficient of variation is a measure of the standard deviation relative to the mean, which provides a dimensionless measure of the spread of the collected data. The results imply that the data collected in Case Study 1 is generally consistent across all the trials and, barring possible outliers, additional runs would likely produce similar results.

Two statements can made based on the overall packet losses of the monitoring tools and the variations in the numbers of dropped packets. First, network traffic created using Ethernet and RoCE operations can be captured using common network monitoring tools; also, both monitoring tools are capable of receiving the network traffic. Second, at bandwidths above 1 Gbps, the monitoring tools are ineffective at capturing all the network traffic. Wireshark and tcpdump begin to drop well over 30% of the incoming packets starting at 3 Gbps and the packet dropping only becomes worse with increasing bandwidth. In summary, while traffic capture is possible, common network monitoring tools are ineffective at high bandwidths.

5.2 Case Study 2 Results

The second case study was designed to determine if the monitoring tools used to capture InfiniBand traffic on the host workstation could

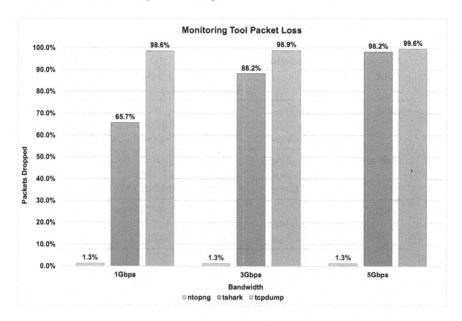

Figure 4. Dropped packets on the SmartNIC at various bandwidths.

capture traffic on the SmartNIC. TCP/IP traffic could not be captured on the SmartNIC when hardware offload was enabled. Therefore, the hardware offload feature was disabled in the experiments.

Figure 4 shows that `tshark` and `tcpdump` were unable to capture all the traffic. Specifically, `tshark` dropped a minimum of 65.7% of packets and `tcpdump` essentially dropped all the packets. Interestingly, `ntopng` incurred minimal packet loss. The `ntopng` tool also enables live captures of packets at specified time intervals.

In order to confirm that the packet loss counts were accurate, the numbers of packets reported by the monitoring tools were compared with those reported by the Linux tool `ethtool`, which provides numerous statistics about traffic received at an interface. The comparisons confirmed that the packet loss counts of the monitoring tools were accurate. The minimal packet loss incurred by `ntopng` was confirmed by examining the PCAP files.

As in Case Study 1, the dropped packet statistics at various bandwidth levels were compared. A total of 45 trials were performed, five trials at each of the three bandwidth levels for each of the three monitoring tools. Note that trials were not performed at the 10 and 25 Gbps levels due to bandwidth limitations imposed by the hardware offload

Table 3.   Case Study 2: Packet loss – data variance.

Monitoring Tool	Bandwidth	Mean of Packets Dropped	SD of Packets Dropped	CV of Packets Dropped
tshark	1 Gbps	65.7%	2,043.18	0.4%
	3 Gbps	88.2%	19,554.85	0.9%
	5 Gbps	98.2%	90,484.81	2.8%
tcpdump	1 Gbps	98.6%	10,687.54	1.5%
	3 Gbps	98.9%	31,744.95	1.3%
	5 Gbps	98.2%	16,916.16	0.5%
ntopng	1 Gbps	1.3%	492.94	5.1%
	3 Gbps	1.3%	1,231.38	4.1%
	5 Gbps	1.4%	1,050.55	2.1%

feature. Table 3 shows that the coefficients of variation were all under 6%. Thus, it is safe to conclude that the collected data was consistent across all the trials and, barring possible outliers, additional trials would likely produce similar results.

Two statements can made based on the overall packet losses of the monitoring tools and the variations in the numbers of dropped packets. First, the hardware offloading feature of the SmartNIC is not available when using the network monitoring tools; therefore, the ability to see individual TCP/IP packet data is lost. Second, network traffic created using Ethernet and RoCE operations can be captured using the network monitoring tools on the SmartNIC with hardware offload is disabled, albeit only at lower bandwidths.

Figure 4 and Table 3 show that tcpdump and ntopng are capable of receiving network traffic. However, tshark and tcpdump are not effective at capturing traffic. In fact, Figure 4 shows that tcpdump and tshark drop more than 99% of the network packets at the maximum bandwidth. Thus, another method is required to monitor network traffic.

Fortunately, the ntopng results are promising. At each bandwidth level, only a small percentage of packets were dropped – a little over 1%. Note that dropped implies that the packets were not captured and processed by the network interface. The consistency and efficacy of the ntopng tool demonstrate that its flow-based traffic monitoring capability is a promising alternative for InfiniBand networks.

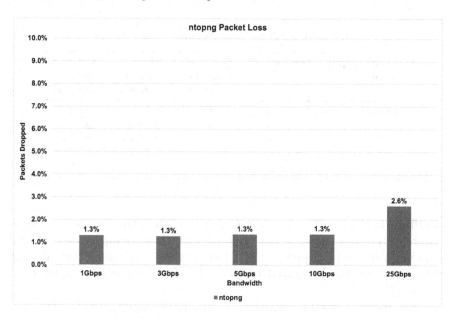

Figure 5. Dropped packets at various bandwidths at the host server using ntopng.

5.3 Case Study 3 Results

The third case study was designed to determine if the promising results obtained using ntopng to monitor InfiniBand traffic on the Smart-NIC in Case Study 2 would persist at higher bandwidths. In the previous case studies, all the other monitoring tools dropped significant percentages of packets as bandwidth increased. This is likely due to the packet capture library being slow, packets being copied between user and kernel space and/or buffer space in the operating system kernel overflowing quickly.

Case Study 2 demonstrated that ntopng, which is a flow-based monitoring tool, captured InfiniBand traffic very effectively up to 5 Gbps. In Case Study 3, ntopng executed on the server host workstation while the flow data was configured on and sent from the SmartNIC via Open vSwitch. Thus, it seemed possible that hardware offload could be leveraged, even at high bandwidths, to monitor traffic at the SmartNIC without losing the ability to see packet data.

The experiments revealed that, not only were TCP/IP packets visible and captured at all bandwidths by ntopng, but very few packets were dropped. Figure 5 shows ntopng only dropped between 1.3% to 2.6% of network packets at bandwidths from 1 Gbps up to 25 Gbps. To

Table 4.   Case Study 3: Packet loss – data variance.

Monitoring Tool	Bandwidth	Mean of Packets Dropped	SD of Packets Dropped	CV of Packets Dropped
ntopng	1 Gbps	1.3%	466.00	5.0%
	3 Gbps	1.3%	1,040.50	3.7%
	5 Gbps	1.4%	347.24	0.7%
	10 Gbps	1.4%	317.27	0.3%
	25 Gbps	2.6%	1,765.02	0.4%

confirm that the packet loss counts were accurate, the numbers of packets reported by ntopng were compared with those reported by ethtool running on the host server. The comparisons confirmed that ntopng was seeing all the generated traffic and that its reported metrics were accurate.

The dropped packet statistics at various bandwidth levels were also compared. A total of 25 trials were performed, five at each of the five bandwidth levels. Table 2 shows that the coefficients of variation were all under 5%. Thus, it is safe to conclude that the collected data was consistent across all the trials and, barring possible outliers, additional trials would likely produce similar results.

In summary, network traffic created by RoCE operations even at high bandwidths is effectively captured by ntopng on the SmartNIC. Specifically, hardware offload could be enabled on the SmartNIC, allowing for high network speeds; also, packet data was observable in the captured files. Second, the results in Figure 5 and Table 4 demonstrate that ntopng and its packet capture library implementation in conjunction with the Nvidia Mellanox hardware drastically reduced packet loss. The packet loss measured for ntopng at the maximum bandwidth was reduced by more than 95% compared with Wireshark and tcpdump in Case Study 1.

6.   Conclusions

This research has attempted to evaluate the capabilities of modern traffic monitoring tools (Wireshark/tshark, tcpdump and ntopng) for monitoring InfiniBand networks. The experimental results demonstrate that the monitoring tools can capture InfiniBand traffic, but are limited to lower bandwidths due to inefficiencies in their packet capture libraries and/or limited buffer space in the operating system kernels. The experimental results also reveal that positioning the monitoring tools on an

InfiniBand network interface incurred significant packet loss except at low bandwidths. In contrast, the `ntopng` flow-based monitoring tool, due to its efficient packet capture library, had very low packet loss at much higher bandwidths. The `ntopng` incurred minor packet loss even at the maximum bandwidth of 25 Gbps, rendering it a viable option for monitoring InfiniBand networks.

The case study results indicate that options exist for monitoring InfiniBand networks. However, additional research is needed to determine the optimal configurations to achieve low-cost, efficient and reliable InfiniBand network monitoring solutions.

The views expressed in this chapter are those of the authors, and do not reflect the official policy or position of the U.S. Air Force, U.S. Department of Defense or U.S. Government. This document has been approved for public release, distribution unlimited (Case #88ABW-2020-3829).

References

[1] J. Corbet, A. Rubini and G. Kroah-Hartman, *Linux Device Drivers*, O'Reilly Media, Sebastopol, California, 2005.

[2] N. Dandapanthula, H. Subramoni, J. Vienne, K. Kandalla, S. Sur, D. Panda and R. Brightwell, INAM – A scalable InfiniBand network analysis and monitoring tool, in *Euro-Par 2011: Parallel Processing Workshops, Part II*, M. Alexander, P. D'Ambra, A. Belloum, G. Bosilca, M. Cannataro, M. Danelutto, B. Di Martino, M. Gerndt, E. Jeannot, R. Namyst, J. Roman, S. Scott, J. Traff, G. Vallee and J. Weidendorfer (Eds.), Springer, Berlin Heidelberg, Germany, pp. 166–177, 2011.

[3] J. Hennessy and D. Patterson, *Computer Architecture: A Quantitative Approach*, Morgan Kaufmann, San Francisco, California, 2011.

[4] InfiniBand Trade Association, InfiniBand Architecture Specification, Volume 1, Release 1.4, Beaverton, Oregon, 2020.

[5] H. Jin, T. Cortes and R. Buyya (Eds.), *High Performance Mass Storage and Parallel I/O: Technologies and Applications*, Wiley-IEEE Press, New York, 2001.

[6] M. Lee and E. Kim, A comprehensive framework for enhancing security in the InfiniBand architecture, *IEEE Transactions on Parallel and Distributed Systems*, vol. 18(10), pp. 1393–1406, 2007.

[7] M. Lee, E. Kim and M. Yousif, Security enhancement in the InfiniBand architecture, *Proceedings of the Nineteenth IEEE International Parallel and Distributed Processing Symposium*, 2005.

[8] Linux Foundation, What is Open vSwitch? San Francisco, California (docs.openvswitch.org/en/latest/intro/what-is-ovs), 2016.

[9] P. MacArthur and R. Russell, A performance study to guide RDMA programming decisions, *Proceedings of the Fourteenth IEEE International Conference on High Performance Computing and Communications and the Ninth IEEE International Conference on Embedded Software and Systems*, pp. 778–785, 2012.

[10] Mellanox Technologies, Introduction to InfiniBand, White Paper, Document No. 2003WP, Santa Clara, California (www.mellanox.com/pdf/whitepapers/IB_Intro_WP_190.pdf), 2003.

[11] Mellanox Technologies, InfiniBand Software and Protocols Enable Seamless Off-the-Shelf Applications Deployment, White Paper, Sunnyvale, California (www.mellanox.com/pdf/whitepapers/WP_2007_IB_Software_and_Protocols.pdf), 2007.

[12] Mellanox Technologies, RDMA Aware Networks Programming User Manual, Rev. 1.7, Sunnyvale, California (www.mellanox.com/related-docs/prod_software/RDMA_Aware_Programming_user_manual.pdf), 2015.

[13] Mellanox Technologies, BlueField SmartNIC Modes, Sunnyvale, California (community.mellanox.com/s/article/BlueField-SmartNIC-Modes), 2019.

[14] Mellanox Technologies, Nvidia Mellanox BlueField SmartNIC for InfiniBand and Ethernet, Sunnyvale, California (www.mellanox.com/files/doc-2020/pb-bluefield-vpi-smart-nic.pdf), 2020.

[15] L. Mireles, S. Graham, S. Dunlap, P. Sweeney and M. Dallmeyer, Securing an InfiniBand network and its effect on performance, in *Critical Infrastructure Protection XIV*, J. Staggs and S. Shenoi (Eds.), Springer, Cham, Switzerland, pp. 157–179, 2020.

[16] ntop, Vanilla PF_RING, Pisa, Italy (www.ntop.org/guides/pf_ring/vanilla.html), 2018.

[17] D. Schmitt, S. Graham, P. Sweeney and R. Mills, Vulnerability assessment of InfiniBand networking, in *Critical Infrastructure Protection XIII*, J. Staggs and S. Shenoi (Eds.), Springer, Cham, Switzerland, pp. 179–205, 2019.

[18] E. Strohmaier, J. Dongarra, H. Simon and M. Meuer, Top 500 The List, Prometeus, Sinsheim, Germany, 2020.

[19] K. Subedi, D. Dasgupta and B. Chen, Security analysis of InfiniBand protocol implementations, *Proceedings of the IEEE Symposium Series on Computational Intelligence*, 2016.

Chapter 10

GPS SIGNAL AUTHENTICATION USING A CHAMELEON HASH KEYCHAIN

Yu Han Chu, Sye Loong Keoh, Chee Kiat Seow, Qi Cao, Kai Wen and Soon Yim Tan

Abstract   Global navigational satellite systems provide accurate time synchronization and location services. Satellites transmit navigation messages that can be used by a receiver to compute its location. However, most navigation messages are not protected and are easily spoofed. Several attacks have been reported that transmit spoofed or replayed GPS signals to divert or hijack autonomous vehicles, ships and drones. Unfortunately, non-cryptographic protection methods that use antenna arrays, pseudorange differences and multi-receivers to detect GPS spoofing tend to be inaccurate due to environmental conditions.

This chapter proposes an efficient GPS signal authentication protocol that engages a dedicated server to continuously compute hash-based message authentication codes of GPS navigation messages received from satellites using the chameleon hash keychain. The keychain is practically unbounded, which enables GPS receivers to easily authenticate the server and verify GPS signals concurrently by checking the hash-based message authentication codes. A proof-of-concept prototype has been developed to demonstrate the feasibility of the authentication scheme. Experimental results demonstrate that the hash key in the keychain can be updated every 30 seconds, enabling every five GPS message subframes to be secured with a different hash key. This makes it difficult for attackers to compromise GPS navigation messages.

Keywords: GPS signals, authentication, integrity, chameleon hashing

1.   Introduction

The proliferation of location services have led to the increased use of the Global Positioning System (GPS) in the automotive, maritime and aviation sectors. Safe and secure navigation are vital. Therefore, it is

© IFIP International Federation for Information Processing 2022
Published by Springer Nature Switzerland AG 2022
J. Staggs and S. Shenoi (Eds.): Critical Infrastructure Protection XV, IFIP AICT 636, pp. 209–226, 2022.
https://doi.org/10.1007/978-3-030-93511-5_10

important to ensure that automobiles, maritime craft and drones are not diverted or hijacked by malicious entities [2, 16].

Global navigation satellite systems such as GPS are easily spoofed [8]. GPS signals have no authentication or integrity protection, enabling them to be replayed and spoofed. An adversary can leverage an inexpensive software-defined radio such as HackRF One to transmit captured GPS signals to receivers mounted on vehicles, ships [1] and drones [20], causing them to move to the wrong locations. Additionally, malicious entities can spoof their locations for nefarious purposes. In such scenarios, GPS devices must be protected from hardware tampering, but the authenticity of the received GPS signals must also be verified to prevent location spoofing.

This chapter proposes a novel and efficient approach to verify the authenticity of GPS signals by continuously computing hash-based message authentication codes (HMACs) of GPS navigation messages received from satellites using the chameleon hash keychain. The generated HMACs serve as fingerprints for GPS receivers mounted on vehicles, ships, drones and mobile devices, enabling their GPS signals to be authenticated in real time. The approach uses a new key to protect every frame of a navigation message. Verifying each frame using a different key in the keychain renders GPS signal tampering and spoofing very difficult. GPS receivers can easily verify keys in the keychain and use the authenticated keys to compute the HMACs of GPS subframes to perform signal authentication.

A principal advantage of the approach is near real-time, secure GPS authentication using the unbounded one-way chameleon hash keychain. Another advantage is fast and efficient authentication of GPS signals by synchronizing the keychain without a public-key infrastructure and GPS message modification. Additionally, the GPS signal authentication is readily supported by existing network infrastructures (e.g., IP networks) without deploying additional satellites.

2.   Background and Related Work

This section discusses GPS signals [22] and chameleon hashing [13]. Also, it describes related work on location spoofing detection.

2.1   GPS Signals

Figure 1 shows the GPS L1 C/A navigation message structure. Each satellite transmits a continuous stream of data at 50 bits per second. The data contains the system time, clock correction values, satellite orbital data (ephemeris), orbital data of all the other satellites (almanac) and

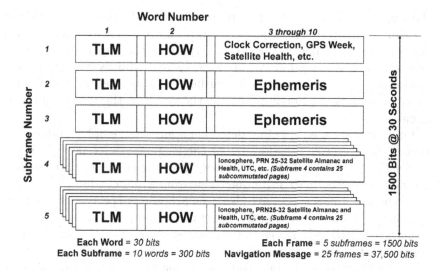

Figure 1. GPS L1 C/A navigation message structure.

satellite system health. The data is grouped into units called frames or pages. A navigation message comprises 25 frames. Each frame contains 1,500 bits and is divided into five subframes, each containing 300 bits. Transmission time from a satellite to a GPS receiver is six seconds. An entire navigation message is transmitted in 12.5 minutes. GPS navigation messages are not protected using cryptography and are, therefore, susceptible to spoofing attacks.

2.2 Chameleon Hashing

Chameleon hashing [13] is a trapdoor collision resistant function that is associated with a public-private key pair. The function is easy to compute in one direction, but very difficult to compute in the reverse direction without the private key (trapdoor). The private key holder can easily detect a collision for every input and can change the input value while computing the same output hash value. Chameleon constructs are based on discrete logarithms and elliptic curve cryptography [12].

Chameleon hashing has been used to secure data integrity in advanced metering infrastructures [21] and industrial control systems [10, 11]. Data tampering is detected by verifying the chameleon hash value.

2.3 Related Work

Liu et al. [14] have proposed a non-cryptographic scheme for computing pseudorange differences to detect meaconing and simple and intermediate spoofing attacks. A signal pseudorange model based on the signal transmission path is constructed to establish the double-difference of the pseudoranges of adjacent epochs. By applying the Taylor expansion to the position relationship between a satellite and GPS receiver or spoofer, the authenticity of a signal can be verified by comparing the result of the spoofing detection algorithm against the result of the traditional least squares method.

Other signal-based spoofing detection approaches employ antenna arrays [9, 23], receiver pseudorange or carrier phase differences [3, 19] or correlation methods [4, 18]. However, these signal-based anti-spoofing methods are often inaccurate due to environmental conditions.

Cryptography schemes have also been proposed to protect global navigational satellite system signals. Wu et al. [25] proposed an anti-spoofing scheme for BeiDou-II navigation messages using the Chinese SM cryptographic standards for message encryption. The integrity of navigation messages is protected by inserting spread spectrum information between subframes 1 and 2 in D2 navigation messages. However, this requires modifications to the navigation message format, which increases the difficulty of deployment. Other schemes use RSA or the Elliptic Curve Digital Signature Algorithm (ECDSA) to secure navigation messages and broadcast the authenticated signals as QZSS L1-SAIF navigation messages [15] or GPS civil navigation (CNAV) messages [24].

The effectiveness of broadcast authentication has led to the use of TESLA [17] to secure navigation messages. In the scheme of Fernandez-Hernandez et al. [6], senders encrypt their navigation messages using TESLA and receivers only need to wait for the senders to reveal the keys in order to authenticate the signals. Ghorbani et al. [7] applied TESLA to GPS L1 C/A navigation messages, but this requires the protocol to be implemented for civil navigation (CNAV-2) signals of GPS L1C. Yuan et al. [26] used ECDSA in conjunction with TESLA to secure BeiDou civil navigation signals; ECDSA ensures signal reliability while TESLA is efficient for broadcast authentication. Although a one-way keychain is very efficient, TESLA is a bounded keychain and, therefore, requires a new keychain to be set up after its keys are exhausted. Additionally, TESLA relies on loosely-synchronized time between a server and receivers to ensure data authenticity. The approach proposed in this chapter addresses these weaknesses using an unbounded keychain.

Table 1. Chameleon hash keychain notation.

$\mathbb{CH}$	Chameleon hash function
$\mathbb{CH}'$	Trapdoor chameleon hash function
$\mathbb{K}$	Trapdoor key
HK	Chameleon hash value or hash key
m	Input message to $\mathbb{CH}$
m'	Message $m' \neq m$
r	Input random prime number to $\mathbb{CH}$
r'	Collision resulting from $\mathbb{CH}'$

3. GPS Signal Authentication

This section presents the threat model and assumptions, along with the chameleon hash keychain. Also, it presents the proposed GPS authentication protocol using an unbounded chameleon hash keychain.

3.1 Threat Model and Assumptions

An adversary intends to spoof the locations of automobiles, ships, drones and mobile devices by transmitting spoofed or replayed GPS signals. The following assumptions are adopted in this work:

- An adversary has access to a software-defined radio or low-cost radio device to capture GPS signals from satellites and broadcast spoofed GPS signals.

- An adversary must use a software-defined radio or low-cost radio device with a transmitter that is proximal to a victim's device in order to launch a location spoofing attack.

- An adversary does not need access to the hardware or software of a victim's GPS receiver to tamper with GPS signals.

- An adversary does not need to control a victim's device in order to launch a location spoofing attack.

3.2 Chameleon Hash Keychain

This section describes the chameleon hash keychain, an unbounded one-way keychain with chameleon hashing that provides fast, efficient authentication between two parties [5]. Table 1 shows the notation used to discuss details about the chameleon hash keychain.

A one-way unbounded chameleon hash keychain $HK_0 \to HK_1 \to HK_2 \to ... \to HK_\infty$ is generated using a random message m_0 and random prime number r_0 by computing HK_n with $n = 0$:

$$HK_n = \mathbb{CH}(m_n, r_n) \qquad (1)$$

The principal property of chameleon hashing is that a hash collision is computed easily when the trapdoor key $\mathbb{K}$ is known. Specifically, it is feasible to derive a pair of messages (m', r') that when hashed using the chameleon hash function yields the same chameleon hash value (hash key):

$$\mathbb{CH}(m_n, r_n) = \mathbb{CH}(m'_n, r'_n) \qquad (2)$$

where $m \neq m'$ and $r \neq r'$.

Each subsequent hash key HK_n $(n = 1, 2, ...)$ is generated using Equation 1 with parameters m_n and r_n. The keychain is formed by linking a new hash key HK_{n+1} with its previous hash key HK_n by finding a collision. This is accomplished by computing the corresponding r' using the trapdoor key $\mathbb{K}$:

$$r'_n = \mathbb{CH}'(\mathbb{K}, m_n, r_n, HK_{n+1}) \qquad (3)$$

where $m'_n = HK_{n+1}$.

The resulting relationship between two consecutive hash keys in the keychain HK_n and HK_{n+1} generated using (m_{n+1}, r_{n+1}) is given by:

$$HK_n = \mathbb{CH}(HK_{n+1}, r'_n) \qquad (4)$$

It is easy to determine the authenticity of HK_{n+1} and r'_n because they yield a hash value equal to the previous hash key HK_n.

Note that $\mathbb{CH}$ is a public function that does not require knowledge of $\mathbb{K}$. Thus, anyone can verify the authenticity of a hash key in the chain, but it is very difficult to derive future hash keys. Additionally, the two communicating parties do not need to synchronize their clocks because new hash keys can be revealed on demand and verified immediately.

3.3   Architecture Overview

Figure 2 shows the proposed GPS signal authentication architecture to combat GPS location spoofing. Because GPS L1 C/A signals are not protected, multiple land-based GPS authentication servers using a chameleon hash keychain are deployed to secure GPS navigation messages transmitted by satellites. All the navigation message frames received are protected by HMACs computed using the latest hash keys in the keychain every 30 seconds. This is done by the main authentication

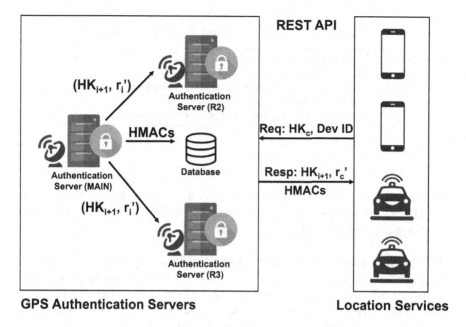

Figure 2. GPS signal authentication architecture.

server, which is housed in a secure facility. Other authentication servers located at different locations can verify the HMACs based on the latest hash keys obtained from the main authentication server. If HMAC verification fails, then the GPS signals of one or more authentication servers have been spoofed.

The proposed GPS authentication protocol has three phases:

- **Hash Key Generation and Distribution:** The chameleon hash keychain is set up on the GPS authentication server, which distributes hash keys HK to clients periodically.

- **GPS Navigation Message Protection:** The GPS authentication server computes the HMACs of message subframes using the latest hash keys in real time.

- **GPS Signal Verification:** The clients verify the hash keys and the GPS signals received from satellites by verifying the HMACs with the GPS authentication server.

Any location-based service can execute the proposed GPS signal authentication protocol to verify the GPS authentication server. The location-based service verifies the GPS signals it receives by checking

Table 2.   GPS signal authentication protocol notation.

SF	Subframe of a GPS navigation message
E	Elliptic curve used by the chameleon hash function
G	Base point of the NIST prime curve secp256r1
Y	Elliptic curve cryptography public key
y	Elliptic curve cryptography private key (trapdoor key $\mathbb{K}$)

the chameleon hashes of the signals using a representational state transfer (REST) interface. Table 2 presents the notation used to specify the GPS signal authentication protocol.

Hash Key Generation and Distribution. The GPS authentication server generates and maintains the chameleon hash keychain that secures GPS navigation messages. The NIST prime curve P-256 E of the form $y^2 \pmod{p} = x^3 + ax + b \pmod{p}$ on the finite field F_p is used to construct the chameleon hash function. First, the elliptic curve cryptography domain parameters are generated, where p is a large prime number, a and b are elliptic curve coefficients and G is a generator selected from the elliptic curve. A random value y is chosen as the private key (trapdoor key) and the corresponding public key is computed as $Y = yG$.

The first hash key HK_0 is generated using a random message m_0 and random prime number r_0 as follows:

$$HK_n = \mathbb{CH}(m_n, r_n) = HMAC(m_n, Y) \cdot Y + r_n \cdot G \qquad (5)$$

where $HMAC(m_n, Y)$ is a keyed message authentication code of m_n (i.e., SHA-256 with input key Y).

Whenever a new hash key HK_{n+1} is generated by the GPS authentication server using $\mathbb{CH}(m_{n+1}, r_{n+1})$, an r'_n is derived to link HK_{n+1} with the previous hash key HK_n as follows:

$$r'_n = y \cdot [HMAC(m_n, Y) - HMAC(HK_{n+1}, Y)] + r_n \qquad (6)$$

Note that only the GPS authentication server can generate a hash collision to obtain r'_n because it is the only entity that possesses the private key y (trapdoor key). HK_{n+1} and r'_n are then distributed to all the clients.

A location-based service that requires GPS authentication can bootstrap its application by registering the device and obtaining the initial hash key or the latest hash key from the GPS authentication server via a TLS session.

GPS Navigation Message Protection. The proposed authentication protocol secures GPS navigation messages received from satellites. Each GPS message frame comprising five subframes is protected using a different hash key in the chameleon hash keychain.

The GPS authentication server is set up with a dedicated GPS signal receiver to collect navigation messages from all the GPS satellites that are detected. This server should be housed in a security facility to prevent attackers from spoofing GPS signals. Upon receiving a complete frame comprising five subframes, the server computes the next hash key in the chameleon hash keychain using Equation 5, where m is the concatenation of subframes 1 to 5 of each message frame and r is a random prime number that is generated securely by the authentication server.

The GPS authentication server executes the following steps:

- HK_0 is generated using a random message m_0 and random prime number r_0, i.e., $HK_0 = \mathbb{CH}(m_0, r_0)$. The GPS authentication server maintains the chameleon hash keychain, generating a hash key every 30 seconds. The current hash key is HK_i.

- The five subframes of a received GPS navigation message are concatenated to create next message m_{i+1}. For example, when $i = 0$, $m_1 = \mathbb{SF}_{1,1} \cdot \mathbb{SF}_{1,2} \cdot \mathbb{SF}_{1,3} \cdot \mathbb{SF}_{1,4} \cdot \mathbb{SF}_{1,5}$.

- The next hash key HK_{i+1} is generated via Equation 5 by selecting a random prime number r_{i+1}. For example, $HK_1 = \mathbb{CH}(m_1, r_1)$.

- The private key y is used to compute r_i' via Equation 6 in order to link HK_{i+1} and HK_i. For example, $HK_0 = \mathbb{CH}(HK_1, r_0')$.

- The HMAC of each subframe is computed using SHA-256 and the new hash key HK_{i+1}. The HMACs are stored in a database to facilitate GPS verification requests by clients.

Algorithm 1 summarizes the chameleon hash keychain generation and GPS message protection computations performed by the GPS authentication server. The hash key is used to compute the HMAC fingerprint of every message subframe that is later verified by clients over the Internet. This means that the hash key is renewed per frame (i.e., every 30 seconds), making it extremely difficult for an attacker to spoof GPS signals without being detected.

Algorithm 1 : Hash keychain generation and GPS message protection.

Initialize public key: $Y = yG$
Choose a random message m_0 and random prime number r_0
Generate initial $HK_0 = HMAC(m_0, Y) \cdot Y + r_0 \cdot G$
$i = 0$
for each complete message frame m_{i+1} received **do**
$//m_{i+1} = \mathbb{SF}_{i+1,1} \cdot \mathbb{SF}_{i+1,2} \cdot \mathbb{SF}_{i+1,3} \cdot \mathbb{SF}_{i+1,4} \cdot \mathbb{SF}_{i+1,5}$
Generate a random prime number r_{i+1}
$HK_{i+1} = HMAC(m_{i+1}, Y) \cdot Y + r_{i+1} \cdot G$
$r'_i = y \cdot [HMAC(m_i, Y) - HMAC(HK_{i+1}, Y)] + r_i$

$//$Generate HMAC for each subframe $\mathbb{SF}_{i+1,j}$ using HK_{i+1}
for j=1; j<6; j++ **do**
$HMAC_{i+1,j} = HMAC(\mathbb{SF}_{i+1,j}, HK_{i+1})$
Store $HMAC_{i+1,j}$ in the database
end for

i++
end for

GPS Signal Verification. Location-based service clients verify GPS navigation messages received from satellites by first synchronizing the hash key with the GPS authentication server as follows:

$$\text{Client} \rightarrow \text{Server:} \quad HK_c, Device_{ID}$$
$$\text{Server} \rightarrow \text{Client:} \quad HK_{i+1}, r'_c$$

A client possessing a hash key $HK_c \neq HK_i$ sends its $Device_{ID}$ and HK_c to the GPS authentication server to obtain the next hash key HK_{i+1}. The server computes r'_c for the requesting client using Equation 6 such that $HK_c = \mathbb{CH}(HK_{i+1}, r'_c)$. The server then sends HK_{i+1} and r'_c to the client, enabling the client to authenticate the server. When this is successful, the client can maintain a synchronized chameleon hash chain with the server to continuously authenticate GPS signals received during a session.

To verify a GPS navigation message, a client sends a request to the GPS authentication server to obtain the HMACs of each message frame by indicating the *Satellite ID* and *Frame ID*. The client also receives the message subframes directly from a satellite and uses the next hash key HK_{i+1} to verify the HMAC of each subframe. The GPS data is authentic if the computed HMACs match the HMACs obtained from the GPS authentication server.

Algorithm 2 : GPS message authenticity verification.

Client maintains the chameleon hash keychain: $HK_0 \rightarrow HK_1 \rightarrow ... \rightarrow HK_i$
Authenticate with the GPS authentication server
Synchronize the keychain
Receive HK_{i+1} and r'_i from the GPS authentication server
Verify HK_{i+1} such that $HK_i = \mathbb{CH}(HK_{i+1}, r'_i)$

for each complete message frame m_{i+1} received **do**
   $//m_{i+1} = \mathbb{SF}_{i+1,1} \cdot \mathbb{SF}_{i+1,2} \cdot \mathbb{SF}_{i+1,3} \cdot \mathbb{SF}_{i+1,4} \cdot \mathbb{SF}_{i+1,5}$
   Request HMACs from the GPS authentication server for $\mathbb{SF}_{i+1,j}$, $j = 1, 2, ..., 5$
   Compute $HMAC'_{i+1,j} = HMAC(\mathbb{SF}_{i+1,j}, HK_{i+1})$, $j = 1, 2, ..., 5$

   for j=1; j<6; j++ **do**
     if $HMAC_{i+1,j} == HMAC'_{i+1,j}$ **then**
       Subframe $\mathbb{SF}_{i+1,j}$ is authenticated
     else
       Subframe $\mathbb{SF}_{i+1,j}$ is spoofed
     end if
   end for

end for

Algorithm 2 summarizes the steps involved in GPS message authentication by a client. The steps in the verification process are:

- The client synchronizes the keychain with the GPS authentication server.

- The client obtains the current hash key HK_i and verifies that the key is authentic, thereby authenticating the GPS authentication server.

- After the keychain is synchronized, the client authenticates the server every 30 secs by verifying that $HK_i = \mathbb{CH}(HK_{i+1}, r'_i)$.

- The client requests the HMACs of each satellite frame m_{i+1} comprising five subframes $\mathbb{SF}_{i+1,1}$, $\mathbb{SF}_{i+1,2}$, ..., $\mathbb{SF}_{i+1,5}$ from the server.

- For all the subframes in frame m_{i+1}, the client computes the corresponding $HMAC(\mathbb{SF}_{i+1,j}, HK_{i+1,j})$ where $j = 1, 2, ..., 5$ and verifies that they all match the respective HMACs provided by the GPS authentication server.

It is crucial that clients ensure the authenticity of hash keys so that the HMAC verification can be trusted. The authenticity of hash keys is provided by the unique chameleon hash keychain property that the $\mathbb{CH}$

of the current hash key equals the previous hash key (Equation 6). Since the HMAC computations are fast, clients can verify a GPS navigation message in every 30 second interval.

4.   Prototype Implementation

A proof-of-concept prototype was constructed to validate the proposed GPS signal authentication protocol. The GPS authentication server running a Linux Ubuntu operating system was deployed in the Amazon Elastic Compute Cloud (EC2). The GPS authentication service was operational 24/7 and was accessible on the Internet.

An Android smartphone was used as a GPS signal receiver for the GPS authentication server, which enabled raw GPS navigation messages to be obtained directly from satellites. In a real deployment, a proper GPS receiver should be used. Node.js and Express.js were used to develop a representational state transfer API that enabled location-based applications and clients to request authenticated GPS signals from the authentication server. GPS navigation messages were received continuously with one subframe received every six seconds. Since each message frame contained five subframes, it took about 30 seconds to collect the five subframes, after which the GPS authentication server computed the subframe HMACs that were stored in a Mongo DB Atlas cloud database.

A C library was developed for chameleon hashing based on elliptic curve cryptography. The OpenSSL library and Bouncy Castle cryptography library were employed. The two main constructs included:

- EC_POINT *generateChameleonHash(EC_GROUP *E,
  EC_POINT *Y, unsigned char *m, BIGNUM *r)

- BIGNUM *computeChameleonRPrime(EC_GROUP *E,
  EC_POINT *Y, BIGNUM *y, BIGNUM *r, unsigned char *m,
  unsigned char *m_prime)

The implementation employed the NIST prime curve P-256. The chameleon hash keychain implementation generated chameleon hash values HK_n and computed collisions r'_n.

An Android application was developed to obtain raw GPS navigation messages using the Android location library. Since GPS navigation messages are continuous streams of data transmitted by satellites, the implementation used GnssNavigationMessage.Callback() to listen for event changes. The onGnssNavigationMessageReceived() and onStatusChanged() functions were triggered to retrieve the raw GPS data received by the smartphone.

Table 3. Navigation signals supported by Samsung Note 8 and Note S8+ models.

Samsung Model	Android Version	Navigation Messages	Accumulated Delta Range	Supported Signals
Note 8	9.0	Yes	Yes	GPS, GLO, GAL, BDS
Note S8+	9.0	Yes	Yes	GPS, GLO, GAL, BDS, QZS

Samsung Note 8 and S8+ Android smartphone models were used to obtain the raw GPS data. One smartphone functioned as the GPS receiver for the GPS authentication server while the other functioned as a client that attempted to verify the received GPS navigation messages. Table 3 shows the signals that can be retrieved by the Samsung Note 8 and Samsung Note S8+ model smartphones.

5.   Evaluation Results and Discussion

This section discusses the evaluation results related to execution time, communications overhead and security aspects.

5.1   Execution Time

Since there are 31 satellites in the GPS constellation, it was important that the GPS authentication server generates hash keys concurrently (although not all the GPS satellites could be detected at a given location).

Table 4. Chameleon hash keychain function and HMAC computation times.

Computation	Time
Chameleon hash key generation: $HK = \mathbb{CH}(m, r)$	$137.2\,\mu s$
Collision generation: $r_i' = \mathbb{CH}'(y, m_i, r_i, HK_{i+1}))$	$20.1\,\mu s$
HMAC computation: $HMAC(m, Y)$	$10.7\,\mu s$

Table 4 shows the average times over 1,000 sequential executions of the chameleon hash keychain generation, collision generation and HMAC computation functions. Hash key generation took $137.2\,\mu s$ and computing r_i' for collision generation took $20.1\,\mu s$. Chameleon hash key generation required more time than collision generation due to its two elliptic curve point multiplication operations compared with one point multiplication for collision generation. The $HMAC(m, Y)$ function was fast and efficient, requiring only $10.7\,\mu s$ to generate five HMACs.

5.2   Communications Overhead

The proposed GPS signal authentication protocol incurs less overhead for a large number of clients compared with the conventional ECDSA digital signature approach that generates a signature for each GPS message subframe. Assuming that an ECDSA signature is 64 bytes, a complete GPS navigation message contains 25 frames (i.e., 125 subframes) and incurs an overhead of 7.81 KB per navigation message per client. In contrast, the HMAC in the GPS signal authentication protocol is 32 bytes and the hash key HK_{i+1} and r'_i are 64 bytes each. The hash key is renewed every frame, which incurs an overhead of 3.12 KB and the HMACs for 125 subframes incur an overhead of 3.91 KB. The total overhead per navigation message per client is 7.03 KB, which is 10% less than the overhead in the ECDSA scheme. Each subframe has to be signed or its HMAC computed separately because some receivers may not have received all the subframes. Therefore, each subframe needs to be verified individually.

5.3   Security Aspects

Based on the trapdoor collision property of chameleon hash functions, an efficient probabilistic polynomial time algorithm exists such that, upon receiving a private key y, message pair (m, r) and m', the GPS authentication server outputs a value r' such that a hash collision occurs (i.e., $\mathbb{CH}(m', r') = \mathbb{CH}(m, r)$). The m' and r' values are sent to clients that wish to verify GPS signals, advance their chameleon hash keychains and renew their hash keys. If a client cannot verify the pair (m', r') it receives, then the new hash key did not originate from the GPS authentication server.

The proposed authentication protocol also has the collision resistant property. No probabilistic polynomial time algorithm exists that, upon input of a hash key HK and without the knowledge of the private key y, would enable the GPS authentication server to find pairs (m, r) and (m', r') where $m \neq m'$ such that $\mathbb{CH}(m', r') = \mathbb{CH}(m, r)$ has a non-negligible probability. This is equivalent to solving the elliptic curve discrete logarithm problem (ECDLP), which is known to be computationally hard. The significance of the collision resistant property is that no entity apart from the GPS authentication server can extend the keychain.

Every frame is protected with a HMAC using a different hash key. Unless the private key y of the GPS authentication server is compromised, it would be very difficult for an attacker to fix the next hash key in advance and use it to compute the HMACs of the next set of GPS frames. By changing the hash key frequently, the authenticity guarantees of the GPS navigation messages increase, but this comes with the overhead of distributing the hash keys more frequently to all the clients.

6.   Conclusions

This chapter has presented a novel approach using a chameleon hash keychain to efficiently protect GPS navigation messages, enabling clients to verify their GPS signals via a web service interface. The approach adopts an unbounded one-way keychain generated using chameleon hash constructs, providing the ability to use a new hash key to protect every frame of a GPS navigation message. The resulting GPS signal authentication protocol is effective because clients can authenticate the GPS authentication server easily by verifying the one-way property of new hash keys they receive. The approach also eliminates the need to loosely synchronize time between the GPS authentication server and clients.

This research has conducted a preliminary evaluation of the prototype implementation. The next step is to work with government agencies to roll out a larger deployment to investigate network latency and system scalability. In a real deployment, the GPS authentication server will have to be hardened and integrated with adequate web security protection measures. Future research will also investigate extensions of the GPS authentication protocol to protect other global navigational satellite systems such as GLO, GAL and BeiDou.

References

[1] J. Bhatti and T. Humphreys, Hostile control of ships via false GPS signals: Demonstration and detection, *Journal of the Institute of Navigation*, vol. 64(1), pp. 51–66, 2017.

[2] M. bin Mohammad Fadilah, V. Balachandran, P. Loh and M. Chua, DRAT: A drone attack tool for vulnerability assessment, *Proceedings of the Tenth ACM Conference on Data and Application Security and Privacy*, pp. 153–155, 2020.

[3] D. Borio and C. Gioia, A sum-of-squares approach to GNSS spoofing detection, *IEEE Transactions on Aerospace and Electronic Systems*, vol. 52(4), pp. 1756–1768, 2016.

[4] A. Broumandan, A. Jafarnia-Jahromi and G. Lachapelle, Spoofing detection, classification and cancellation (SDCC) receiver architecture for a moving GNSS receiver, *GPS Solutions*, vol. 19(3), pp. 475–487, 2015.

[5] R. Di Pietro, A. Durante, L. Mancini and V. Patil, Practically un-
    bounded one-way chains for authentication with backward secrecy,
    *Proceedings of the First IEEE International Conference on Security
    and Privacy for Emerging Areas in Communications Networks*, pp.
    400–402, 2005.

[6] I. Fernandez-Hernandez, V. Rijmen, G. Seco-Granados, J. Simon, I.
    Rodriguez and J. Calle, A navigation message authentication pro-
    posal for the Galileo Open Service, *Journal of the Institute of Nav-
    igation*, vol. 63(1), pp. 85–102, 2016.

[7] K. Ghorbani, N. Orouji and M. Mosavi, Navigation message authen-
    tication based on a one-way hash chain to mitigate spoofing attacks
    on GPS L1, *Wireless Personal Communications*, vol. 113(4), pp.
    1743–1754, 2020.

[8] T. Humphreys, B. Ledvina, M. Psiaki, B. O'Hanlon and P. Kint-
    ner Jr., Assessing the spoofing threat: Development of a portable
    GPS civilian spoofer, *Proceedings of the Twenty-First International
    Technical Meeting of the Satellite Division of the Institute of Navi-
    gation*, pp. 2314–2325, 2008.

[9] K. Jansen, N. Tippenhauer and C. Popper, Multi-receiver GPS
    spoofing detection: Error models and realization, *Proceedings of the
    Thirty-Second Annual Computer Security Applications Conference*,
    pp. 237–250, 2016.

[10] S. Keoh, K. Au and Z. Tang, Securing industrial control systems:
     An end-to-end integrity verification approach, presented at the *In-
     dustrial Control System Security Workshop of the Thirty-First An-
     nual Computer Security Applications Conference* (www.acsac.org/
     2015/workshops/icss), 2015.

[11] S. Keoh, H. Tan and Z. Tang, Authentication and integrity protec-
     tion for real-time cyber-physical systems, in *Handbook of Real-Time
     Computing*, Y. Tian and D. Levy (Eds.), Springer, Singapore, chap-
     ter 3, 2020.

[12] N. Koblitz, Elliptic curve cryptosystems, *Mathematics of Compu-
     tation*, vol. 48(177), pp. 203–209, 1987.

[13] H. Krawczyk and T. Rabin, Chameleon Hashing and Signatures,
     Cryptography ePrint Archive, Report 1998/010 (eprint.iacr.org/
     1998/010), 1998.

[14] K. Liu, W. Wu, Z. Wu, L. He and K. Tang, Spoofing detection
     algorithm based on pseudorange differences, *Sensors*, vol. 18(10),
     article no. 3197, 2018.

[15] D. Manandhar and R. Shibasaki, Authenticating Galileo Open Service signals using QZSS signals, *Proceedings of the Thirty-First International Technical Meeting of the Satellite Division of the Institute of Navigation*, pp. 3995–4003, 2018.

[16] J. Noh, Y. Kwon, Y. Son, H. Shin, D. Kim, J. Choi and Y. Kim, Tractor Beam: Safe-hijacking of consumer drones with adaptive GPS spoofing, *ACM Transactions on Privacy and Security*, vol. 22(2), article no. 12, 2019.

[17] A. Perrig and J. Tygar, TESLA broadcast authentication, in *Secure Broadcast Communication*, A. Perrig and J. Tygar (Eds.), Springer, Boston, Massachusetts, pp. 29–53, 2003.

[18] M. Psiaki, B. O'Hanlon, J. Bhatti, D. Shepard and T. Humphreys, GPS spoofing detection via dual-receiver correlation of military signals, *IEEE Transactions on Aerospace and Electronic Systems*, vol. 49(4), pp. 2250–2267, 2013.

[19] D. Radin, P. Swaszek, K. Seals and R. Hartnett, GNSS spoof detection based on pseudoranges from multiple receivers, *Proceedings of the Twenty-Eighth International Technical Meeting of the Institute of Navigation*, pp. 657–671, 2015.

[20] J. Su, J. He, P. Cheng and J. Chen, A stealthy GPS spoofing strategy for manipulating the trajectory of an unmanned aerial vehicle, *IFAC-PapersOnLine*, vol. 49(22), pp. 291–296, 2016.

[21] H. Tan, K. Lim, S. Keoh, Z. Tang, D. Leong and C. Sum, Chameleon: A blind double trapdoor hash function for securing AMI data aggregation, *Proceedings of the Fourth IEEE World Forum on the Internet of Things*, pp. 225–230, 2018.

[22] J. Van Sickle and J. Dutton, GEOG862: GPS and GNSS for Geospatial Professionals, Department of Geography, Pennsylvania State University, University Park, Pennsylvania (`www.e-education.psu.edu/geog862/home.html`), 2014.

[23] W. Wang, G. Chen, R. Wu, D. Lu and L. Wang, A low-complexity spoofing detection and suppression approach for ADS-B, *Proceedings of the Integrated Communications, Navigation and Surveillance Conference*, 2015.

[24] K. Wesson, M. Rothlisberger and T. Humphreys, A proposed navigation message authentication implementation for civil GPS anti-spoofing, *Proceedings of the Twenty-Fourth International Technical Meeting of the Satellite Division of the Institute of Navigation*, pp. 3129–3140, 2011.

[25] Z. Wu, Y. Zhang and R. Liu, BD-II NMA&SSI: A scheme for anti-spoofing and open BeiDou II D2 navigation message authentication, *IEEE Access*, vol. 8, pp. 23759–23775, 2020.

[26] M. Yuan, Z. Lv, H. Chen, J. Li and G. Ou, An implementation of navigation message authentication with reserved bits for civil BDS anti-spoofing, in *China Satellite Navigation Conference (CSNC) 2017 Proceedings: Volume II*, J. Sun, J. Liu, Y. Yang, S. Fan and W. Yu (Eds.), Springer, Singapore, pp. 69–80, 2017.

IV

INFRASTRUCTURE SECURITY

Chapter 11

SECURITY ANALYSIS OF SOFTWARE UPDATES FOR INDUSTRIAL ROBOTS

Chun-Fai Chan, Kam-Pui Chow and Tim Tang

Abstract   Robots are widely deployed in industrial manufacturing environments. Cyber compromises of industrial robots pose threats to products and services, to the robots as well as to human workers. Previous security studies of robots have focused on network service vulnerabilities and privileged execution. However, research has not examined robot software updates and their security features. This chapter investigates the security features of software updates for a Universal Robots UR3 cobot, one of the most commonly-used collaborative industrial robots.

Keywords: Industrial robots, Universal Robots UR3 cobot, software updates

1.   Introduction

Robots are widely deployed in industrial manufacturing environments. Cyber compromises of industrial robots pose threats to products and services, to the robots as well as to human workers. Security studies of robots have focused on network service vulnerabilities and privileged execution. However, research has not examined robot software updates and their security features.

This chapter investigates the security features of software updates for a Universal Robots UR3 cobot, one of the most commonly-used collaborative industrial robots. The security analysis reveals four hitherto unknown vulnerabilities in the software update process that can lead to total compromise of the cobot. Several recommendations for the cobot manufacturer and cobot operators are presented to reduce or mitigate the risks.

© IFIP International Federation for Information Processing 2022
Published by Springer Nature Switzerland AG 2022
J. Staggs and S. Shenoi (Eds.): Critical Infrastructure Protection XV, IFIP AICT 636, pp. 229–245, 2022.
https://doi.org/10.1007/978-3-030-93511-5_11

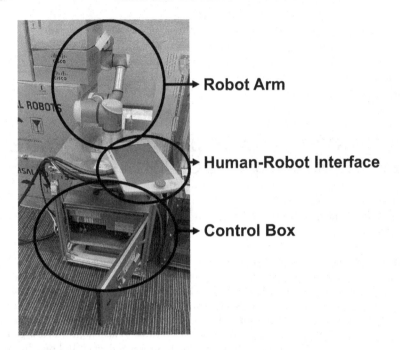

Figure 1.   Principal UR3 cobot components.

2.   Collaborative Robot

Collaborative robots, called cobots, are designed to operate in a shared space with human workers [2]. Universal Robots, based in Odense, Denmark, is a leading manufacturer of industrial cobots. The company sold its first cobot in 2008 [14] and continues to dominate the cobot sector. The industrial research firm, Interact Analysis [11], reports that Universal Robots had a global market share of almost 50% in 2017. In 2020, Universal Robots sold its 50,000th cobot [3].

Figure 1 shows a UR3 cobot manufactured by Universal Robots. Its principal components are a robot arm, human-robot interface and control box:

- **Robot Arm:** The robot arm, made of extruded aluminum, comprises tubes and joints that can be controlled on three or more axes, and moved flexibly according to pre-defined instructions [13]. The wrist joints in the arm can rotate 360 degrees and the end joints have infinite degrees of freedom.

- **Human-Robot Interface:** The human-robot interface (HRI) is a touchscreen device similar to a tablet with a wired connection

Figure 2. Control box lock and key.

to a cobot's control box. The human-robot interface houses a Polyscope graphical user interface, which enables a human operator to execute programs and monitor the status of the cobot.

- **Control Box:** The control box of a cobot is enclosed in a chassis. It contains the physical input/output ports and electronic components that connect to the robot arm, human-robot interface and other peripherals. The computer and communications systems for the robot arm and human-robot interface are located in the control box. An operator powers on the control box before booting and controlling the robot arm. Universal Robots provides software resources that support human-robot interactions, cobot programming and cobot movement visualization. These resources can be downloaded from the Universal Robots website [14].

A UR3 cobot incorporates pre-installed safety and security features to protect the cobot and human operators:

- **Physical Security:** A physical lock on the control box prevents tampering with the internal components of the cobot (Figure 2). However, the control box key has only two simple teeth, enabling the lock to be opened with a suitable screwdriver.

- **Software-Defined Safety Settings:** A human operator can specify safety planes that a cobot cannot breach. These safety settings

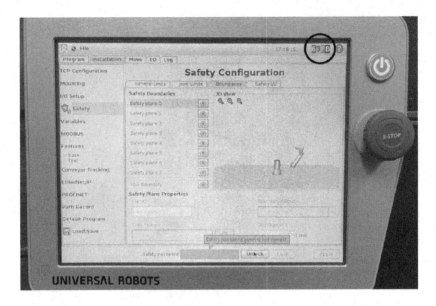

Figure 3. Safety settings and safety settings modification checksum.

cannot be overwritten by other programmed actions, which reduces the potential harm caused by the cobot.

- **Safety Settings Modification Checksum:** The safety settings are protected by a checksum that is computed automatically. The checksum, which is circled in Figure 3, enables a human operator to verify that the settings have not been changed. When an authorized user modifies the safety settings, the checksum is changed accordingly.

- **Human-Robot Interface Password Protection:** In addition to the Linux shell password, the Polyscope software has two additional password protection mechanisms. One is the system password, which a cobot operator is required to input before performing restricted operations such as changing the system settings and programming the robot arm. The other is the safety password, which protects the safety settings that restrict the locations and movements of the robot arm from being modified. As shown in Figure 4, both the passwords cannot be changed without entering the current passwords.

- **Encrypted Software Update:** The cobot software update file is available at the Universal Robots website. The software update

Figure 4. System and safety passwords.

file, which is encrypted using 3TDES, contains the cobot joint firmware update, Polyscope update and update scripts.

3. Previous Work

A growing body of research has focused on the security aspects of industrial robot firmware. Quarta et al. [9] show how attackers can gather information about robot firmware and develop attacks. Information about robots can be obtained without having to purchase them. Many vendors post official support materials on their websites and even allow interested parties to download them free of charge. The most common materials are manuals that provide general information about robots. In the case of advanced robots, additional materials such as software for controlling and simulating robots, as well as drivers and firmware are available. For example, the RobotStudio suite for ABB robots includes a portion of the firmware in the RobotWare distribution [1]. The suite also contains a simulator in the form of a shared library with the entire codebase, which can be analyzed for vulnerabilities. Additionally, platform-specific technical information is available without purchasing a robot.

Researchers have discussed firmware components and how firmware attacks can be performed. Eclypsium [3] describes key firmware components, including system firmware and boot firmware (BIOS, UEFI, EFI and MBR), along with the system management mode and baseboard management controllers that are common components of digital devices.

Rieck [10] discusses the reverse engineering of fitness tracker firmware. The firmware protection mechanism in the fitness tracker analyzed by Rieck is similar to that used by Universal Robotics for software update protection. The fitness tracker firmware comprises two parts, a header and content. The header part has a `table_checksum` field whose value is computed automatically from the content part to verify that no errors occurred during firmware transmission. However, no mechanism is in place to maintain the integrity of the header. Thus, an attacker with access to the firmware can modify the firmware, generate the new checksum and store it in the firmware header. The manipulated firmware can be installed successfully because the checksum and `table_checksum` match.

Shim et al. [12] leveraged Rieck's research to access the firmware of a mobile application that controls a wearable fitness tracker. The firmware was disassembled using the IDA Pro reverse engineering tool. The firmware code was shown to be modifiable by changing the bitmaps of certain characters. The modified firmware was subsequently inserted in the fitness tracker without any warnings or errors.

Apart from research on firmware vulnerabilities, a Robot Vulnerability Database has been created for the public to submit vulnerabilities discovered in industrial robots, which are subsequently verified by experts [7]. A total of 92 vulnerabilities relating to the Universal Robotics UR3 cobot are recorded in the database. Eighty-one vulnerabilities relate to unpatched libraries or binaries in the Linux distribution and eleven relate to the software and firmware. Five of the eleven software/firmware vulnerabilities relate to unauthenticated communications, two to buffer overflows and four to unbounded local privilege execution. None of the reported UR3 cobot vulnerabilities relate to software/firmware integrity.

4.   Experiments and Results

A cobot simulation environment was created by downloading and installing Universal Robots offline simulators as virtual machines [15]. The virtual machines were executed in VMWare under a Windows 10 Pro operating system. Experiments were performed with Universal Robots virtual machine CB version 3.14.3 on an i686 architecture running an

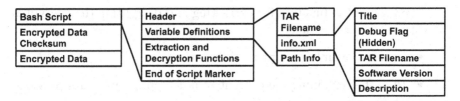

Figure 5. URUP file structure.

Ubuntu 14.04.3 Linux distribution. In addition, experiments were conducted with Universal Robots CB update file versions 3.5.4, 3.6.1, 3.12.1 and 3.14.3. The simulated results were then verified using a Universal Robots UR3 cobot executing CB versions 3.5.1 and 3.5.4 on an i686 architecture with a Debian 7 Linux distribution.

4.1 Software Update File

The software update file (URUP) was examined with the Linux `file` tool to determine if it matched a known file signature. The tool suggested that the update file was a bash script. However, inspection of the update file using a `vim` editor showed that it had bash script text and binary data. Static analysis of the bash script and reverse engineering of the Polyscope program (discussed below) revealed that the URUP update file has the structure shown Figure 5.

A URUP file has three parts. The first part of the update file is a bash script. The first line of the script is a typical bash script header that indicates the bash interpreter file location. After the header line, multiple variables are defined, which include the output TAR filename and the `info.xml` file and extraction path locations. The `info.xml` file content was extracted and read using the Polyscope software update routine (described later).

The `info.xml` file contains its title and description, which are displayed on the human-robot interface screen. The XML file also contains the software version of the URUP update file (which is checked against the existing installed version) and the output TAR filename (same as the TAR filename in the bash script variable definition). Additionally, the XML file may contain flags such as debug and remote server flags that could be used by the update routine, but they were not seen in the URUP update file. Following the variable definitions is a function for extracting `info.xml` from the URUP file and a function for extracting and decrypting the encrypted binary data.

The logic of the function for extracting and decrypting the encrypted binary data is as follows:

- Locate the end of script marker.

- Pipe the remaining file content to a decryption program provided by OpenSSL.

- Decrypt the binary encrypted data using the 3TDES algorithm and symmetric key stored in an environment variable.

- Save the decrypted stream to a file.

- Locate the encrypted data checksum in the update file.

- Compute the MD5 hash of the decrypted file.

- Compare the MD5 checksums.

- Move the decrypted TAR file to a location specified in the input argument.

The second part of the update file is a single line that stores the MD5 checksum of the data contained in the third part of the file.

The third and last part of the update file is a chunk of binary data. According to its binary data header, it corresponds to salted encrypted data. Analysis of the bash script decryption function revealed that the data is encrypted using 3TDES in the CBC mode with a 24 byte key and salt.

4.2 Symmetric Key

Armed with knowledge about the structure and execution flow of the URUP update file, attempts were made to extract the encrypted data in the last part of the update file using the same decryption parameters in the bash script. However, the critical symmetric key was missing. Analysis of the bash script indicated that the symmetric key should be stored in an environment variable. However, examination of the bash shell consoles in the physical and simulated environments did not reveal the presence of the environment variable.

Since the Universal Robots documentation did not have any related information, the only option was to reverse engineer the Polyscope software that provides a graphical user interface to trigger the software update process (Figure 6).

The Universal Robots Polyscope software was developed in Java. The JD-GUI tool [4] was used to decompile the class files in the JAR files.

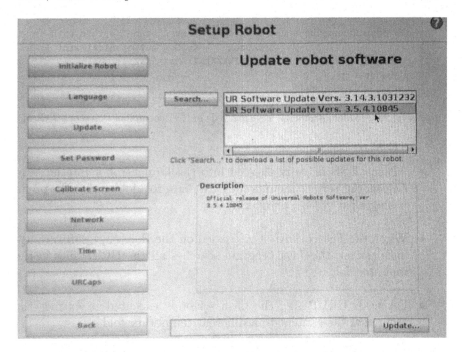

Figure 6. Updating software via the Polyscope graphical user interface.

The decompiled source code was searched for a subroutine that triggers the loading of the URUP update file – this revealed the location where the environment variable is defined. It turned out that the variable is defined just before the bash script is invoked, which is why it could not be located in the bash shell console environment. Surprisingly, the analysis revealed that the symmetric key is saved as a hardcoded string in the Java program (Figure 7).

Multiple versions of the Universal Robots software (version 3.5.4 to the latest version 3.14.3) were decompiled and analyzed. The analyses revealed that all the versions have the same symmetric key saved as a hardcoded string in their Java programs.

4.3   Software Update Process Flow

The decompiled Java source code and other custom system script files were reverse engineered to determine the details of the software update process. The general software update process flow was determined to be as follows:

```
BashScriptRunner bs = new BashScriptRunner("bash " + this.path +
                      " --unpack " + tmpDir.getCanonicalPath());
bs.addEnvVar("RUR", "XXXXXXXXXXXXXXXXXXXXXXXXXXX");
bs.execute();
```

Figure 7. Hardcoded symmetric key (masked) in the decompiled Polyscope JAR file.

- After a USB drive is plugged into the human-robot interface, an automount service mounts the USB drive to a folder with the prefix (usbdisk*) under /programs.

- When the Search button is pressed on the Polyscope software update screen, the Java program searches all the URUP files in the mounted folder.

- For each URUP file, the bash script is executed to extract the info.xml file content to a different temporary folder.

- The related information of each info.xml file is displayed on the human-robot interface screen.

- When a file is selected and the Update button is clicked, the Java program invokes the bash script of the file to extract, decrypt and move the binary data to a temporary folder.

- Major and minor software update versions are checked against the current version and only the compatible version is permitted to be updated.

- The untarred files are saved to /root/update and a system reboot is performed.

- After the reboot, the post upgrade script post.sh is invoked to copy the files to the appropriate locations.

5.   Software Update Process Vulnerabilities

Insights gained from the URUP update file structure and software update process flow supported the vulnerability discovery efforts. This section describes four new vulnerabilities of the UR3 cobot software update mechanism and their exploitation.

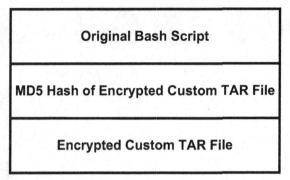

Figure 8. Rogue software update file structure.

5.1 Malicious Software Update File Creation

Because the symmetric key is known and shared by multiple versions of update files, malicious update files with encrypted content can be created to masquerade as legitimate update files.

Two methods were attempted:

- **Method 1:** The first method created an encrypted custom TAR file using the symmetric key that was discovered. An MD5 checksum was computed for the TAR file. The original bash script, new MD5 checksum and encrypted TAR file were concatenated to produce a rogue update file with the structure shown in Figure 8.

- **Method 2:** The second method rewrote the bash script in the first part of the update file. This bypassed the decryption process without needing the symmetric key. At a triggering point in the update process, the content was dumped to a temporary folder and the update process continued its execution.

Method 1 is stealthier than Method 2. Method 2 is easier to perform than Method 1. Also, it enables other actions to be executed that lead to another vulnerability discussed below.

Additionally, an update file with an arbitrary version number can be created by modifying the variables in the bash script as shown in Figure 9. This could mislead a cobot operator to believing that the rogue file is actually a more recent update file. Since the UR3 cobot does not permit software to be downgraded, once a new rogue version is installed, the cobot cannot be rolled back to the previous official version.

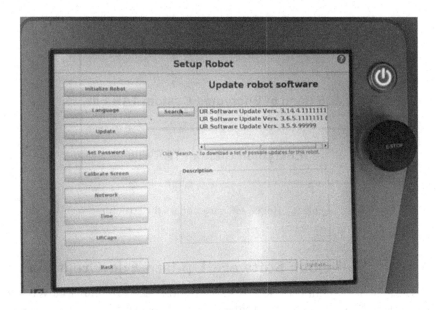

Figure 9. Arbitrary update file version.

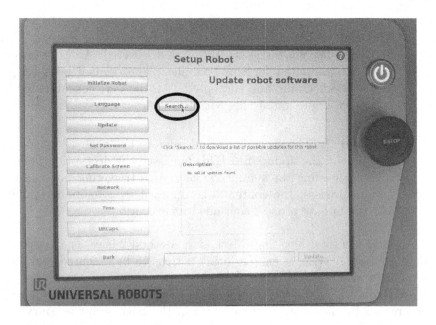

Figure 10. Search function in the software update user interface.

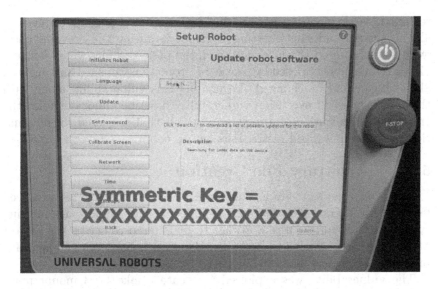

Figure 11. Arbitrary script execution after pressing the Search button.

5.2 Arbitrary Script Execution

The software update process flow analysis revealed that the Search function attempts to locate all the URUP files at the USB mount point (Figure 10). Following this, it tries to extract the info.xml files from the URUP files.

However, the info.xml extraction function is also in the bash script in the update file. Rewriting the extraction function in the bash script enables the execution of an arbitrary script when a user presses the Search button. Figure 11 shows an example of arbitrary script execution. In the example, the extraction function was modified to dump the symmetric key on the screen.

5.3 Password Integrity

Forensic analysis of the cobot system revealed that two files are modified when the system password and safety password are changed. Both are hidden files with filenames starting with "." and located in the root directory. Each file has only one line corresponding to the encrypted password string.

Experiments were conducted to change content by replacing the encrypted string with another encrypted string for which the plaintext password was known. It was discovered that, after the user interface is reloaded, the system accepts the new password and permits changes to all the system and safety settings without requiring the previous passwords to be entered. Even worse, when the password files were removed, all the restrictions imposed by password protection vanished and any and all settings could be changed. Leveraging this vulnerability along with the arbitrary script execution vulnerability described above enabled the creation and execution of a rogue update file that triggered the elimination of all the password restrictions on the cobot.

5.4   Arbitrary File Creation

The Polyscope software has an Expert Mode that provides advanced features for users. The features include creating folders and editing system files. A correct password has to be entered to access the Expert Mode, but the password is available because it is hardcoded in the Java program and is also listed in the user manual.

The vulnerability was exploited to create a fake USB mount point directory and implant a rogue URUP update file in the directory. The arbitrary script execution vulnerability described above was exploited to write a script to execute arbitrary commands. Additionally, the password integrity vulnerability described above was leveraged to remove all the password-imposed restrictions.

These exploits enable any user with physical access to the human-robot interface screen to execute any command and change the system and safety settings of the robot arm even when the USB and network ports are blocked. The impacts are serious – potentially causing harm to the cobot and its products and services as well as its human operators.

6.   Discussion

In theory, a carefully-crafted rogue update file would leave minimal, if any, traces in the cobot filesystem by removing and overwriting all its intermediate files after execution. The digital forensic method proposed by Gong et al. [5] may not be able to discover the execution of the rogue script. This is because script execution does not require system login and, therefore, no records exist in bash_history and the system login record. Additionally, a log would not be written in log_history.txt because it is not a Polyscope software operation.

Based on the severity of the vulnerabilities discovered in the software update process, the following actions are recommended:

- Authenticity checks should be enforced at multiple levels. First, a software update file should not use a hardcoded symmetric key to encrypt content; the cobot manufacturer should consider using public key cryptography to validate software update signatures before installing the software update. Second, all human-robot interface users should be authenticated before gaining access or performing any operations, especially invoking functions that can modify the filesystem.

- The logic flow of the software update process should be reviewed and modified with security in mind. For example, `info.xml` file extraction and software update decryption should be implemented by functions within Polyscope. Additionally, software updates should not be trusted until their authenticity is verified.

- The operating system and network services should be hardened to minimize the attack surface.

- Finally, physical access to the cobot should be restricted, including blocking or locking USB ports and the human-robot interface until users are authenticated and only if access is needed.

7. Conclusions

This chapter presents a security analysis of the software update protection mechanisms of the Universal Robots UR3 cobot, one of the most popular industrial cobots. The security analysis has revealed four hitherto unknown vulnerabilities in the software update process that can lead to total compromise of the cobot. Several recommendations for the cobot manufacturer and cobot operators are presented to reduce or mitigate the risks.

Future research will to employ digital forensic and reverse engineering techniques to identify new vulnerabilities that could be exploited to cause harm to the cobot and its products and services as well as its human operators.

Acknowledgement

The authors wish to thank the Logistics and Supply Chain MultiTech R&D Centre for providing Universal Robots equipment and for sharing its previous research results, both of which have contributed to the research described in this chapter.

References

[1] ABB, Download RobotStudio with RobotWare and Power-Pacs, Zurich, Switzerland (new.abb.com/products/robotics/ro botstudio/downloads), 2021.

[2] L. Apa, Exploiting Industrial Collaborative Robots, IOActive, Seattle, Washington (`www.ioactive.com/exploiting-industrial-co llaborative-robots`), August 22, 2017.

[3] Eclypsium, Anatomy of a Firmware Attack, Portland, Oregon (`eclypsium.com/wp-content/uploads/2020/09/Anatomy-of-a-Firmware-Attack-2020.pdf`), 2020.

[4] emmanuel, A Standalone Java Decompiler (JD-GUI 1.6.6), GitHub (`github.com/java-decompiler/jd-gui`), 2019.

[5] Y. Gong, K. Chow, Y. Mai, J. Zhang and C. Chan, Forensic investigation of a hacked industrial robot, in *Critical Infrastructure Protection XIV*, J. Staggs and S. Shenoi (Eds.), Springer, Cham, Switzerland, pp. 221–241, 2020.

[6] International Federation of Robotics, Record 2.7 million robots work in factories around the globe, Frankfurt, Germany (`ifr.org/ifr-press-releases/news/record-2.7-million-robots-w ork-in-factories-around-the-globe`), September 24, 2020.

[7] V. Mayoral Vilches, L. Usategui San Juan, B. Dieber, U. Ayucar Carbajo and E. Gil-Uriarte, Introducing the Robot Vulnerability Database (RVD), arXiv: 1912.11299 (`arxiv.org/abs/1912.11299`), 2020.

[8] I. Priyadarshini, Detecting and mitigating robotic cyber security risks, in *Cyber Security Risks in Robotics*, R. Kumar, P. Pattnaik and P. Pandey (Eds.), IGI Global, Hershey, Pennsylvania, pp. 333–348, 2017.

[9] D. Quarta, M. Pogliani, M. Polino, F. Maggi, A. Zanchettin and S. Zanero, An experimental security analysis of an industrial robot controller, *Proceedings of the IEEE Symposium on Security and Privacy*, pp. 268–286, 2017.

[10] J. Rieck, Attacks on Fitness Trackers Revisited: A Case Study on Unfit Firmware Security, arXiv: 1604.03313 (`arxiv.org/abs/1604.03313`), 2016.

[11] A. Sharma, Universal Robots continues to dominate cobot market but faces many challengers, Interact Analysis, Irthlingborough, United Kingdom (`www.interactanalysis.com/univer sal-robots`), November 6, 2018.

[12] J. Shim, K Lim, J. Jeong, S. Cho, M. Park and S. Han, A case study on vulnerability analysis and firmware modification attack on a wearable fitness tracker, *IT Convergence Practice*, vol. 5(4), pp. 25–33, 2017.

[13] Universal Robots, User Manual: UR3/CB3, Version 3.5.5, Odense, Denmark (`s3-eu-west-1.amazonaws.com/ur-support-site/323 40/UR3_User_Manual_en_Global-3.5.5.pdf`), 2018.

[14] Universal Robots, About Universal Robots, Odense, Denmark (`www.universal-robots.com/about-universal-robots`), 2021.

[15] Universal Robots, Legacy Download Center, Odense, Denmark (`www.universal-robots.com/articles/ur/documentation/leg acy-download-center`), 2021.

Chapter 12

A SECURITY FRAMEWORK FOR RAILWAY SYSTEM DEPLOYMENTS

Raymond Chan

Abstract   Railway systems are critical transportation infrastructure assets that must be protected from cyber attacks. However, deployments and upgrades of operational technology systems are always challenging due to the short timeframes available for maintenance. Specifically, there is insufficient time to test the safety and robustness of software updates and patches during railway system operation. Cyber security guidelines have been specified for the railway sector. However, the guidelines only mention the security requirements, not how they should be implemented in railway systems. This chapter proposes a security framework for railway system deployments. The framework can also be used as a reference for cyber security testing.

Keywords: Railway systems, cyber security, deployment

1.   Introduction

Railway systems are critical transportation assets. The recent SolarWinds attacks demonstrate the vulnerabilities of the transportation infrastructure.

Although cyber security solutions are available, it is difficult to deploy them in operational railway systems. The principal challenge is the limited time available for maintaining and repairing railway systems. For example, they may not be enough time to test the safety and robustness of a software patch during operating hours. Also, when existing devices are upgraded and new devices are installed, concerns are raised about whether the deployments are secure and are not beset by human error.

This chapter proposes a security framework for railway system deployments. The framework can also be used as a reference for cyber security testing.

© IFIP International Federation for Information Processing 2022
Published by Springer Nature Switzerland AG 2022
J. Staggs and S. Shenoi (Eds.): Critical Infrastructure Protection XV, IFIP AICT 636, pp. 247–253, 2022.
https://doi.org/10.1007/978-3-030-93511-5_12

2.   Related Work

The CYRAIL Project [4] supported by the European Commission has released cyber security guidelines for the railway sector. The guidelines cover methodologies for adding new equipment and replacing old equipment while maintaining the safety and security levels. Also covered are deployment agreements established between suppliers and railway managers related to product security requirements and support for products over their lifetimes. However, no details are provided about implementing the security requirements in railway systems.

Wi-Fi jamming attacks pose significant risks to railway system deployments [8]. Since communications-based train control in a railway system operates at a similar frequency as normal Wi-Fi, the reliability of control signals decreases when many passengers attempt to connect to a Wi-Fi access point on a train. Indeed, a well-resourced attacker could leverage the Wi-Fi access point to connect to a train control system.

Researchers have demonstrated that similar techniques have been used to access elevator control systems [3]. Gransart et al. [6] and Frangie et al. [5] discuss threats to railway systems that leverage wireless communications. Alguliyev et al. [2], Huq et al. [7] and Thaduri et al. [10] discuss various threats to railway systems.

Unfortunately, the trend in transportation systems, including railway systems, is to incorporate smart devices that rely on wireless communications [9]. However, few, if any, studies address the concerns raised by deploying such devices in railway systems.

3.   Security Framework

This section describes the proposed security framework for railway system deployments. The framework has four phases: (i) procurement phase, (ii) testing phase, (iii) deployment phase and (iv) post-deployment phase.

3.1   Procurement Phase

The procurement phase is the important first phase of the deployment framework. During this phase, vendors are selected and checks are made to identify and mitigate security issues. Railway system operators must conduct the following analyses to ensure that railway systems and devices meet the security requirements:

- **Supply Chain Analysis:** A railway system operator should verify the provenance and trust levels of the procured systems and devices. The operator should maintain a trusted vendors list and perform annual auditing to ensure that vendors adhere to the security requirements. The costs of products and services should factor in the decision making, but security should have higher priority. The systems should be maintained and supported by trusted local service teams where possible because it difficult to guarantee 24/7 support by remote, let alone, overseas personnel.

- **Product Lifecycle Analysis:** A railway system operator should ensure that systems and devices are supported by vendors and maintained and replaced by service providers over their lifecycles. Vendors should continue to support their products for at least ten years. Service providers should provide security patches and updates to ensure that applications are secure.

- **Security Requirements Analysis:** A railway system operator should develop security requirements before procuring products. Since railway systems are typically regulated by government agencies, all systems and devices should be procured by issuing tenders to ensure transparency. Bids should not be accepted unless the vendors and service providers satisfy all the security requirements considered in the supply chain analysis and product lifecycle analysis.

  The CYRAIL Project [4] has identified the following security requirements for railway systems:

  - *Personnel Requirements:* Requirements must be imposed on the personnel involved in operating railway automation and telemechanical systems and devices. A railway operator must collect requirements from the stakeholders involved in developing, administering and operating the railway system. Additional security requirements should be solicited from cyber security experts.

  - *Physical Protection Requirements:* Systems and devices must be isolated and protected from access by unauthorized staff and passengers. The physical protection requirements should include video monitoring, physical locks and alarms, and periodic checks by staff.

  - *Access Management Requirements:* Access to operational technology systems must be managed securely and effectively to prevent misuse and mitigate human error. A railway operator must define system access rights for all personnel and ensure that the rights are managed and controlled properly.

- *Data Protection Requirements:* A railway system has to collect large quantities of data for regulatory and analytic purposes. Data collection, access, dissemination and retention must follow the applicable government and industry data protection requirements. The requirements should be considered carefully during the procurement phase.

- *Software Requirements:* Software must be compatible in existing and new operating environments. Software must be supported by vendors and updates and patches provided regularly for at least ten years.

- *Intrusion Detection Requirements:* Adequate measures must be taken to detect and alert to cyber attacks. Data related to railway system operation and potential anomalies and attacks should be archived and secured, and passed promptly to relevant personnel and organizations.

- *Incident Response Requirements:* Requirements for effective incident response, especially incident analysis and mitigation activities, must be specified to reduce risk and negative impacts to railway system operations.

- *Reliability Requirements:* Reliability requirements must be imposed on systems and devices to ensure reliable operation over their lifecycles.

3.2   Testing Phase

Activities during the testing phase ensure that newly-installed systems and devices interoperate seamlessly in the operational environment. Although testing can be conducted using an experimental testbed or simulated environment, it is important to ensure that the testing environment models the operational environment with high fidelity to provide assurance.

The following activities should be conducted during the testing phase:

- **Vulnerability Assessment and Penetration Testing:** Vulnerability assessments and penetration tests are routinely conducted for information technology systems. To enhance reliability and resilience and reduce operational risk, the assessments and tests should be performed for information and operational technology assets in railway systems.

- **Simulation and Digital Twin Testing:** It may not be possible to test a new system or device in an operational environment before their deployment. In such cases, a high-fidelity simulation or digital twin should be used for testing. The tests should be performed in an integrated environment with and without the new system or device.

3.3 Deployment Phase

In a railway system, the timeframe for deployment and maintenance may be only a few hours starting at midnight. The following activities must be performed during the deployment phase:

- **Security Deployment Checklist:** Security deployment checks must be conducted to verify the configurations and settings of systems and devices. If the time required for deployment is more than the maintenance timeframe, the checklist should include the configurations and settings that must be verified every time the checks are conducted.

- **Rollback Procedure:** A rollback procedure must be performed to stop a deployment and return the system to the previous state if the deployment cannot be completed within the maintenance timeframe. The rollback procedure should also verify that the system is working properly after the rollback.

- **Deployment Verification:** Deployment verification checks that a deployment has been completed and the newly-installed system or device is working as expected. Deployment verification should also use the security deployment checklist to ensure that the configurations and settings are correct.

3.4 Post-Deployment Phase

During the post-deployment phase, a railway operator should perform the appropriate procedures for maintaining and monitoring the systems and devices:

- **Patch and Upgrade Procedure:** This procedure includes the testing and deployment phase activities to ensure that the patch or update does not affect system functionality and reliability. The patch and upgrade procedure may require an additional deployment to address follow-up actions.

- **Drill Procedure:** Drills must be conducted periodically in the experimental and production environments during the maintenance timeframe, if possible. The drills must be performed after new systems and devices are deployed, patched or upgraded. They should also simulate intruder attacks and the operator should be able to react appropriately to the simulated attacks and mitigate the impacts on the railway system.

■ **Monitoring and Open-Source Intelligence Workflow:** A railway operator must implement standard operating procedures to react to security alerts and security incidents. A decision to apply a quick fix and monitor system behavior must be made before a patch is deployed.

4.   Conclusions

Railway systems are critical transportation infrastructure assets that must be protected from cyber attacks. The security framework for railway system deployments presented in this chapter covers activities that must be performed during the procurement, testing, deployment and post-deployment phases of systems and devices. The framework also serves as a reference for cyber security testing.

The security framework was intended to be applied to transportation systems operated by the Singapore Land Transport Authority (LTA) and Mass Rapid Transit (SMRT), but discussions were suspended due to the COVID-19 pandemic and may resume in the near future.

Future research will extend the work to apply continuous integration and delivery concepts in software development to railway systems. Additionally, research will attempt to apply modified versions of the security framework to deployments of other critical infrastructure assets such as building management systems and industrial control systems.

References

[1] Acute Market Reports, Railway Signaling Systems Market Size, Market Share, Application Analysis, Regional Outlook, Growth Trends, Key Players, Competitive Strategies and Forecasts, 2020 to 2028, Report ID: 5232539, New York, 2020.

[2] R. Alguliyev, Y. Imamverdiyev and L. Sukhostat, Cyber-physical systems and their security issues, *Computers in Industry*, vol. 100, pp. 212–223, 2018.

[3] R. Chan and K. Chow, Threat analysis of an elevator control system, in *Critical Infrastructure Protection XI*, M. Rice and S. Shenoi (Eds.), Springer, Cham, Switzerland, pp. 175–192, 2017.

[4] CYRAIL Project, Cybersecurity in the Railway Sector, Evoleo Technologies, Maia, Portugal (`cyrail.eu`), 2017.

[5] R. Frangie, A. Mihalic, T. Chehab, J. Kan, C. Luk and S. Perin-pacumarasamy, Smart railways ... or not so smart: A cyber security perspective, *Proceedings of the Conference on Railway Excellence*, pp. 230–239, 2018.

[6] C. Gransart, V. Deniau, E. Simon, A. Fleury, S. Lecoeuche, P. Millot and E. Masson, Cyber security of the railway wireless system: Detection, decision and human-in-the-loop, *Proceedings of the Seventh Transport Research Arena*, 2018.

[7] N. Huq, R. Vosseler and M. Swimmer, Cyberattacks Against Intelligent Transportation Systems, TrendLabs, Trend Micro, Tokyo, Japan, 2017.

[8] S. Lakshminarayana, J. Karachiwala, S. Chang, G. Revadigar, S. Kumar, D. Yau and Y. Hu, Signal jamming attacks against communications-based train control: Attack impacts and countermeasures, *Proceedings of the Eleventh ACM Conference on Security and Privacy in Wireless and Mobile Networks*, pp. 160–171, 2018.

[9] P. Radanliev, D. De Roure, J. Nurse, R. Nicolescu, M. Huth, S. Cannady and R. Mantilla Montalvo, New Developments in Cyber Physical Systems, the Internet of Things and the Digital Economy – Discussion on Future Developments in the Industrial Internet of Things and Industry 4.0, Unpublished Manuscript (www.preprints.org/manuscript/201903.0094/v1), 2019.

[10] A. Thaduri, M. Aljumaili, R. Kour and R. Karim, Cybersecurity for e-maintenance in the railway infrastructure: Risks and consequences, *International Journal of System Assurance Engineering and Management*, vol. 10(2), pp. 149–159, 2019.

Printed in the United States
by Baker & Taylor Publisher Services